Group Financial Statements

Roy Dodge

Faculty of Business and Management
University of Westminster

CHAPMAN & HALL
London · Glasgow · Weinheim · New York · Tokyo · Melbourne · Madras

Published by Chapman & Hall, 2–6 Boundary Row, London SE1 8HN, UK

Chapman & Hall, 2–6 Boundary Row, London SE1 8HN, UK

Blackie Academic & Professional, Wester Cleddens Road, Bishopbriggs, Glasgow G64 2NZ, UK

Chapman & Hall GmbH, Pappelallee 3, 69469 Weinheim, Germany

Chapman & Hall USA, 115 Fifth Avenue, New York, NY 10003, USA

Chapman & Hall Japan, ITP-Japan, Kyowa Building, 3F, 2-2-1 Hirakawacho, Chiyoda-ku, Tokyo 102, Japan

Chapman & Hall Australia, 102 Dodds Street, South Melbourne, Victoria 3205, Australia

Chapman & Hall India, R. Seshadri, 32 Second Main Road, CIT East, Madras 600 035, India

First edition 1996

© 1996 Roy Dodge

Typeset in 11/12 Goudy by Best-set Typesetter Ltd., Hong Kong
Printed in England by Clays Ltd, St Ives plc

ISBN 0 412 63930 0

A catalogue record for this book is available from the British Library

Library of Congress Catalog Card Number: 95-74624

∞ Printed on permanent acid-free text paper, manufactured in accordance with ANSI/NISO Z39.48-1992 and ANSI/NISO Z39.48-1984 (Permanence of Paper).

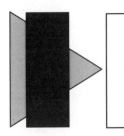

Contents

Preface

This book attempts to provide a bridge between two extremes: at one level of the subject we have the purely technical aspects of preparing group financial statements, at another we can find lofty academic dissertations that are written as if the real world did not exist. Somewhere in-between is the practical task of ensuring that the public are given useful information regarding the financial affairs of the most common form of entity in a modern economy: a group. The task of providing this information falls on the practitioner where the various technical and intellectual skills are developed through professional training and examinations.

As a subject, group accounts tends to appear in the final stages of most accounting courses and this might suggest it is an advanced and difficult topic. This is not so; there is a lot to learn but none of it is difficult. In any event it is wrong for any student (technician, professional or academic) to approach this subject as if it were little more than learning how to prepare the accounts. There is nothing complicated in the actual construction of group financial statements; the main problem is in making sense of the various conceptual and regulatory aspects of the subject.

Admittedly a fair part of this book is concerned with 'how to do it' but the methodology is constantly underpinned by the relevant concepts, objectives and accounting regulations at each stage of the subject. Since the introduction of the Companies Act 1989, and FRSs 1–7, the regulatory aspects of the subject are fairly well defined. We are now told what to do but do we understand why we are being told to do it? This questioning approach is essential if students are to develop sound professional judgement.

It seemed to me that students (particularly professional students) are not very well served by existing texts on this subject. There are books that concentrate on the mechanics of preparing the accounts. Some of these give the impression that the subject can be learned by memorizing a series of double-entry manoeuvres and are written as if the problems which the Accounting Standards Board has been trying to resolve do not exist. Then we have excellent books, such as UK GAAP (see 'Sources and Acknowledgements'), which provide the reader with well researched technical information together with practical and conceptual discussions but are not designed to instruct readers on the mechanics of preparing the accounts.

Between these two extremes there are a host of study manuals that provide excellent technical instruction based on current regulations and practice but which seem to do very little to nourish the intellectual development of their readers. This book attempts to fulfil that need.

The range of subjects covered is such that the entire book will meet the demands of the most advanced professional accounting syllabus. The sequence of chapters has been arranged so that the book can be adapted for any preliminary or intermediate syllabus. Some guidance on this is given in the section called 'Using the book'.

Roy Dodge
London

Sources and acknowledgements

The task of trying to make sense of all the concepts and regulations affecting group accounts would be almost impossible without some kind of reliable reference such as UK GAAP, written by authors from Ernst & Young and published by Macmillan Publishers Ltd. I have made several references to this book throughout the text and I constantly use it as a source of information when teaching the subject to professional students.

I also found the FRS Reviews published by KPMG Peat Marwick to be a useful source of guidance and have made textual references to them where appropriate.

Apart from these specific publications, my main sources of reference were the actual regulations, such as the Companies Act 1985 and the accounting standards published by the Accounting Standards Board. In some cases there are extracts from these regulations in an appendix to the chapter and in some cases the text of a chapter includes a summary of the relevant regulation. There are ample references in the text should readers wish to locate the actual wording of the regulations concerned if this has not been provided.

I am also most grateful to various examining bodies for permission to reproduce their examination questions. The bodies concerned are:

The Association of Accounting Technicians (AAT)
The Chartered Association of Certified Accountants (ACCA)
The Institute of Chartered Accountants in England and Wales (ICAEW)
The Chartered Institute of Bankers (CIB)
The Chartered Institute of Management Accountants (CIMA)

In many cases it was necessary to adapt the past questions set by these bodies because regulations affecting the subject had changed since the date that the questions were set. The answers to these questions as published in this book are my own responsibility and not those of the professional body concerned.

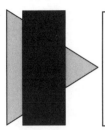

Abbreviations

The use of abbreviations when discussing the regulatory aspects of financial reporting has become so common that most readers of this book will not require any explanation of their meaning. In cases of doubt, the following list explains the abbreviations used.

ASB **Accounting Standards Board**. A subsidiary of the Financial Reporting Council. It is responsible for setting accounting standards in the UK.

ASC **Accounting Standards Committee**. A committee set up by the main accountancy bodies to develop accounting standards in the UK. This process was taken over by the ASB in 1990.

CA **Companies Act** (usually the Companies Act 1985).

FRS **Financial Reporting Standard**. Accounting standards issued by the ASB.

IAS **International Accounting Standard**. An accounting standard issued by the International Accounting Standards Committee.

SSAP **Statement of Standard Accounting Practice**. Accounting standards issued by the accountancy bodies following development by the former ASC. The extant SSAPs were adopted as accounting standards by the ASB at the time it came into existence. Some of them have since been revised or superseded.

UITF **Urgent Issues Task Force**. A sub-committee of the ASB. It considers issues that emerge from time to time and publishes accounting directions called *Abstracts*.

Abbreviations used to identify the source of various examination questions are given in the section called 'Sources and acknowledgements'.

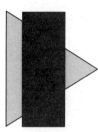

Using the book

1. Interactive learning

An interactive learning approach has been used throughout this book. The learning principles are the same as in my two previous books, *Foundations of Business Accounting* and *Foundations of Cost and Management Accounting*. Any readers who are new to this type of text will soon see how it works.

The activities within the text are not posed as a test of memory, they are an integral part of the learning process. They encourage you to become actively involved in discovering the principles by experimenting with figures or responding to thought provoking questions. The equivalent of feedback that tutors give during a live tutorial will be found in the key to the activites. This key has been placed at the end of each chapter in order to encourage you to make some attempt at each activity before referring to the feedback given.

In most cases the work that you do on each activity forms an essential link to the text which follows. It is important, therefore, that you clear each activity as you reach it, otherwise it might be difficult to make sense of the ensuing text. It does not matter if you make mistakes or your mind goes blank when working an activity. We all have these problems when trying to learn a new subject. The important point is to make an attempt before resorting to the key.

There is always somewhere for you to write down your response. This might be a space within the activity box or, in the case of financial statements, an outline format following the activity box. In many cases you will be developing your own illustrations which, in a traditional text book, are presented by the author. In some cases you might find it helpful to draft out your answer on a rough piece of paper before checking with the key and writing in the book.

2. Self-assessment questions

The questions at the end of each chapter provide additional practice at applying the principles. The questions are capable of being answered based on the material provided up to the end of the chapter concerned. In some cases, particularly at the end of Chapter 1, additional tutorial guidance is given in the question if this was considered to be necessary. Tutorial guidance is also provided in some of the answers and so you should think of the questions and answers as being a continuation of the learning process.

3. Reference material

There is an appendix to most chapters containing extracts from the regulations relating to the subject matter of that chapter. You will find that some of the activities require you to refer to these extracts. This is an attempt to simulate how an accountant has to work in practice. A practitioner does not know all the answers, but a practitioner is capable of locating the relevant regulations and forming a judgement on the matter being considered. Being able to interpret the relevant regulations is an important skill that accountancy students must develop.

Being asked to interpret an official regulation or guideline is an excellent way of learning but, as with all the best learning techniques, it does tend to slow down progress. In view of this, the instances where you are required to read the reference material have been kept to a minimum. In some cases a compromise approach has been used whereby the extracts from the regulations are included in the appendix but the text of the chapter contains an interpretation or paraphrase of the relevant points. In these cases students can refer to the actual wording should they wish to do so.

4. Adapting the book to your own syllabus

As mentioned in the Preface, the book covers the entire range of subjects demanded by even the most advanced of professional accounting syllabuses. The sequencing of chapters has been devised to enable students to find a suitable cut-off point for their own syllabus. In view of the diversity of these syllabuses, and the fact that they change from time to time, no attempt has been made to produce a schedule showing which chapters to read for which syllabus.

It should, however, be possible to correlate the chapter titles with the subject headings in your own syllabus. For example, a technician grade syllabus similar to the old AAT Final is covered by Chapters 1 to 3. Students preparing for the new Paper 10 in the ACCA syllabus should read the entire book with the exception of Chapters 9 and 10. These students should, however, study SSAP 20 on foreign currency transactions (the first part of Chapter 10) and also be aware of the impact on group accounts of a disposal (Chapter 9). Students preparing for the new Paper 13 should study the entire book and use their own judgement over skipping the subjects with which they are familiar. You must take care with this skipping though; some important conceptual matters (which tend to crop up in Paper 13) are covered in Chapter 2.

Allow something like 3 hours for the study of each chapter, plus additional commitment for working the end of chapter questions.

The conceptual and regulatory framework

1

Objectives

After completing this chapter you should be able to:

- explain the economic substance of a group and contrast this with its legal status;
- describe the objectives of group accounts as seen by accounting regulators;
- explain why the practice of preparing group accounts was developed, and why some companies attempted to avoid the regulations by setting up 'quasi-subsidiaries';
- demonstrate the effect of inter-company transactions;
- describe what is meant by equity accounting;
- summarize the accounting regulations that affect group accounts and outline their historical development;
- explain the circumstances in which the merger accounting method of consolidation is permitted;
- analyse the structure of a group.

Introduction

The mechanics of preparing group accounts are quite easy to learn providing you have a clear idea of the principles on which they are based. This chapter attempts to provide a basic framework of the concepts, principles and regulations that influence the accounting practice.

In order to find a starting point, I have made a few assumptions regarding prior knowledge. These include assumptions that you have some idea of what is meant by a group, and that you have a broad knowledge of the regulatory framework that affects financial reporting. If you have any difficulty with the abbreviations that are now a part of our everyday language on these regulations (such as: ASC, ASB, SSAP, FRS, and so on), they are explained on p. xi. Some of the comments in this chapter also assume that you know there are statutory regulations affecting the amount of profit available for distribution to shareholders, but it is not necessary to know the details of this legislation in order to appreciate the points covered.

Concepts, objectives and practices

The group concept

A group is not a separate legal person, it is a concept that treats a number of separate companies as a single entity for the purposes of financial reporting. Each company in 'the group' keeps its own accounting records and produces its own financial statements. It is not possible to enter into a legal contract with the group because it does not exist as a separate entity; contracts are made with individual companies in the group. A group is not a taxable person; corporation tax is levied on individual companies in the group although some tax provisions (such as those that deal with losses and advance corporation tax) recognize the economic reality of a group.

Activity 1.1

In January 1995 a radio reporter on a business news programme announced that 'the Dixons group will be paying an interim dividend of 1.8p per share'. There was nothing misleading in this statement but, in a technical sense, it was nonsense. Based on what you have read up to now, make a note here of why this statement does not make sense.

Each company in the group is responsible for payment of dividends to its own shareholders. If we think of the group as being owned by the shareholders of the parent company then any dividends paid to these shareholders will be paid by the parent company. Dividends paid by a subsidiary will be paid to whoever owns the shares in that company.

Throughout your studies on group accounts it is vital not to lose sight of the distinction between the individual companies in the group (each of which is a separate legal entity) and the group as a whole which is merely a concept. This is something which is so basic that it could be thought of as obvious, and yet it is easily forgotten when working on the techniques of consolidation.

Concepts and objectives of group accounts

Financial reporting practices are based mainly on conventions and regulations rather than on concepts. Accounting concepts are sometimes publicized by the regulatory bodies when a new accounting standard is being established but in many cases we have no choice other than to discuss concepts and objectives in the light of practices already established.

This state of affairs certainly exists in the case of group accounts. When these accounts were first prepared in the UK (round about the 1930s) it is unlikely that they were the result of any serious thought on accounting concepts. Accountants simply worked out a practical way of doing things. Even the idea of establishing a clear objective for these accounts seems to have had a shaky start. Earlier text books show that the objectives ranged from the naïve, such as 'being a good idea', through to more concrete suggestions, such as:

- to amplify the information contained in the accounts of the parent company; or
- to portray the financial affairs of a group as if it were a single entity.

Today, the objectives of group accounts are given official status in the accounting standard known as: _FRS 2: Accounting for subsidiary undertakings._ This standard describes the objectives of the FRS and the objectives of consolidated financial statements. It also includes several definitions, including paragraph 5 which states what is meant by consolidation. The objectives and some of the definitions in FRS 2, together with an extract from the Companies Act 1985, are set out in the appendix to this chapter.

Activity 1.2

Read paragraphs 1 and 5 of FRS 2 (and the Companies Act extract) as set out in the appendix and make a note here of the objective of consolidated financial statements as seen by the regulators.

Despite the apparent clarity of this objective it is riddled with conceptual problems. For example, how do we look at the so-called single economic entity? Do we look at it through the eyes of those who own shares in the parent company? Or do we look at the group as a single economic entity that has various ownership interests, including people who own shares in the subsidiaries other than the parent company? Should we ignore ownership interests altogether and simply look at the total entity?

Various concepts have been identified that help to explain these different viewpoints (such as the **entity concept** and the **proprietary concept**) but it will be difficult for beginners to see how these result in different figures without relating them to established practices. Since these different ways of looking at a group are more relevant when the group includes **partly owned** subsidiaries, a detailed discussion will be postponed until Chapter 2.

The discussion of concepts in relation to group accounts seems to be relatively new. If we look at text books written by respected accounting academics as late as 1980, we find virtually no discussion of concepts specific to group accounts. We can find discussions of the different methods of consolidation, such as the acquisition (or purchase) method and the merger (or pooling) method but that was as far as any kind of intellectual discourse had progressed. The difference between these two methods will become apparent by the time you reach the end of Chapter 5.

Group accountability

The modern practice of preparing consolidated financial statements probably grew out of a need to combat creative accounting devices that were being practised during the 1920s. It is quite easy to imagine that without any rules on consolidation, some transactions could have been hidden from the eyes of shareholders by conducting them through the medium of a wholly owned subsidiary. Even if this speculation is unfounded (and accounting historians will find it difficult to refute the idea) you should be aware that despite many years of accounting regulations, our present regulators are still struggling to prevent companies from devising schemes that are aimed at avoiding the requirement to consolidate the results of two or more separate entities.

The main problem stems from the definition of a subsidiary. This is important because if a parent company and subsidiary company relationship exists, the financial accounts of the subsidiary must be consolidated with those of the parent company in order to present financial statements that reflect the combined operations of the group. If the relationship between two entities can be constructed in such a way as to fall outside the scope of the legal definition of a group, the requirement to consolidate the results of each entity can be avoided. Despite a number of attempts by the regulators to define subsidiaries, some companies continue to find ways of establishing separate entities that escape being classed as subsidiaries under these regulations. Entities of this type are known as **quasi-subsidiaries**.

A quasi-subsidiary is usually established to hide certain types of transaction that would otherwise be included in the reporting company's own accounts. The latest initiative taken by the Accounting Standards Board (ASB) to combat this problem is contained in an accounting standard known as *FRS 5: Reporting the substance of transactions.* This standard defines a quasi-subsidiary and requires the results of such a company to be consolidated with those of the reporting entity. This particular aspect is discussed more fully in Chapter 11 of this book. In the meantime, you will appreciate why consolidated accounts were originally thought to be necessary by considering a highly contrived example.

Assume that a new company, A Ltd, is formed and raises funds of £100 000 through the issue of ordinary shares. A Ltd does not use the £100 000 cash for acquiring physical assets such as plant and stocks; instead, another company called B Ltd is formed and A Ltd pays the whole of the £100 000 to B Ltd in exchange for the shares issued by that company. The directors of B Ltd are the same people as the directors of A Ltd.

At this stage the balance sheet of A Ltd will be as follows:

Investment in B Ltd at cost	£100 000
Share capital	£100 000

B Ltd used the whole of the £100 000 received from A Ltd for investment in plant and machinery. The following is a summary of the financial transactions that occurred during the first year of trading:

1. B Ltd made a profit of £30 000. This was derived from sales of £300 000 less operating costs of £270 000. Operating costs included directors' salaries of £40 000.
2. B Ltd paid dividends to A Ltd of £10 000.
3. A Ltd incurred operating expenses of £8000.
4. All transactions were on a cash basis and so any retained profits are represented by an increase in the cash resources of each company.

For the sake of clarity in the explanation, taxation and depreciation will be ignored.

Activity 1.3

Prepare the separate financial statements of A Ltd based on the above information. Use the outline formats below this box. Remember that you are simply looking at the transactions of A Ltd as an individual company.

A Ltd: *profit and loss account for the year*

£

* Dividends received
  Expenses _____
  Profit ========

A Ltd: *balance sheet at the end of the year*

Investment in B Ltd
Cash at bank _____
========

Share capital
Profit and loss account _____
========

B Ltd would produce financial statements as follows:

Profit and loss account

	£
Turnover	300 000
Operating costs	270 000
Profit	30 000
Dividends paid	10 000
Profit retained	20 000

Balance sheet

	£
Plant and machinery	100 000
Cash at bank	20 000
	120 000
Share capital	100 000
Profit and loss account	20 000
	120 000

The shareholders of A Ltd would not see these accounts because the financial statements of B Ltd are presented to its sole shareholder, A Ltd. There is no doubt that the shareholders of A Ltd are being misled by this separation of trading activities. The assets of their own company show an increase of £2000 over the year whereas the combined assets of the group have increased by £22 000 (£20 000 in B Ltd and £2000 in A Ltd). Moreover, the shareholders in A Ltd have not been informed that the directors of their company were paid £40 000 as remuneration by B Ltd.

If we think of the two separate companies as being a singly entity we will find that combined assets owned by the group have a book value of £122 000, as follows:

	£
Plant and machinery at cost	100 000
Cash balance in B Ltd	20 000
Cash balance in A Ltd	2 000
	122 000

The investment owned by A Ltd (shown at a cost of £100 000 in A Ltd's balance sheet) is not an asset of 'the group'. It would be an asset of the group if it were an investment in a company outside of the group but this is not the case here; it is an inter-company shareholding.

The combined profit of the two companies for the year is £22 000. This is represented by the profit of £30 000 made by B Ltd less A Ltd's expenses of £8000. If we were to produce a consolidated profit and loss account, it would be on the following lines:

	£
Sales	300 000
Operating costs (£270 000 + £8000)	278 000
Group profit	22 000

Since none of this profit has been paid to the shareholders of A Ltd, the full amount of £22 000 has been retained by the group. The dividend of £10 000 paid by B Ltd is not a dividend of the group because it was paid to another company (A Ltd) within the group. Inter-company dividends are a means of transferring some of the profit from one company in the group to another; they do not represent a distribution of profit to shareholders outside of the group.

The above discussion gives an insight into the basic mechanics of preparing consolidated financial statements. The two separate companies are considered to be a single economic entity. In order to reflect the operating results and financial position of this single (albeit artificial) entity in so far as it concerns users outside of the group, it is necessary to cancel out inter-company shareholdings and inter-company transactions.

Accounting regulations require the directors of A Ltd to provide its shareholders with consolidated financial statements of the group in addition to its own financial statements. In the case which we have been discussing, the consolidated balance sheet will be on the following lines:

Consolidated balance sheet at the end of the year

	£
Plant and machinery	100 000
Cash at bank (£20 000 + £2000)	22 000
	122 000
Share capital	100 000
Profit and loss account	22 000
	122 000

As you can see, this presents a somewhat different picture to that given by the separate accounts of A Ltd as an individual company. In addition, the notes to the consolidated financial statements would have to disclose the fact that the directors of A Ltd received remuneration of £40 000 (although the fact that this was paid by B Ltd does not have to be mentioned).

Equity accounting

The type of balance sheet outlined in the previous section is derived from the objective of presenting the financial information of a group as if it were a single economic entity. If the objective were merely to 'amplify the information contained in the accounts of the parent company', a different approach to preparing the financial statements for A Ltd could have been taken. Various methods other than consolidation have been devised for preparing group accounts and one of these, known as **equity accounting**, is now required by statute for certain types of investment, including investments in certain types of subsidiary whose results are not consolidated in the normal way.

In particular, equity accounting is required for investments in companies known as **associated companies**. A substantial investment in another company which is not a subsidiary might have to be treated as an investment in an associated company. For example, an investment that represents 40% of the equity shares in another company is unlikely to be classed as an investment in a subsidiary but it is likely to be classified as an investment in an associated company. This subject is covered in Chapter 3. Equity accounting is also required when certain types of subsidiary company are excluded from consolidation. A discussion of which companies can (or must) be excluded from consolidation is dealt with in Chapter 11.

The idea of equity accounting received official recognition following the publication off *SSAP 1: Accounting for associated companies* in 1971, but it had been used by some companies as a basis for preparing group accounts much earlier. The requirement for group accounts in the UK to be in the form of consolidated accounts did not apply until SSAP 14 was issued in 1978. The underlying approach to equity accounting is to recognize that an investment in the equity shares of another company provides the investor with an interest in the net assets of that company. The value of this equity interest will change as time progresses. If the investee company earns and retains profits, the net assets of the investee will increase and so the equity interest of the investor will increase. Under equity accounting, the carrying value of the investment in the investor's balance sheet should reflect its current equity value.

The investor will account for the increase in the equity value between two accounting dates by including a share of the investee's profit in its own profit and loss account. This share of profits is based on the proportion of equity shares owned and is substituted for any dividends received from the investee. Dividends received from the investee have the effect of increasing the tangible assets of the investor and decreasing the equity value of the investment (the investee's assets are reduced when dividends are paid). Since dividends received merely change the composition of the investor's assets, they are not included in the profit reported by the investor when equity accounting is used.

If equity accounting had been applied to the situation described in 1.3 above, the financial statements of A Ltd (as an individual company) would have been presented to its shareholders as follows:

Profit and loss account of A Ltd

	£
Share of profits of subsidiary (100% × £30 000)	30 000
Less expenses (incurred by A Ltd)	8 000
	22 000

Balance sheet of A Ltd

	£
Investment in B Ltd at equity value:	
Share of net assets (100% × £120 000)	120 000
Cash at bank (A Ltd)	2 000
	122 000

	£
Share capital	100 000
Profit and loss account	22 000
	122 000

Although these figures give more information than the individual accounts of A Ltd when equity accounting is not used, they do not show the composition of the group's assets. The equity value of the investment (shown as a single figure of £120 000) is represented by plant of £100 000 and cash at bank of £20 000. A further criticism of equity accounting is related to the concept of prudence. The above financial statements are presented as the financial statements of A Ltd (not an artificial entity known as a group) and as such they include profits that have not actually been realized by A Ltd. These profits will not be realized by A Ltd until they are paid to A Ltd by B Ltd as a dividend. This criticism is still valid when it comes to considering equity accounting for associated companies, but this will be discussed in Chapter 3.

In the meantime you might be able to see why this criticism does not apply to group accounts that are prepared as consolidated accounts. The problem of identifying realized profits is usually related to the statutory regulations that require dividends to be paid out of realized profits. But these regulations relate to individual companies; they cannot relate to a group because a group (as stated previously) is an artificial entity. Since a group does not exist as a separate legal entity it cannot pay dividends.

We usually think of the shareholders of the parent company as being the shareholders of the group, but any dividends paid to these shareholders are paid by the parent company. It is the position in the parent company's accounts that must be considered when calculating the amount of realized profits available for distribution, not the figures produced by a memorandum exercise of combining the results of several companies.

Activity 1.4

The terms 'group accounts' and 'consolidated accounts' are sometimes used (somewhat carelessly) as synonyms. State why these two terms do not necessarily mean the same thing.

Preview of the regulatory framework

The device of operating a total entity through the medium of a parent company and subsidiary companies has existed in the UK since the 1920s (some 30 years earlier in the USA). The first requirements in the UK for companies to prepare group accounts were made by the London Stock Exchange in 1939 as a condition of listing. The first statutory requirements for group accounts were made in the Companies Act 1947, later consolidated into the Companies Act 1948.

The basic legal position on group accounts did not change very much between 1948 and 1989. The provisions in the Companies Act 1948 allowed group accounts to be in a form other than consolidated accounts but (as stated earlier) an accounting standard was issued in 1978 (SSAP 14) requiring group accounts to be prepared as consolidated accounts. The publication of SSAP 14 was justified at the time on the grounds that an international standard (IAS 3) had been published in 1976 requiring group accounts to be in the form of consolidated accounts.

Historical events eventually required SSAP 14 to be withdrawn in July 1992 when it was replaced by FRS 2. There were very few rules on consolidation principles in SSAP 14 although there were some that attempted to codify practices when investments in subsidiaries were acquired or sold during the year. The approach taken by SSAP 14 on the basic consolidation process was to assume that accountants already knew what to do (an explanatory note stated the procedures were 'well understood'). Unfortunately, this left several aspects open to interpretation.

Acquisition and merger accounting

There was one important change in company law before 1989 that affected the legality of a method of consolidation known as 'merger accounting'. The two main methods for preparing consolidated accounts are usually called **acquisition accounting** and **merger accounting**. You need not worry too much about the difference between these two methods at the moment; you will soon discover the difference as your studies progress. Prior to 1980 some companies in the UK had been preparing group accounts by using the merger method but this practice was deemed to be illegal following a case that came before the courts in 1980 (see Chapter 5 for more details).

Since merger accounting was considered to be an appropriate method of consolidation in certain cases, the government introduced regulations in the Companies Act 1981 which had the effect of removing this illegality when certain conditions were satisfied. This was followed by an accounting standard *SSAP 23: Accounting for acquisitions and mergers*, issued by the former Accounting Standards Committee in 1985. This SSAP included rules to ensure that merger accounting was confined to particular forms of business combination. Similar (but not identical) rules were later introduced into company law by the Companies Act 1989.

However, some companies found ways of flouting these qualifying rules so that subsidiaries could be consolidated by using merger accounting in situations that were at odds with those intended by the regulators. Consequently, the ASB replaced SSAP 23 with *FRS 6: Acquisitions and Mergers* in September 1994. This new standard takes a conceptual approach to the qualifying conditions for merger accounting rather than prescribing a number of specific rules.

In general terms, merger accounting is considered to be an appropriate method of consolidation when the shareholders of a subsidiary become shareholders of the parent company as a result of a share for share exchange (i.e. shareholders in the subsidiary have accepted shares in the parent company in exchange for their shares in the subsidiary). FRS 6 requires this to have been the result of a genuine combination of interests rather than a take-over. In most cases the amount paid for the subsidiary's shares will include something other than shares in the parent company, such as cash. Even if the consideration consists entirely of shares in the parent company, the arrangement will often be seen as an acquisition (a take-over) rather than a merger. The practical effect of this is that the consolidated accounts for most group relationships must be based on acquisition accounting. Throughout most of this book, the principles of consolidation are based on the acquisition method. The merger accounting method is dealt with in Chapter 5.

Activity 1.5

Puffedup plc eventually acquired the entire share capital of Squeaky plc on a share for share exchange. The board of Squeaky plc were hostile to the original terms offered by Puffedup plc and sought competitive bids from other interested companies. As a result of this, Puffedup plc increased its original offer of 1 Puffedup share for 4 Squeaky shares by offering 1 Puffedup share for 3 Squeaky shares.

State whether Puffedup plc will be able to consolidate the accounts of Squeaky plc by using the merger method of accounting.

Changes since 1989

Apart from the rules on merger accounting, the Companies Act 1989 included a substantial amount of law on all aspects of group accounts. This Act implemented the provisions of the EC Seventh Directive which had been issued in 1983 in order to harmonize accounting practices on groups throughout all member states. The main impact of the 1989 legislation on UK practices stemmed from a wider definition of a subsidiary.

These changes to company law took place at a time when the procedure for setting accounting standards was also changing. By 1990 the old Accounting Standards Committee (ASC) had been replaced by the Accounting Standards Board (ASB). At the time when the ASB took over the standard setting process, the extant SSAPs relating to group accounts were out of line with the 1989 legislation and in order to rectify this the ASB issued an interim statement on group accounts in December 1990. This was followed by a specific standard (FRS 2) in July 1992 which replaced SSAP 14. Unlike previous regulations, both FRS 2 and the Companies Act 1989 contain many specific rules affecting the way that consolidated accounts are prepared.

As you can see from the above outline, the existing rules and regulations on group accounts have been built up piecemeal over a long period of time. Unfortunately, these regulations are not all in one place and during your study of group accounts it will be necessary to refer to a number of regulatory documents. The following is a list of the more important sources that will be covered as you progress through this book.

- Companies Act 1985 as amended by the Companies Act 1989
- SSAP 1: *Accounting for associated companies* (originally issued in 1971 but subject to a number of later revisions)
- FRS 2: *Accounting for subsidiary undertakings* (issued in 1992)
- SSAP 20: *Foreign currency translation* (issued in 1983)
- SSAP 22: *Accounting for goodwill* (issued in 1984 and revised in 1989)
- FRS 5: *Reporting the substance of transactions* (issued in April 1994)
- FRS 6: *Acquisitions and mergers* (issued September 1994 to replace SSAP 23)
- FRS 7: *Fair values in acquisition accounting* (issued September 1994)

Some of the provisions in the following two accounting standards will also have to be studied:

- FRS 3: *Reporting financial performance*
- FRS 4: *Capital instruments*

In addition to studying the relevant aspects of the regulations listed above, we will have to review some of the proposals contained in Exposure Drafts (EDs and FREDs). These documents deal with a number of issues on group accounts which, at the time of writing this edition, have not been resolved.

Try not to be discouraged by what might seem like a daunting task. You will be learning the principles and regulations in a series of logical and gentle steps. This is a subject that requires patience rather than a superior intellect.

An outline of group structures

Until we reach Chapter 11 we are going to assume that a subsidiary company is one in which more than 50% of its ordinary share capital is owned by a parent company. If one company owns more than 50% of the ordinary shares of another company it is possible for the company that owns the investment to control the affairs of the company in which the investment has been made. This is because a holding of more than 50% of the ordinary shares in a company enables the investor to pass resolutions regarding the composition of the board of directors of that company. The ability of one company to control another creates a parent company and subsidiary relationship.

The most basic of all groups will consist of a parent company with one direct subsidiary. This type of group will be used as a learning model and can be represented by Figure 1.1.

The rules for consolidating the accounts of these two companies are relatively easy to learn. In practice, the parent company is likely to have more than one direct subsidiary and this kind of group can be represented by Figure 1.2.

The principles of consolidation in this case are no different to when there is one direct subsidiary. The only impact is that the amount of accounting work is increased. In some cases we might find that one subsidiary owns a controlling interest in the ordinary shares of another company. In this case the group can be represented by Figure 1.3.

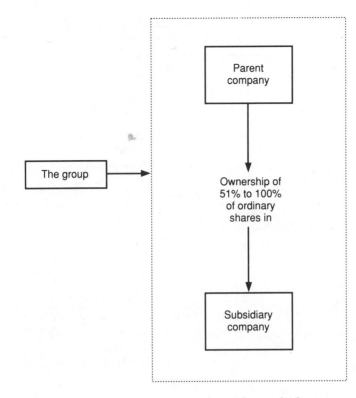

Figure 1.1 Group structure: parent company with one direct subsidiary

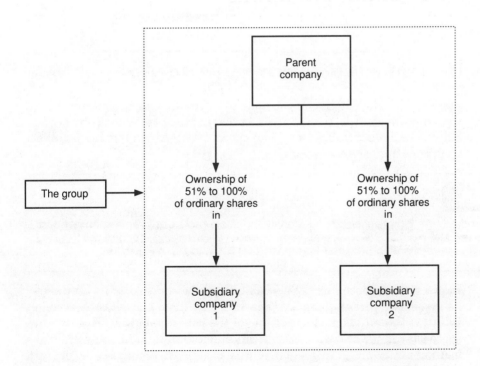

Figure 1.2 Group structure: parent company with more than one direct subsidiary

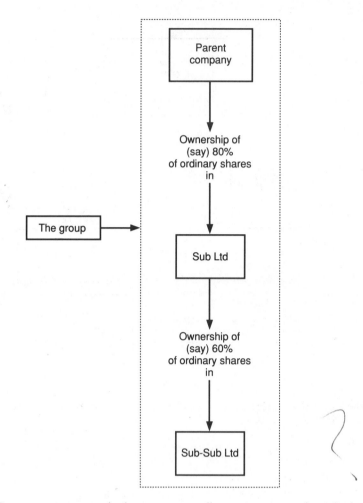

Figure 1.3 Group structure: one subsidiary owns controlling interest in another subsidiary ✗

In this case, the parent company has no direct interest in Sub-Sub Ltd but this company must be treated as a subsidiary of the parent company because Sub-Sub Ltd is controlled by a company (Sub Ltd) which is under the direct control of the parent company.

Activity 1.6

We have used the term 'direct subsidiary' to identify the relationship between the parent company and Sub Ltd. Make a guess (if you do no know already) at identifying the term which is used when explaining the relationship between Parent Ltd and Sub-Sub Ltd in Figure 1.3.

In practice, the accounts of Sub-Sub Ltd will be consolidated with those of its immediate parent company (Sub Ltd) and these consolidated accounts will then be consolidated with those of the parent company. This two-step approach cannot be used in examination questions and so you will learn a method in Chapter 8 (devised purely for examination purposes) to get over this problem.

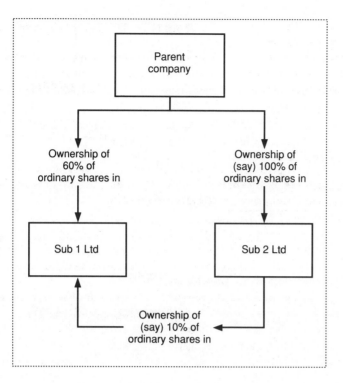

Figure 1.4 Group structure: cross-holding (one direct subsidiary owns shares in another direct subsidiary)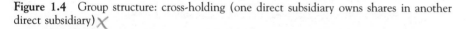

There is nothing to prevent one direct subsidiary from owning shares in another direct subsidiary. This creates what is known as a cross-holding and the relationships can be depicted by Figure 1.4.

In the above case, the parent company has a direct interest of 60% in Sub 1 Ltd and an indirect interest in that company that arises through its control of Sub 2 Ltd. The techniques for dealing with this kind of situation are also dealt with in Chapter 8.

As you can imagine, the above illustrations are merely outlines of the different types of relationship that can exist in a group. In practice, most groups are quite complex and are often a permutation of these relationships. In addition, most parent companies also own investments in companies that are classified as associated companies (as mentioned on p. 8). In these cases the results of the associated company must also be consolidated with those of the group by using the equity method of accounting.

Summary

The main learning points in this chapter can be summarized as follows:

- a group is not a separate legal entity, it is a concept devised for the purposes of financial reporting;

- a group does not pay dividends because a group does not exist as a separate entity;
- group accounts are a single set of financial statements that present information about the group as if it were a single entity;
- group accounts must be in the form of consolidated accounts;
- the definition of a quasi-subsidiary in FRS 5 should help to eliminate the practice of setting up separate entities that fall outside the legal definition of a subsidiary in order to avoid the need to consolidate the results of that entity;
- equity accounting is a modified form of consolidation in which the investment in another company is carried in the balance sheet of the investing company at its equity value;
- equity values are based on a proportion of net assets of the investee company according to the proportion of equity shares owned;
- changes in equity value between two reporting dates are accounted for by including a proportion of the investee's profits or losses in the investor's own profit and loss account;
- the problem of distributable profit does not apply to groups because a group is an artificial entity and does not pay dividends;
- the regulatory framework for group accounts is spread over a large number of separate accounting standards, combined with many detailed regulations in the Companies Act 1985 that were introduced by the Companies Act 1989;
- the two main methods of preparing consolidated accounts are known as acquisition accounting and merger accounting;
- FRS 6 has confined the circumstances in which merger accounting will be permitted;
- group structures can take various forms and a group can include subsidiaries in which the ultimate parent company has no direct interest;
- the mechanics of consolidation are quite easy providing the basic concepts and principles are well understood.

Key to activities

Activity 1.1

Because a group does not exist as a separate legal entity it cannot pay dividends. The reporter was referring to the interim dividend being paid by the parent company of the group.

Activity 1.2

To present financial information of a group as if it were a single entity.

Activity 1.3

A Ltd: *profit and loss account for the year*

	£
Dividends received	10 000
Expenses	8 000
Profit	2 000

A Ltd: *balance sheet at the end of the year*

	£
Investment in B Ltd	100 000
Cash at bank	2 000
	102 000
Share capital	100 000
Profit and loss account	2 000
	102 000

Activity 1.4

Group accounts could be in one of several forms; consolidated accounts is one of these (and is the form required by regulations).

Activity 1.5

Probably not. Although the former shareholders of Squeaky plc are now shareholders in Puffedup plc, the combination will be seen to have resulted from a take-over rather than a merger of interests.

Activity 1.6

Indirect subsidiary.

Appendix

Extracts from FRS 2 (published December 1992)

Objective

1. The objective of this FRS is to require parent undertakings to provide financial information about the economic activities of their groups by preparing consolidated financial statements. These statements are intended to present financial information about a parent undertaking and its subsidiary undertakings as a single economic entity to show

the economic resources controlled by the group, the obligations of the group and the results the group achieves with its resources.

Definitions (extracts)

4. *Consolidated financial statements*
The financial statements of a group prepared by consolidation.

5. *Consolidation*
The process of adjusting and combining financial information from the individual financial statements of a parent undertaking and its subsidiary undertakings to prepare consolidated financial statements that present financial information for the group as a single economic entity.

9. *Group*
A parent undertaking and its subsidiary undertakings.

Note: legislation does not normally state its objectives but the following extract from the Companies Act 1985 does help to confirm the objectives and nature of group accounts:

Extract from Schedule 4A, Companies Act 1985 — Form and Content of Group Accounts (introduced by Companies Act 1989)

1(1)   Group accounts shall comply so far as practicable with the provisions of Schedule 4 as if the undertakings included in the consolidation ("the group") were a single company.

Questions

Past examination questions that could be included here will not help much with the learning process; most of them can be answered by repeating blocks of text from the chapter. The following questions are intended to be an extension of the learning process and most of them include explanatory text that does not normally appear in examination questions.

Questions for self-assessment

Answers to self-assessment questions are given at the end of the book.

1.1 Group structures

Statutory accounting regulations require a parent company to publish its own financial statements together with the financial statements of the group. These two sets of financial statements are normally presented in a single annual report. In the case of the balance sheets, the usual form of presentation is to show figures for the parent company and the group in adjacent columns.

The following is an extract from page 35 of the annual report of Imperial Chemical Industries PLC (ICI) for 1992 which shows how ICI has presented information on fixed assets in the balance sheets for the group and the parent company (the column headed 'Company' relates to the parent company). Comparative figures have been excluded for the sake of clarity.

Balance sheets

At 31 December	Notes	Group 1992 £m	Company 1992 £m
Assets employed			
fixed assets			
Tangible assets	12	5634	353
Investments			
Subsidiary undertakings	13		5800
Participating interests	14	455	255
		6089	6408

Required

(a) Write a short explanation for someone who has not been trained in accounting that will help them to understand why the balance sheet for the company shows £5800 m invested in subsidiaries and yet the corresponding amount shown in the group balance sheet is nil.

(b) Note 14 shows that most of the £255 m invested in participating interests by the company represents investments in associated undertakings that are being carried at cost. This note also shows that most of the £455 m invested in participating interests by the group is represented by investments in associated undertakings. There are many factors that account for the difference between these two figures but from your study of this chapter you should be able to identify two. Make a note of two factors that might account for the difference in the two carrying values.

(c)   The balance sheet for the ICI group at 31 December 1992 shows that £302 m of the group's net assets are attributable to what are called 'minority interests'. State what you think this term means (it was not explained in the chapter but you can probably derive an explanation from the text on group structures).

1.2 Significant investments

Schedule 5 of the Companies Act 1985 (paragraphs 7 to 9) requires companies to disclose information regarding significant investments in undertakings **other than subsidiary undertakings**. That information does not have to be given if the investment is presented in the accounts by means of the equity method of accounting.

A significant investment is defined as one that:

- amounts to 10% or more of the nominal value of any class of share, or
- the carrying value exceeds one-tenth of the investing company's assets.

The information that must be disclosed regarding each investment is as follows:

- the name of the undertaking;
- the country of incorporation, and if this is Great Britain, whether it is registered in England and Wales or in Scotland;
- if it is unincorporated, the principal place of business;
- the identity, and proportion of the nominal value, of each class of share held.

Required

Review the legal provisions outlined above and explain why the information disclosed for significant investments (other than subsidiaries or investments dealt with by the equity method of accounting) might be relevant to a user of the accounts.

1.3 Shareholder voting control

The Companies Act 1985 describes various situations where the relationship between two companies must be treated as that of a parent and a subsidiary. One of these is:

'An undertaking is a parent undertaking in relation to another undertaking, a subsidiary undertaking, if it holds a majority of the voting rights in the undertaking…' (Section 258).

Holding a majority of the shareholders' voting power is the most common way in which one company is able to control another. Shareholder voting rights are usually attached to the ordinary shares, although there can be different classes of ordinary shares with different voting rights for each class. The following details are based on part of a question in Paper 10 the ACCA examinations for June 1994.

The share capital of Fortran plc consists of the following:

Ordinary £1 shares class 'A'	£6 000 000
Ordinary £1 shares class 'B'	£4 000 000
	£10 000 000

Holders of 'A' ordinary shares are assigned one vote per share and holders of 'B' ordinary shares are assigned two votes per share.

On 1 April 1993 Jasmin (Holdings) plc acquired 80% of Fortran's 'A' ordinary shares and 10% of the 'B' ordinary shares. The 'A' ordinary shares and 'B' ordinary shares carry equal rights to share in the company's profits and losses.

Required

(a) Produce a calculation to establish whether or not Fortran plc should be treated as a subsidiary of Jasmin (Holdings) plc based on the information provided.

(b) Write brief notes on any factors you consider appropriate to the way that Jasmin (Holdings) plc should account for its investment in Fortran plc.

Questions without answers

Answers to these questions are published separately in the *Teacher's Manual*.

1.4 Users
Consolidated accounts are prepared primarily for the parent company's shareholders.

Required

Discuss whether you consider that consolidated accounts provide useful information to bankers and creditors. Your discussion should extend to two or three paragraphs.

1.5 Consolidated figures
The following list gives details of certain items that appear in the individual financial statements of a parent company and its wholly owned subsidiary:

	Parent	Subsidiary
1. Closing stock in the balance sheets	£2000	£4000

The stock of the subsidiary includes items that were purchased from the parent company at a price of £500. The transfer price charged by the parent company was based on cost plus a mark-up of 25%

2. Turnover in the profit and loss accounts	£8 000 000	£2 000 000

The turnover of the parent company includes sales of £500 000 to the subsidiary

3. Inter-company balances in the balance sheet

Amount due from subsidiary	£10 000 debit	
Amount due to parent		£10 000 credit

4. Investment income in the profit and loss accounts:

Dividends received from subsidiary	£20 000	
Dividends from other investments	£5 000	£1 000

Neither company has investments in associated undertakings

5. Dividends paid in the profit and loss accounts   £80 000   £20 000

6. Investments at cost in the balance sheets

Investment in subsidiary	£500 000	
Other fixed asset investments	£100 000	£20 000

7. Called up share capital

    £1 ordinary shares   £1 000 000   £300 000

8. Plant and machinery at cost   £400 000   £50 000

The plant of the parent company includes an item purchased from the subsidiary at a price of £22 000. The transfer price charged by the subsidiary was based on cost plus a mark-up of 10%.

Required

For each class of item listed, state the amount that should be disclosed in the consolidated financial statements according to the concepts and principles discussed in this chapter. Add a brief note to explain why you consider each amount appropriate. **(It is recognized that some items in this question require the application of principles which have not been fully discussed in the chapter. In these cases it is sufficient to make an intelligent guess.)**

2 ▶ Acquisition accounting

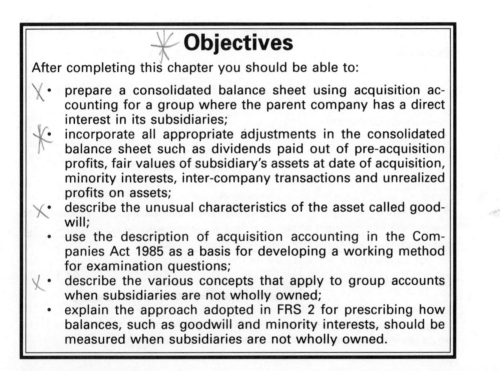

✳ Objectives

After completing this chapter you should be able to:

- prepare a consolidated balance sheet using acquisition accounting for a group where the parent company has a direct interest in its subsidiaries;
- incorporate all appropriate adjustments in the consolidated balance sheet such as dividends paid out of pre-acquisition profits, fair values of subsidiary's assets at date of acquisition, minority interests, inter-company transactions and unrealized profits on assets;
- describe the unusual characteristics of the asset called goodwill;
- use the description of acquisition accounting in the Companies Act 1985 as a basis for developing a working method for examination questions;
- describe the various concepts that apply to group accounts when subsidiaries are not wholly owned;
- explain the approach adopted in FRS 2 for prescribing how balances, such as goodwill and minority interests, should be measured when subsidiaries are not wholly owned.

Introduction

The most common method of preparing consolidated accounts is called **acquisition accounting.** You will appreciate the origins of this term in a moment. In order to discover the basic mechanics of acquisition accounting you will be working through a series of activities based on the abbreviated balance sheets of two companies. The circumstances will be constantly changed in order to build up a series of learning points. This is essentially a practical chapter but the various techniques are underpinned by references to concepts (particularly on pp. 40–42, below, on partly owned subsidiaries) and to the relevant accounting regulations.

Wholly owned subsidiary

The basic process

The balance sheets of two companies are set out below. At the time of preparing these balance sheets the two companies were not connected in any way.

	Company A		Company B	
	£	£	£	£
Tangible fixed assets		30 000		9 000
Current assets	25 000		3 000	
Current liabilities	11 000		2 000	
		14 000		1 000
		44 000		10 000
Ordinary share capital		35 000		7 000
Profit and loss reserve		9 000		3 000
		44 000		10 000

Company A wishes to acquire the business owned by Company B. There are two ways in which Company A could do this. It could either make an offer to purchase the business from Company B, or it could make an offer to the shareholders of Company B to acquire their shares.

In the first activity, we will assume that Company A decides to acquire the business by making an offer to Company B to purchase its net assets. For the sake of simplicity we will also assume that the net current assets of Company B do not include any cash or bank balances. Since cash balances would be retained by the seller, this assumption allows us to see what happens if the entire set of assets and liabilities in the above balance sheet of Company B are acquired by Company A.

Activity 2.1

Assume that Company B agrees to transfer its assets and liabilities to Company A at a price equal to the book value of £10 000. Company A pays cash of £10 000 to Company B. Assume that the current assets of Company A include sufficient cash to make this payment.

There are no group accounts to prepare as a result of this transaction because there is no group. Company A has simply exchanged £10 000 cash for the assets and liabilities of Company B which have a net book value of £10 000.

Construct the balance sheet of Company A to show its position immediately following this acquisition. Use the outline format shown below this box.

Balance sheet of Company A following the acquisition of Company B's assets and liabilities

Tangible fixed assets		£
Current assets	£	
Current liabilities	£	
	———	
		———
		═══
Share capital		£
Profit and loss reserve		£
		———
		═══

Following the acquisition, Company B will have no operating assets. Its only asset is £10 000 cash. It can either go into liquidation and pay this cash to the shareholders, or it can use the money to start up (or buy) another business.

You will notice that the transaction dealt with in this activity did not involve Company A in purchasing the profits previously earned by Company B. This might seem like an odd comment to make but you will see the point of making it in a moment. The reason why the comment seems odd is because it is quite easy to see how assets can be acquired (and liabilities taken over) but the term 'profits' does not refer to any particular thing that can be purchased; it is merely an accounting description of a source of funds that contributes to the creation of assets. It is possible to purchase assets that will produce profits in the future, but it is not possible to purchase past profits that helped to create those assets in the first place. In terms of group accounting we refer to the profits earned by a subsidiary prior to acquisition as **pre-acquisition** profits.

In the next activity we will assume that instead of paying the £10 000 to Company B the money is offered to the shareholders of Company B. As a result of the offer, all shareholders in Company B agree to sell their shares to Company A. After completing the transaction, Company A owns 100% of the shares in Company B at a cost of £10 000.

Activity 2.2

Construct the balance sheet of Company A following the purchase of these shares. Keep in mind that Company A has not purchased any assets from Company B; it has made an investment by purchasing the shares in another company. The cash paid has been exchanged for an investment. Use the outline format provided below this box.

Balance sheet of Company A

Fixed asset investments:

Investment in Company B Ltd at cost		£
Tangible fixed assets		£
		————
Current assets	£	
Current liabilities	£	
	———	
		————
		════
Share capital		
Profit and loss account reserve		
		————
		════

In this case, the only thing that needs to be done in the books of Company B is to change the name of the shareholder in the register of members. The entire share capital is now owned by Company A whereas previously it was owned by a number of individuals. Company B continues to exist and operate as a separate company with its own operating assets. We have reached a point where there are two companies in existence, and whose separate balance sheets are as follows:

		Company A £		Company B £
Fixed asset investments:				
Investment in Company B at cost		10 000		—
Tangible fixed assets		30 000		9 000
Current assets	15 000		3 000	
Current liabilities	11 000		2 000	
	————	4 000	————	1 000
		44 000		10 000
		════		════
Ordinary share capital		35 000		7 000
Profit and loss reserve		9 000		3 000
		44 000		10 000
		════		════

Company A now owns a controlling interest in Company B. It can appoint and remove the directors of Company B and, in this particular example, it could even pass a resolution to put Company B into voluntary liquidation. Company B has become a subsidiary of Company A and a group exists. In these circumstances the accounting regulation require Company A to produce a consolidated balance sheet of the group in addition to its own financial statements. Since Company A owns the entire share capital of Company B we can think of the owners of 'the group' as being the shareholders in Company A. It is for the benefit of these shareholders that the consolidated accounts will be prepared.

A balance sheet for the group will combine the various assets and liabilities of each company in the group. If we look at this group through the eyes of the shareholders in Company A we can use the balance sheet of their own company as a starting point. By doing this we notice that the balance sheet of Company A includes an investment in Company B which is not an asset of the group; it is an investment in another company within the group. This investment gives Company A the right to control the assets and liabilities of Company B. We can, therefore, think of the investment as being represented by the individual assets and liabilities of Company B controlled through that investment.

In the consolidated balance sheet for the group we will simulate what the position of Company A would be if it had acquired the assets and liabilities of Company B instead of acquiring an investment that gave control over those net assets. The investment in Company A's balance sheet is, therefore, eliminated and replaced by the assets and liabilities of Company B. These assets and liabilities are combined with their corresponding class of asset and liability in the balance sheet of Company A.

Activity 2.3

Use the above explanation to prepare the first consolidated balance sheet of Company A and its subsidiary Company B. Use the outline format below this box.

Consolidated balance sheet of Company A and Company B

Tangible fixed assets		£
Current assets	£	
Current liabilities	£	
	———	
		———
		———
Share capital		
Profit and loss reserve		
		———
		———

If you now compare this consolidated balance sheet with the individual balance sheet of A Ltd that you prepared following Activity 2.1 (when Company A actually acquired net assets rather than an investment in shares) you will notice that the two balance sheets are identical. This is why the consolidation process outlined above is called the acquisition method. It is based on the idea that the acquisition of a controlling interest in another company is, in economic reality, the acquisition of the net assets owned by the controlled company at the time when the investment was made.

You must, however, keep in mind that the consolidated balance sheet prepared above is purely the result of a paper exercise. The assets and liabilities presented in this balance sheet are not owned by one company; they are a combination of items that appear in the balance sheets of two separate companies. The only items in the above consolidated balance that represent those of a single company in the group are the share capital and the profit and loss reserve. In the example so far, these two figures are those of the parent company. You will find it helpful to stop and think about these two items a little further before we move on to any further explanation of how consolidated accounts are prepared.

In the case of the share capital, the external shareholders with an interest in this group are the shareholders of Company A. There are no external shareholders in Company B because its entire share capital is owned by Company A. (We will see what happens when there are external shareholders in the subsidiary in a moment.) If we think of the group as being a single economic entity owned by the shareholders in the parent company, it is logical to show the share capital of the group as being represented by the share capital of the parent company.

As regards the profit and loss reserve in the consolidated balance sheet, you must keep in mind that we have presented the position at the date of acquisition. When acquisition accounting is used, the profit and loss reserve of the group at the date of acquisition is represented by the balance on the profit and loss account of the parent company. The consolidated profit and loss reserve will include profits earned by the subsidiary following acquisition, but profits earned by the subsidiary prior to acquisition must be excluded. This reflects the position that would have applied if Company A had acquired the net assets of Company B. (Company A would have acquired rights over the net assets of Company B, not the sources of funds that had created those net assets.)

Dividends from pre-acquisition profits

There are no legal provisions to prevent Company B from remitting its pre-acquisition profits to Company A in the form of a dividend, but the principles of acquisition accounting will prevent Company A from including these dividends as income in its own profit and loss account.

Dividends paid by the subsidiary out of profits earned prior to acquisition must be treated as capital receipts by the parent company and credited to the cost of the investment. The receipt has to be seen as a refund of part of the amount paid for the investment. The same situation would have applied if the business combination had been achieved by Company A purchasing the net assets of Company B. If Company A had paid £10 000 to Company B for its net assets and then, a few weeks later, had received a cash payment from Company B of (say) £1000, it would have to treat this receipt as a reduction of the amount paid.

A change of viewpoint

Up to now we have looked at the basic technique of acquisition accounting in the context of substituting an investment in a subsidiary with the net assets controlled through that investment. This is a practical way of looking at the technique because it gives some indication of why it is called acquisition accounting and also helps to explain the principles that apply when the amount paid for the investment exceeds the net assets of the subsidiary. But it is not the only way of looking at the basic technique. It is not even the way that acquisition accounting is described in the Companies Act 1985. We need to look at the basic technique in a slightly different way because it will provide a basis for a method of working when dealing with examination questions.

You will notice the consolidated balance sheet that you prepared following Activity 2.3 was a combination of everything in the two balance sheets apart from two things, namely:

- the cost of the investment (in Company A's books) at £10 000; and
- the share capital and reserves in Company B which, at the date of acquisition, total £10 000.

In terms of double-entry accounting, what we have done is to set off the cost of the investment (a debit balance of £10 000) against the capital and reserves of the subsidiary at the date of acquisition (two credit balances totalling £10 000). The remaining items in each company's balance sheet have then been combined. This idea of setting off the cost of the investment against the capital and reserves of the subsidiary at the time of acquisition forms the basis of the legal description of acquisition accounting.

Prior to the Companies Act 1989 the description of accounting methodology was usually left to the authors of text books. We rarely found accounting methods being described in company law. In the case of group accounts this situation has changed. Schedule 4A of the Companies Act 1985 (introduced by the Companies Act 1989) includes descriptions of both acquisition accounting and merger accounting. These descriptions have now been incorporated in FRS 6 although the wording used is slightly different. The relevant paragraphs (8 to 9) of Schedule 4A, and paragraph 20 from FRS 6, are reproduced in Section A of the appendix to this chapter. It will not be very easy for you to make sense of everything in these paragraphs at this stage (unless you have studied the subject previously) but you should glance through them before attempting the next activity.

Activity 2.4

In our consolidated balance sheet following Activity 2.3 we have combined the book values of Company B's assets and liabilities with those of Company A. If you read Paragraph 9(2) of Schedule 4A, and paragraph 20 of FRS 6, you will see that it is wrong to use the book values in the case of the subsidiary. Make a note here of the basis that should be used.

Make sure that your notes in the above box include the words 'at the date of acquisition'. These words are quite important, and form a key to certain aspects of acquisition accounting. They will also help you to appreciate the nature of the balancing figure known as 'goodwill arising on consolidation' as discussed in the next section.

Goodwill

What is goodwill?

The total value of a business entity is unlikely to be the same as the book value of the net assets shown in its balance sheet. A balance sheet provides some information about the financial position of an entity but it does not show how much that entity is worth as a going concern. Even if we substituted realizable values for book values (particularly for the assets), we are unlikely to arrive at a value of the business as a 'going concern'. We would finish up with a value based on the total amount that might be realized if each type of asset were sold separately and the liabilities were discharged.

In order to determine a value for 'the business' we need to think about the business as a single unit which produces income in the form of profits. The amount that someone would be prepared to pay in order to acquire the income-producing potential of a business is likely to be influenced by two main factors, namely:

- the level of profits capable of being generated by the business; and
- the rate of return expected by an investment in that type of business.

Activity 2.5

An investor is considering the value of a business that is capable of producing profits of £10 000 a year. Considering the risks involved in this type of business, the investor requires a return of 25% per annum on the amount paid to acquire that business. How much would the investor be prepared to pay for this business?

The various factors that would influence a potential investor's perception of future profits, and the rate of return required, are not matters for discussion in this book. It is sufficient for you to appreciate that the value of a business as a whole is likely to be different to a total value found by aggregating the identifiable assets and liabilities of that business. The difference between these two values is called **goodwill**. The term **purchased goodwill** is used to describe a balancing figure that arises when the amount paid for the acquisition of a business is different to the aggregate value of the identifiable assets and liabilities acquired.

Unfortunately, this is an oversimplification of the problem. If the amount paid in order to acquire a business is settled entirely in cash, the cost of the acquisition is an established fact; but the value of each identifiable asset owned by the business acquired will depend on what is meant by value. Even the cost of the acquisition is also open to interpretation when the amount paid includes something other than cash, such as an issue of shares. For the time being, however, we will assume that all acquisitions are settled by a payment of cash and that the main difficulty in establishing an amount for 'purchased goodwill' is related to how the identifiable assets acquired should be valued. We also need to take a closer look at the word 'identifiable'.

Although FRS 6 describes acquisition accounting in a slightly different way to the Companies Act 1985, the concepts in both regulations are identical. In both cases the value of the identifiable assets acquired should be brought into the consolidated balance sheet at their 'fair values' at the date of acquisition. You will recall reading about this when working Activity 2.4 above. Any difference between the amount paid for the acquisition, and the fair values attributed to the identifiable assets and liabilities of the undertaking on the date acquired, must be treated as goodwill.

Unfortunately, there is no definition of fair value in the Companies Act. There is a weak definition of fair value in SSAP 22 (*Accounting for goodwill*) but this leaves a great deal open to interpretation and abuse. The various attempts by the accounting regulators to prevent these abuses culminated in the issue of *FRS 7: Fair values in acquisition accounting* in September 1994.

In this chapter we will not be getting bogged down with the problem of what is meant by fair value. To do so would interrupt the learning process. It is sufficient for you to realize that the concept of fair value did result in a number of creative accounting devices which FRS 7 has attempted to prevent. These aspects will be dealt with in Chapter 11. For the time being we will be satisfied with the former definition of fair value as contained in SSAP 22. This stated that fair value is 'the amount for which an asset (or liability) could be exchanged in an arm's length transaction'.

Companies Act help for students

There is an interesting difference in the language (but not the concepts) between the description of acquisition accounting in the Companies Act and that contained in FRS 6. This difference (which is also reflected in the definition of goodwill as stated in SSAP 22) provides a focal point on the way that you will have to calculate goodwill in examination questions. The relevant paragraphs for the next activity are set out in Section A of the appendix to this chapter.

Activity 2.6

Compare paragraph 20 of FRS 6 (and paragraphs 26 to 28 of SSAP 22) with paragraph 9(4) and 9(5) of Schedule 4A to the Companies Act 1985. In both cases the provisions are aimed at identifying the amount to be treated as purchased goodwill. Although these two sets of regulations look at goodwill from two different angles, they amount to the same thing. Make a note of the difference here:

1. FRS 6 and SSAP 22 identify goodwill as the difference between the acquisition cost and:

2. The Companies Act identifies goodwill as the difference between the acquisition cost and:

These are two different ways of looking at the same thing. The term **net assets** looks at one side of the balance sheet; the term **capital and reserves** looks at the other side of the balance sheet.

Consequently, the fair value of the net identifiable assets acquired (as mentioned in FRS 6) is the same as the 'adjusted capital and reserves' as stated in Schedule 4A of the Companies Act. This is because the term 'adjusted capital and reserves' as used in the Companies Act is the total of the capital and reserves of the acquired company (at the date of acquisition) after creating a revaluation reserve for the difference between book values and fair values of the identifiable assets and liabilities of the acquired company. The way that the Companies Act identifies the amount to be treated as goodwill (comparing acquisition cost with adjusted capital and reserves at the date of acquisition) is the one that you will have to use for examination questions.

Admittedly FRS 6 (and SSAP 22) describe the nature of purchased goodwill (the difference between acquisition cost and the aggregate of the fair values of the separable net assets in the acquired entity at the date of acquisition) but if we use this approach in exam questions on group accounts we will hit a slight snag. This is because exam questions on group accounts are usually based on the financial statements of each company in the group at a date which is later than the date of acquisition. These details do not state (directly) what the fair value of the **net assets** in the acquired entity were at the date of acquisition. Instead, they give information that will allow you to determine the **adjusted capital and reserves** of the acquired entity at the date of acquisition.

Providing you are happy with the idea that the figure for 'adjusted capital and reserves' is the same as 'the fair value of the net identifiable assets', you should not encounter any difficulty when sorting out an approach to be used with exam questions. We will practise using both approaches in a moment.

Identifiable or separable

There is one further aspect on the nature of the asset called goodwill that we should look at before continuing with the mechanics of consolidation. You might have noticed that in the description of acquisition accounting, both FRS 6 and the Companies Act refer to all assets other than goodwill as **identifiable** assets. (SSAP 22 refers to them as **separable** assets.) If you refer to paragraph 9(2) in the Companies Act again (Section A of the appendix) you will see that identifiable assets are defined as those that can be disposed of separately without any need to dispose of the whole business. Goodwill is, therefore, an unusual asset in the sense that it cannot be identified as a separate asset; it is an integral part of the whole business and can be realized only if the whole business is sold.

There are a number of other intangible assets, such as 'brand names', which are similar in nature to goodwill but with one important difference: they can usually be separated from the business and sold as specific assets. This has led to a number of controversial practices which to some extent are aimed at avoiding the accounting standard on goodwill. If an accounting value can be attributed to an identifiable intangible, such as a brand name, it will not be subject to the regulations on goodwill. We will, however, not be considering this problem in this chapter.

Calculating goodwill

We will continue using the details of Company A and Company B as used in previous activities. These were based on the balance sheets of two companies which, prior to any form of business combination, were as follows:

	Company A		Company B	
	£	£	£	£
Tangible fixed assets		30 000		9 000
Current assets	25 000		3 000	
Current liabilities	11 000		2 000	
		14 000		1 000
		44 000		10 000
Ordinary share capital		35 000		7 000
Profit and loss reserve		9 000		3 000
		44 000		10 000

Activity 2.7

Assume that Company A acquires the business of Company B by purchasing the net assets of that company for £12 000 (paid out of Company A's current assets). In considering the price to be paid for the business, Company A considered the fair value of Company B's tangible fixed assets to be £10 000, and that the fair value of current assets and current liabilities was the same as their book value. Set out a schedule (using the outline format provided below) showing the make-up of the assets and liabilities that Company A has acquired as a result of spending £12 000.

Assets and liabilities acquired for £12 000

Goodwill		£
Tangible fixed assets		£ 10 000
Current assets	£	
Current liabilities	£	
		———
		£12 000

The next activity requires you to show the balance sheet of Company A following the acquisition of the above net assets from Company B. When doing this, remember that Company A's current assets will be reduced by the £12 000 spent on acquiring the net assets of Company B but will be increased by an amount of £3000 in respect of the current assets acquired.

Activity 2.8

Prepare the balance sheet of Company A following the acquisition. Use the outline format provided below. This format shows goodwill as an intangible fixed asset; we will consider the alternative methods of accounting for goodwill in a later part of this section.

Balance sheet of Company A following the acquisition of net assets from Company B

Fixed assets
    Intangible (goodwill)   £
    Tangible   £

Current assets   £

Current liabilities   £

Capital and reserves
    Share capital
    Profit and loss reserve

In the next activity we will see what happens if Company A acquires the entire share capital from the shareholders of Company B at a total cost of £12 000. The same facts regarding fair values of identifiable assets and liabilities of Company B will apply. In this situation there are no regulations that require Company B to revalue its assets to the fair values as perceived by Company A. In practice these revaluations would probably be written up in the subsidiary's books but they are very rarely dealt with this way in examination questions. If we assume that no adjustment for fair values is made in the subsidiary's books, the balance sheet of Company A and Company B after the acquisition of these shares will be as follows:

	Company A £	Company A £	Company B £	Company B £
Fixed asset investments:				
Investment in Company B at cost		12 000		—
Tangible fixed assets		30 000		9 000
Current assets	13 000		3 000	
Current liabilities	11 000		2 000	
		2 000		1 000
		44 000		10 000
Ordinary share capital		35 000		7 000
Profit and loss reserve		9 000		3 000
		44 000		10 000

In order to produce a consolidated balance sheet of Company A and Company B we look at Company A's balance sheet and pretend that instead of Company A owning an investment costing £12 000, it owns the assets and liabilities of Company B that are controlled through that investment. In this new situation the various assets and liabilities of Company B that are controlled by Company A will have the same values that you assigned to them in Activity 2.8. These values included £1000 for an asset called goodwill, and tangible fixed assets with a fair value of £10 000.

Activity 2.9

Produce the consolidated balance sheet of the group based on the above details. Use the format below this box.

Consolidated balance sheet of Company A and Company B

Fixed assets
   Intangible (goodwill arising on consolidation)   £
   Tangible fixed assets   £

                                 _____

Current assets   £
Current liabilities   £

Capital and reserves:
   Share capital
   Profit and loss reserve

In the above activities we determined the figure for goodwill arising on consolidation by comparing the cost of the investment with the fair value of the net assets acquired, as follows:

	£
Cost of investment	12 000

Fair value of net assets at date of acquisition:

	£	
Tangible fixed assets	10 000	→ *fair value*
Current assets	3 000	
Current liabilities	(2 000)	
	11 000	
Goodwill arising on consolidation	1 000	

Although this identifies the true nature of the asset called goodwill it is unlikely that you will be able to use this approach in exam questions. In the examination you are usually presented with the balances sheets for each company at an accounting date that falls after the date of acquisition. In these circumstances the balance sheet of the subsidiary will not show its assets and liabilities at the date of acquisition. You will, however, be given

---

sufficient information to determine what are called (by the Companies Act 1985) the 'adjusted capital and reserves' at the date of acquisition. The information given that will enable you to calculate the total adjusted capital and reserves will include the balance on the subsidiary's profit and loss reserve at the date of acquisition, and any difference between book values and fair values of the subsidiary's net assets at the date of acquisition. By using this information in the above case, the computation would be as follows:

	£	£
Cost of investment		12 000
Adjusted capital and reserves of subsidiary at date of acquisition		
Share capital	7 000	
Profit and loss account	3 000	
Revaluation reserve (£10 000 – £9000)	1 000	
		11 000
Goodwill arising on consolidation		1 000

You should note that neither the profit and loss account reserve, nor the revaluation reserve, will be included in the consolidated balance sheet. Both reserves are pre-acquisition. The profits of £3000 were earned prior to acquisition, and the revaluation reserve recognizes economic factors that relate to the period before the date of acquisition.

You might be a little concerned over the fact that consolidated balance sheets will include items that are on different valuation bases. The various assets and liabilities of the parent company are included at book values whereas those for the subsidiary's will be based on their fair value at the date of acquisition. In order to see the rationale for this you need to think in terms of an acquisition.

If a business is acquired by the purchase of net assets, the cost of each asset would not be recorded in the purchaser's books at book values shown in the seller's books; the cost would be based on a value attributed to each asset by the purchaser. The same concept is adopted for consolidated accounts under acquisition accounting. We must think of the assets of the new subsidiary as having being acquired at a cost equal to their fair value at the date of acquisition. Although we have used the term 'fair value' when discussing the amounts to be allocated to each asset, the assets will be described as being at cost when they are brought into the consolidated balance sheet.

Accounting for goodwill

There is an accounting standard for goodwill (SSAP 22) although this has been subject to a great deal of criticism and debate. The subject of accounting for goodwill is one of the areas in group accounts which continues to perplex the efforts of our accounting regulators. One of the problems is related to other intangibles which are similar to goodwill (such as brand names) as mentioned earlier. For the time being, however, we will have to work on the basis of regulations in SSAP 22.

The standard accounting practice as prescribed in SSAP 22 can be paraphrased as stated below. The paragraph numbers are those in SSAP 22. The comments in brackets are mine, they do not appear in the actual standard.

35 No amount should be attributed to non-purchased goodwill [note how this does not stop companies from attributing values to non-purchased intangibles such as brand names].

37 The amount attributed to purchased goodwill should not include amounts for separate intangibles.

38 Purchased goodwill should not be carried as a permanent item.

39 Purchased goodwill should normally be eliminated by an immediate write-off against reserves [this is often called the preferred treatment].

41 Purchased goodwill may be eliminated from the accounts by amortization through the profit and loss account [as an ordinary item] over the useful economic life as estimated at the time of acquisition.

42 The accounting policy may differ for each acquisition; companies can adopt the immediate write-off policy for one acquisition and the amortization policy for another.

There are two important points that are worth thinking about at this stage. The first is that there is no help in SSAP 22 as to which reserves are available for the immediate write-off. For the purposes of this chapter we will assume that the reserves available for an immediate write-off are those that are represented by the balance on the profit and loss account. The second point is that there will be a difference in reported profits depending on whether goodwill is written off against the balance on the profit and loss account, or whether it is amortized through the profit and loss account.

Activity 2.10

Most listed companies prefer to adopt the immediate write-off method for goodwill arising on consolidation. This preference appears to be more concerned with the effect on profits rather than on the balance sheet. The amortization method would affect a profit indicator to which investors pay particular attention. Make a note of this indicator here.

Partly owned subsidiaries

In this section we will have to dispense with the idea of comparing the purchase of a business with the purchase of shares in the company owning the business. It would be almost impossible to purchase a percentage of a business, but it is possible to acquire a controlling interest in another company by purchasing less than 100% of its shares.

A controlling interest is one that carries a majority (i.e. more than 50%) of the voting rights in another company. This particular aspect is codified in Section 258 (and Schedule 10A) of the Companies Act 1985, and is also repeated in paragraph 14 of FRS 2. There is no need to refer to these provisions for this chapter because we will assume that the subsidiary has one class of ordinary shares only and that the voting rights attached to each share are equal. In this situation we can refer to a controlling interest as being the ownership of more than 50% of the ordinary shares.

The practice

The alternative concepts for looking at a group become relevant when a subsidiary is not wholly owned by the parent company. We will, however, delay any study of this aspect until we have seen how the current regulations require a partly owned subsidiary to be consolidated.

We will use our rolling series of activities (for Company A and Company B) to sort out the principles and assume that Company A acquires control of Company B by purchasing 80% of the ordinary shares in Company B. For the purposes of this explanation we will assume that since Company A was prepared to pay £12 000 for a 100% interest, the amount paid for an 80% interest was £9600. This assumption is not necessarily realistic but it will help to explain certain principles.

In this new situation there will be 20% of the shares in the subsidiary owned by shareholders external to the group (the internal shareholder being Company A). These external shareholders are called **minority interests**. The basic approach to the consolidation will be the same as before except that the consolidated balance sheet must recognize that 20% of the net assets in the subsidiary are attributable to minority interests. The effect of current regulations is such that the following three principles must be applied to this new situation:

1. We must consolidate 100% (not 80%) of the subsidiary's assets and liabilities and then show the minority interests' share of these net assets as a separate credit balance.
2. The net assets attributable to minority interests in the subsidiary must be based on the fair values assigned to them by the parent company (even if these fair values are not written into the subsidiary's books).
3. Minority interests are not credited with any share of goodwill arising on consolidation.

The effect of point 3 is that the amount shown as goodwill in the consolidated balance sheet for our example will be based on comparing the cost of the investment with 80% of the fair value of the net identifiable assets at the date of acquisition. We will, however, calculate the amount by using the 'adjusted capital and reserves' at the date of acquisition (rather than net identifiable assets) since this is the method you will have to adopt in examination questions. The approach is the same as before except that after finding the total of adjusted capital and reserves, it will be necessary to attribute 20% of this total to the minority interests.

Activity 2.11

Complete the schedule shown below for the calculation of goodwill. This relates to the new situation in our rolling example where Company A has acquired an 80% interest in Company B at a cost of £9600. All other facts and figures relating to Company B are the same as before. Some of the figures have been included in this computation in order to save you the task of referring back to previous pages.

Goodwill arising on consolidation

Cost of investment £

Adjusted capital and reserves of subsidiary
    at date of acquisition:

Share capital	£7 000
Profit and loss account	3 000
Revaluation reserve	1 000
	11 000

20% X 11000

Less amount attributed to minority interests

Parent company's interest (balance) £

Goodwill arising on consolidation £

You should note that the amount attributed to minority interests in this calculation is in accordance with the principle described in point 2 above, i.e. the net assets attributable to minority interests in the subsidiary must be based on the fair values assigned to them by the parent company.

The only other question that we need to consider at this point is: where should the amount for minority interests be presented in the consolidated balance sheet? This was addressed in the Companies Act 1989 which included provisions to enable the official formats (in Schedule 4 of the Companies Act 1985) to be adapted for group accounts. The effect of these provisions (Paragraph 17 of Schedule 4A) is that the amount for minority interests should be presented in Format 1 (the most popular format) in one of two places, namely:

1. As the last item on the net asset side of the balance sheet (after item J). In this case minority interests will be shown as a deduction from the sub-total of net assets.
2. As the last item on the capital and reserves side of the balance sheet (after item K). In this case minority interests will be added to the sub-total of capital and reserves attributable to members of the parent company.

In this text book we will present minority interests as an additional item in the capital and reserves side of the balance sheet. In order to enable you to work the next activity, the balance sheets of Company A and Company B at the date of acquisition for this new situation are reproduced below:

	Company A		Company B	
	£	£	£	£
Fixed asset investments:				
Investment in Company B at cost		9 600		—
Tangible fixed assets		30 000		9 000
Current assets	15 400		3 000	
Current liabilities	11 000		2 000	

	Company A £	Company B £
	4 400	1 000
	44 000	10 000
Ordinary share capital	35 000	7 000
Profit and loss reserve	9 000	3 000
	44 000	10 000

Company A's investment in Company B represents an 80% interest. Company A considers the fair value of Company B's tangible fixed assets to be £10 000.

Activity 2.12

Complete the consolidated balance sheet for Company A and Company B based on the situation described above. You have already calculated the figure for goodwill and for minority interests in Activity 2.11. The outline formats are provided below this box. Remember to consolidate 100% of Company B's assets and liabilities (not 80%) at the fair values assigned to them by Company A and show the interests of the minority shareholders in these net assets as an addition to capital and reserves.

Consolidated balance sheet of Company A and Company B

Fixed assets
    Intangible (goodwill arising on consolidation)   £
    Tangible   £

Current assets   £
Current liabilities   £

Capital and reserves
    Share capital
    Profit and loss account

    Minority interests

The concepts

The above balance sheet was prepared according to rules in accounting standards and legislation (as summarized in points 1 to 3 at the start of this section). These rules are based on a concept of the group which falls under a general heading known as the 'proprietary concept'. The basic idea of the proprietary concept is that it looks at the group from the viewpoint of ownership.

There are several variations to the proprietary concept, some of which recognize that ownership of the group is represented entirely by shareholders in the parent company. The concept adopted by regulations does, however, extend the concept of ownership of the group to include minority interests in the subsidiary as well as members of the parent company. This is reflected by the requirement to show the minority interests in the subsidiary's net assets on the same basis as the parent company. This is sometimes called the 'parent company extension concept'.

An alternative to the proprietary concept is known as the entity concept. This looks at the group as an economic unit and considers ownership interests as of secondary importance. The practical effect of this concept is that the value of goodwill is recorded in the consolidated balance sheet at an amount that reflects its total value. This total value is based on what it would have been if the parent company had acquired a 100% interest in the subsidiary. The minority shareholders are then credited with their proportionate share of this total goodwill.

In the consolidated balance sheet produced for Activity 2.12, it could be argued that the amount of £800 for goodwill represents 80% of its total value. This argument is based on the notion that if Company A paid £9600 for an 80% interest, it would have been prepared to pay (£9600 ÷ 0.8) £12 000 for a 100% interest. If Company A considers the total value of the business owned by Company B to be £12 000, then the value of goodwill in Company B must be (£12 000 – £11 000) £1000. On this basis the cost of the investment of £9600 would be substituted for the following in the consolidated balance sheet:

	£	£
Goodwill arising on consolidation		1 000
Tangible fixed assets (at fair value)		10 000
Current assets	3 000	
Current liabilities	2 000	
		1 000
		12 000
Minority interests (20% × £12 000)		2 400
		9 600

You will notice that both goodwill and minority interests are £200 greater than what they were in Activity 2.12. The effect of this concept is, therefore, to assume a total amount for goodwill based on a transaction of the parent company, and to credit the minority interests with a share of this assumed value.

This basis would contravene the standard practice set out in paragraph 38 of FRS 2. This particular paragraph has not been reproduced in the appendix to this chapter because some of the wording might seem a little confusing until after you have studied merger accounting. It is, however, interesting to consider the reasons why the ASB discarded this concept. Their reasons are explained in paragraph 82 which has been reproduced in the appendix (Section B) to this chapter.

Activity 2.13

Read paragraph 82 from FRS 2 as set out in Section B of the appendix to this chapter. Make a note here of the reasons why the FRS requires goodwill in partly owned subsidiaries to be recognized only in respect of the parent company's interest.

Another conceptual aspect that is worth considering relates to the fact that paragraph 38 of FRS 2 requires that the amount attributed to minority interests for the net identifiable assets (assets other than goodwill) in their company should be on the same valuation basis as that adopted by the parent company. In other words, minority interests are credited (or debited) with a share of the total revaluation surplus (or deficit) resulting from the procedure of establishing fair values at the date of acquisition. This does not accord with a pure interpretation of the 'proprietary concept' which looks at the group principally through the eyes of shareholders in the parent company. Financial statements produced on this basis would make no attempt to produce information which is relevant to the minority shareholders in a subsidiary.

If a strict interpretation of the proprietary concept is applied, the amounts attributed to minority interests would be based on book values of the net identifiable assets in their company. The problem with this concept is that it would result in a mixture of valuation bases in the consolidated accounts. The proportion of identifiable assets and liabilities attributable to the parent company would be based on fair values at the date of acquisition, and the proportion attributable to minority interests would be based on book values. The reasons why the ASB discarded this basis is explained in paragraph 80 of FRS 2. Extracts from this paragraph have been included in Section B of the appendix to this chapter.

Activity 2.14

Read paragraph 80 from FRS 2 as set out in Section B of the appendix to this chapter. Make a note here of the reason why the FRS requires the amount attributed to minority interests (for the identifiable assets and liabilities in their company) to be on the same basis as those attributed to the parent company's interest.

Further reading

Students whose syllabus requires a detailed analysis of the concepts relating to group accounts will find that the foregoing explanations provide a useful foundation study of the problem. It is not, however, a complete exposition of all concepts relating to group accounts because the text was aimed at underpinning the standard practice required by regulations. For example, no attempt has been made to explain concepts such as **partial consolidation** whereby minority interests are excluded altogether by consolidating only the parent company's percentage of each identifiable asset and liability in a partially owned subsidiary. If you wish to pursue your study of the concepts further, you should refer to a standard book on accounting principles such as *UK GAAP* written by Ernst & Young and published by Macmillan Press Ltd.

Post-acquisition profits

Exam questions requiring preparation of consolidated accounts are likely to be for a date which is at least one year after acquisition. You will notice that **none** of the profits earned by a subsidiary **prior to acquisition** is included in the consolidated balance sheet when the acquisition method is used. Neither is the revaluation reserve that results from attributing fair values to the identifiable assets and liabilities in the subsidiary at the date of acquisition. This is in keeping with the position that would apply if the business assets had been acquired instead of the shares.

If the combination had been achieved by acquiring the assets, any profits earned by those assets since acquisition would form part of the profits available for distribution to the shareholders of the acquiring company. The same concept is applied on consolidation of a subsidiary; post-acquisition profits earned by the subsidiary are consolidated and included in the group profits attributable to shareholders in the parent company. The word 'attributable' should not be confused with the word 'distributable'. In reality (in contrast to the fiction of a group) the post-acquisition profits of the subsidiary would have to be distributed to the parent company before they could be distributed to the shareholders of the parent company.

In cases where the parent company owns less than 100% of the shares in the subsidiary, the amount of **post-acquisition** profit consolidated will be based on the proportion of shares held. The remaining proportion is attributable to the minority interests in the subsidiary. This leads to the idea that three key figures have to be calculated when preparing consolidated balance sheets, as follows:

Goodwill	Minority interests	Profit and loss reserve
The difference between the cost of the investment, and the parent company's share of net identifiable assets in the subsidiary at the **date of acquisition**. Net identifiable assets must be based on **fair values** at acquisition.	Share of net assets in the subsidiary at the date of **consolidation**. This will include any adjustment needed to reflect the **fair values** as recognized by the parent company at the date of acquisition.	Balance on the parent company's own profit and loss account, plus the parent company's share of **post-acquisition profits of the subsidiary** (share being based on proportion of shares held).
The figure for net identifiable assets at acquisition is the same as	Notice how the above description refers to minority interests at the	The amount found by this process might have to be reduced to reflect

Goodwill	Minority interests	Profit and loss reserve
the **adjusted capital and reserves** at acquisition.	date of **consolidation**, not at the date of acquisition.	goodwill written off (either through the profit and loss account or against the balance on the profit and loss account).

In order to consolidate the balance sheets that are for a date beyond the date of acquisition, the amount for goodwill will have to be based on information regarding the capital and reserves of the subsidiary at the date of acquisition. Unless there is information to the contrary we can assume that the share capital of the subsidiary at the date of acquisition was the same as it is in the current balance sheet. The examiner will always give you the balance on the subsidiary's profit and loss account at the date of acquisition, and also provide information regarding the difference between book values and fair values at the date of acquisition. You need this information for two reasons: (1) to calculate goodwill, and (2) to determine post-acquisition profits of the subsidiary.

The profit and loss reserve might be subject to adjustments for unrealized profits on stocks and for additional depreciation when fixed assets are revalued. These aspects are discussed on pp. 46–48.

Details for Activity 2.15

The balance sheets for our rolling exercise (Company A and Company B) one year after acquisition are as follows:

	Company A		Company B	
	£	£	£	£
Tangible fixed assets		32 000		10 000
Investment in Company B		9 600		
Current assets	17 400		4 000	
Current liabilities	11 000		2 000	
		6 400		2 000
		48 000		12 000
Share capital		35 000		7 000
Profit and loss reserve		13 000		5 000
		48 000		12 000

Company A's investment in Company B represents an 80% holding which was acquired one year earlier when B's profit and loss account had a balance of £3000. The fair value of B's fixed assets at the date of acquisition was £1000 in excess of the book value. This revaluation has not been written into B's books. The group's accounting policy for this acquisition is to write off the goodwill arising on consolidation over its estimated useful economic life of five years.

When working the next activity you should pretend that you have never seen the financial statements of each company at the date of acquisition and that you are working entirely from the above data. Try to avoid the temptation of looking back to see what you did on previous activities by using the working principles provided in the table set out above the data.

Activity 2.15

Prepare the three working schedules below, and prepare the consolidated balance sheet.

Goodwill	Minority interests	Profit and loss

Now prepare the consolidated balance sheet.

Consolidated balance sheet of A and B

Activity 2.16

Reconcile the figure for 'Minority interests' by identifying what has caused it to change from the balance at the date of acquisition, to the balance shown in the consolidated balance sheet above.

Balance at acquisition	£2200
Balance at date of consolidation	£2600

Unrealized profits on inter-company transactions

Transactions between separate companies within the group will be reflected in the individual financial statements of the companies concerned but the effect of such transactions must be eliminated when producing consolidated financial statements. If the group is to be presented as a single entity, these transactions do not represent dealings between the group and parties outside of the group. There are usually two aspects that require adjustment for the consolidated balance sheet:

1. Balances for unsettled inter-company transactions must be eliminated. These balances will be represented by a debtor in one company's books and a creditor for the same amount in another. These debtors and creditors do not represent amounts owing to or by the group as a single entity.

2. The cost of assets (such as stock) in one company's books might include items that have been purchased from another company in the group at a price in excess of original cost (the transfer price included a profit margin). The consolidated balance sheet must show assets at cost to the group. The transfer price usually includes an element of profit added to cost by the supplying company. This does not cause a problem providing the stock acquired by the purchasing company has been sold; as far as the group is concerned the total profit on the transaction will simply be divided between two companies. If, however, the stock has not been sold it will be included in the assets of the purchasing company at a price that exceeds cost to the group. The profit that has not been realized by the group must be eliminated when preparing consolidated accounts.

The basic process of eliminating inter-company balances is simply a matter of setting off a debit balance in one company's books against the corresponding credit balance in the other company's books. Both balances are excluded from the consolidated balance sheet. In some exam questions (and very nearly always in practice) adjustments are needed in order to bring the two balances into agreement before they can be eliminated. This is usually due to 'cut-off' problems such as a remittance by one company in the old accounting period being recorded by the receiving company in the subsequent period.

There was no standard practice for the elimination of unrealized profits on assets acquired from another company in the group prior to the introduction of FRS 2. The policy adopted when the stock arose from a transaction with a partly owned subsidiary was either arbitrary or depended upon an interpretation of the various ways of looking at a group in such circumstances.

In this book we will not be relating former practices to the various concepts of a group. Students who are interested in this will find ample reference in the book previously mentioned. The standard practice required by current regulations is clearly stated in FRS 2. The effect of these regulations is as follows:

1. The unrealized profit must be eliminated in full even where the transactions involve a subsidiary company with minority interests.
2. The profit should be eliminated by reducing both the parent company's interest and the minority shareholder's interest in the profits of the company whose accounts have recorded the profit.

The above wording is not, by any means, a replica of the wording in FRS 2. Students who wish to study the actual wording must read paragraph 39 which invokes the standard, and paragraph 83 which gives an explanation of why this basis was prescribed. (These paragraphs are not included in the appendix.) The practical effect of these regulations is as follows:

If the parent company's balance sheet includes stock purchased from a subsidiary at a price in excess of cost to the subsidiary, the whole of the profit must be eliminated, even if the subsidiary is partly owned. In this case the profit has been recorded by the subsidiary and so the parent company's share will be debited to consolidated profit and loss reserve and the minority's share will be debited to minority interests. If the balance sheet of a partly-owned subsidiary includes stock purchased from the parent company, the profit has been recorded by the parent company and so the whole of the unrealized profit must be eliminated by reducing the consolidated profit and loss reserve.

In this chapter we are looking at the effect of these adjustments on the consolidated balance sheet. In Chapter 3 you will see how the adjustment is achieved through the consolidated profit and loss account.

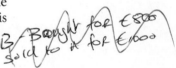

Details for the next activity

The following details are now available in respect of the consolidated accounts produced for Activity 2.15:

(a) Current assets of Company A include £1000 owing by Company B. The corresponding creditor in Company B's books is £800. The difference is accounted for by the fact that Company B had sent a remittance of £200 to Company A on the last day of the accounting period; this was not recorded by Company A until after the balance sheet date.

(b) Current assets of Company A include stock purchased from Company B at a transfer price of £800. Transfer prices are calculated by adding one-third to the original purchase price.

Activity 2.17

Prepare the consolidated balance sheet taking account of these details.

Additional depreciation

When the fixed assets of the subsidiary are revalued as a part of the fair value exercise, the revalued amounts represent the cost to the group of the assets acquired. This is in keeping with the position that applies when an unincorporated business is acquired. The cost of the assets is based on the values assigned to them by the acquirer, not on the book values shown in the accounts of the acquired business.

The annual depreciation of these fixed assets must, therefore, be based on the values assigned to them at the time of acquisition. If the fair values at acquisition have not been incorporated in the subsidiary's books, the depreciation provided by the subsidiary will be based on the original book values. In these circumstances it will be necessary to make an adjustment in the group accounts for any differences between the depreciation provided and the amount that should have been provided on the fair values.

In some ways this is similar to the requirement in SSAP 12 for depreciation on revalued assets to be based on the revised carrying values. In a technical sense, however, the situation is different because the fair values on an acquisition represent the cost to the acquirer. Depreciation is simply being calculated on a cost that differs from the cost in the subsidiary's books.

Most of the learning activities in the early stages of this book ignore adjustments to depreciation in order to focus attention on the basic principles. Some of the end of chapter exercises will, however, included depreciation adjustments. These are quite easy to handle providing you have a clear idea of how group accounts are constructed. For example, if you had been told in Activity 2.17 that there was additional depreciation of £100 to be provided on the subsidiary's fixed assets, you would have made the following adjustments:

- reduce fixed assets by £100;
- reduce minority interests by (20% × £100) £20;
- reduce consolidated profit and loss reserve by (80% × £100) £80.

Summary

The key learning points in this chapter are as follows:

- acquisition accounting is based on the principle that the purchase of a controlling interest in the voting shares of a subsidiary can be likened to the purchase of the business owned by that subsidiary;
- the essential features of acquisition accounting are:
  - the difference between the acquisition cost and the parent company's interest in the fair values of the net identifiable assets in the subsidiary at the date of acquisition is goodwill (positive or negative);
  - profits earned by the subsidiary are consolidated only from the date of acquisition;
- dividends paid to the parent company out of pre-acquisition profits must be treated as capital receipts and should be credited to the cost of the investment;
- in the case of a subsidiary that is not wholly owned there are several concepts which look at the group in different ways, such as: the pro-

prietary concept, the parent company extension concept, the entity concept, and partial consolidation;

- the practical effect of these concepts as adopted in FRS 2 is as follows:
  - minority interests are not credited with any goodwill arising on consolidation;
  - the interests of minority shareholders in the net identifiable assets of the subsidiary are based on the same values as assigned to those assets by the parent company;
  - partial consolidation (consolidating the parent company's proportionate interest in the net identifiable assets) is not permitted; *100% net Assets*
- goodwill arising on consolidation must be either written off immediately against reserves or treated as an intangible asset and amortized through the profit and loss account over its estimated useful economic life;
- the Companies Act description of acquisition accounting provides the basis for dealing with examination questions because it identifies goodwill as being the difference between the acquisition cost and the parent company's interest in the adjusted capital and reserves at the date of acquisition;
- unsettled inter-company balances must be eliminated on consolidation;
- unrealized profits on assets such as stock must be eliminated in full by reducing both the parent company's interest and the minority shareholders' interest in the profits of the company whose accounts have recorded the profit. *→ sub.*

Key to activities

Activity 2.1

	£	£
Tangible fixed assets (£30 000 + £9000)		39 000
Current assets (£25 000 − £10 000 + £3000)	18 000	
Current liabilities (£11 000 + £2000)	13 000	
		5 000
		44 000
Share capital		35 000
Profit and loss reserve		9 000
		44 000

We paid £10000 for the ord. share capital.
We got £9000 + £3,000 Asset
Less £2,000 liabilities.

Activity 2.2

	£	£
Fixed asset investments:		
Investment in Company B at cost		10 000
Tangible fixed assets		30 000
Current assets	15 000	
Current liabilities	11 000	
		4 000
		44 000
Share capital		35 000
Profit and loss reserve		9 000
		44 000

Activity 2.3

Consolidated balance sheet of Company A and Company B

Tangible fixed assets (£30 000 + £9000)		39 000
Current assets (£15 000 + £3000)	18 000	
Current liabilities (£11 000 + £2000)	13 000	
		5 000
		44 000
Share capital		35 000
Profit and loss reserve		9 000
		44 000

Activity 2.4

At their fair values **at the date of acquisition.**

Activity 2.5

£10 000 ÷ 0.25 = £40 000.

Activity 2.6

1. The fair values of the net identifiable assets acquired (although SSAP 22 uses the term 'separable' rather than identifiable).
2. The adjusted capital and reserves.

Activity 2.7

	£	£
Goodwill		1 000
Tangible fixed assets		10 000
Current assets	3 000	
Current liabilities	2 000	
		1 000
		12 000

Activity 2.8

	£	£
Fixed assets		
Intangible (goodwill)		1 000
Tangible (£30 000 + £10 000)		40 000
		41 000
Current assets (£25 000 – £12 000 + £3000)	16 000	
Current liabilities (£11 000 + £2000)	13 000	
		3 000
		44 000
Capital and reserves:		
Share capital		35 000
Profit and loss reserve		9 000
		44 000

Activity 2.9

The balance sheet will be the same as for Activity 2.8 except that the workings for current assets will be slightly different (i.e. £13 000 + £3000).

Activity 2.10

Earnings per share.

Activity 2.11

	£	£
Cost of investment		9 600
Adjusted capital and reserves at date of acquisition:		
Share capital	7 000	
Profit and loss account	3 000	
Revaluation reserve	1 000	
	11 000	
Less attributable to minority interests	2 200	
Parent company's interest		8 800
Goodwill arising on consolidation		800

Activity 2.12

	£	£
Fixed assets		
Intangible (goodwill)		800
Tangible (£30 000 + £10 000)		40 000
		40 800
Current assets (£15 400 + £3000)	18 400	
Current liabilities (£11 000 + £2000)	13 000	
		5 400
		46 200
Capital and reserves:		
Share capital		35 000
Profit and loss reserve		9 000
		44 000
Minority interests		2 200
		46 200

Activity 2.13

Any other amount would be hypothetical since the minority interests were not a party to the transaction.

Activity 2.14

To present assets and liabilities on a consistent basis for the group as a whole.

Activity 2.15

Working schedules

1. *Goodwill*

Cost of investment		9 600
Adjusted capital and reserves at date of acquisition:		
Share capital	7 000	
Profit and loss account	3 000	
Revaluation reserve	1 000	
	11 000	
Less attributable to minority interests	2 200	
Parent company's interest		8 800
Goodwill arising on consolidation		800

2. *Minority interests*

20% × £12 000 (the book values)	2 400
20% × £1000 (the unrecorded revaluation reserve)	200
	2 600

3. Consolidated profit and loss reserve

	£	£
Company A's balance		13 000
Post-acquisition of Company B (80% × (£5000 – £3000))		1 600
		14 600
Less amortization of goodwill (1/5 × £800)		160
		14 440

Consolidated balance sheet

		£
Fixed assets		
Intangible (goodwill) (£800 – £160)		640
Tangible (£32 000 + £10 000 + £1 000)		43 000
		43 640
Current assets (£17 400 + £4000)	21 400	
Current liabilities (£11 000 + £2000)	13 000	
		8 400
		52 040
Capital and reserves:		
Share capital		35 000
Profit and loss reserve		14 440
		49 440
Minority interests		2 600
		52 040

Activity 2.16

Balance at acquisition	2 200
Share of post-acquisition profits (20% × £2000)	400
Balance at date of consolidation	2 600

Activity 2.17

Commentary on the adjustments:

1. Company A will debit bank with £200 and credit its account with Company B. The effect of this adjustment on total current assets will be nil. The current assets of Company A to be consolidated will be reduced by £800 (the revised debit balance for Company B). The current liabilities of Company B to be consolidated will be reduced by £800.

2. The unrealized profit is (1/4 of £800) £200. The profit was recorded by Company B which has minority interests. Current assets (stock) will be reduced by £200, consolidated profit and loss will be reduced by (80% × £200) £160, and minority interests will be reduced by (20% × £200) £40.

Consolidated balance sheet

	£	£
Fixed assets		
Intangible (goodwill) (as before)		640
Tangible (as before)		43 000
		43 640
Current assets (£17 400 − £800 − £200 + £4000)	20 400	
Current liabilities (£11 000 + £2000 − £800)	12 200	
		8 200
		51 840
Capital and reserves:		
Share capital		35 000
Profit and loss reserve (£14 440 − £160)		14 280
		49 280
Minority interests (£2600 − £40)		2 560
		51 840

(handwritten annotations: "−stock", "−unrealised profit" over the current assets line; "stock" under the current liabilities line; "−profit" over the profit and loss reserve line)

Appendix

Section A

Extracts from legislation and accounting standards on acquisition accounting

Schedule 4A Companies Act 1985 (extracts)

8   An acquisition shall be accounted for by the acquisition method of accounting unless the conditions for accounting for it as a merger are met and the merger method of accounting is adopted.

9(1) The acquisition method of accounting is as follows.

9(2) The identifiable assets and liabilities of the undertaking acquired shall be included in the consolidated balance sheet at their fair values as at the date of acquisition.
In this paragraph the "**identifiable**" assets or liabilities of the undertaking acquired means the assets or liabilities which are capable of being disposed of or discharged separately, without disposing of a business of the undertaking.

9(3) The income and expenditure of the undertaking acquired shall be brought into the group accounts only as from the date of the acquisition.

9(4) There shall be set off against the acquisition cost of the interest in the shares of the undertaking held by the parent company [. . .] the interest of the parent company in the adjusted capital and reserves of the undertaking acquired.

For this purpose —

"**the acquisition cost**" means the amount of any cash consideration and the fair value of any other consideration, [. . .], and

"**the adjusted capital and reserves**" of the undertaking acquired
means its capital and reserves at the date of the acquisition after
adjusting the identifiable assets and liabilities of the undertaking to fair values as at that date.

9(5)   The resulting amount if positive shall be treated as goodwill, and
if negative as a negative consolidation difference.

FRS 6: Acquisitions and mergers (extracts) – published September 1994

20   Business combinations not accounted for by merger accounting
should be accounted for by acquisition accounting. Under acquisition accounting, the identifiable assets and liabilities of the companies acquired should be included in the acquirer's consolidated
balance sheet at the fair value at the date of acquisition. [. . .] The
difference between the fair value of the net identifiable assets acquired and the fair value of the purchase consideration is goodwill,
positive or negative.

SSAP 22 Accounting for goodwill (extracts) – published 1984, revised 1989, and revised by FRS 7 in 1994

Part 2 – Definition of terms

26   *Goodwill* is the difference between the value of a business as a whole
and aggregate of the fair values of its separable net assets.

27   *Separable net assets* are those assets (and liabilities) which can be
identified and sold (or discharged) separately without necessarily
disposing of the business as a whole. They include identifiable
intangibles.

28   *Purchased goodwill* is goodwill which is established as a result of the
purchase of a business accounted for as an acquisition. Goodwill
arising on consolidation is one form of purchased goodwill.

29   *Non-purchased goodwill* is any goodwill other than purchased goodwill.

30   *Fair value* is the amount for which an asset (or liability) could be
exchanged in an arm's length transaction.

[*Note*: para. 30 has now been replaced by a new but similar definition in FRS
7, para. 2; see Chapter 11. Para. 27 has been superseded by FRS 7.]

Section B

Extracts from the explanation paragraphs in FRS 2 – published 1992

82　The FRS requires that the goodwill arising on acquisition of a subsidiary undertaking that is not wholly owned should be recognised only in relation to the group's interest and that none should be attributed to the minority interest. Although it might be possible to estimate by extrapolation or valuation an amount of goodwill attributable to the minority when a subsidiary undertaking is acquired, this would in effect recognise an amount for goodwill that is hypothetical because the minority is not a party to the transaction by which the subsidiary undertaking is acquired.

80　[. . .] The effect of the existence of minority interests on the returns to investors in the parent undertaking is best reflected by presenting the net identifiable assets attributable to minority interests on the same basis as those attributable to group interests. Using the same basis for including group assets and liabilities, irrespective of the extent to which they are attributable to the minority interest, presents the assets and liabilities on a consistent basis for the group as a whole.

Questions

Questions for self assessment

Answers to self-assessment questions are given at the end of the book

2.1 Kilgour group
The following summarized balance sheets relate to the Kilgour group of companies as at 30 June 1994:

	Kilgour plc £000	Lynn Ltd £000	Norr Ltd £000
Tangible fixed assets (net book value)	6 200	1 050	450
Investments in subsidiaries (at cost)			
Lynn Ltd	1 000 .		
Norr Ltd	500		
Current assets	14 000	250	150
Current liabilities	(6 000)	(300)	(200)
	15 700	1 000	400
Capital and reserves:			
Share capital (£1 ordinary shares)	12 000	800	300
Revenue reserves	3 700	200	100
	15 700	1 000	400

Additional information
1. Kilgour acquired a 70% holding in Lynn on 1 July 1990. At that date, Lynn's revenue reserves were £400 000, and they were in credit.
2. Kilgour acquired a 60% holding in Norr on 1 July 1993. Norr's revenue reserves at that date were £150 000, and they were in credit.
3. Kilgour amortizes any goodwill arising on consolidation on a straight-line basis over a ten-year period.

Required

Prepare the consolidated balance sheet of the Kilgour group of companies as at 30 June 1994.

> *Author's note: Since no information is given on the fair values of net identifiable assets at acquisition, you will have to assume that they are the same as book values.*
>
> AAT Final, December 1994

2.2 Pagg group
The following question has been altered slightly from the original in order to allow the provisions in FRS 2 for unrealized profit on stock to be applied.
The following summarized information relates to the Pagg Group of companies:

Balance sheet at 31 March 1990

	Pagg plc £000	Ragg Ltd £000	Tagg Ltd £000
Tangible fixed assets at net book value	2000	900	600
Investments			
800 000 ordinary shares in Ragg Ltd	3000		
300 000 ordinary shares in Tagg Ltd	1000		
Current assets			
Stocks	1300	350	100
Debtors	3000	200	300
Cash	200	20	50
Current liabilities			
Creditors	(4000)	(270)	(400)
	6500	1200	650
Capital and reserves			
Called up share capital (all ordinary shares of £1 each)	5500	1000	500
Profit and loss account	1000	200	150
	6500	1200	650

Additional information

1. Pagg acquired its shareholding in Ragg Ltd on 1 April 1985. Ragg's profit and loss account balance at that time was £600 000.
2. The shares in Tagg Ltd were acquired on 1 April 1989 when Tagg's profit and loss account balance was £100 000.
3. All goodwill arising on consolidation is amortized in equal amounts over a period of 20 years commencing from the date of acquisition of each subsidiary company.
4. At 31 March 1990, Ragg had in stock goods purchased from Tagg at a cost to Ragg of £60 000. These goods had been invoiced by Tagg at cost plus 20%.
5. Inter-company debts at 31 March 1990 were as follows:
   Pagg owed Ragg £200 000, and Ragg owed Tagg £35 000.

Required

Prepare the consolidated balance sheet of the Pagg Group of companies as at 31 March 1990.

Author's note: Since no information is given on the fair values of net identifiable assets at acquisition, you will have to assume that they are the same as book values.

AAT Final, December 1990

Questions without answers

Answers to these questions are published separately in the *Teacher's Manual*.

2.3 Notable group

The following balance sheets relate to the Notable Group of companies as at 30 September 1992.

	Notable plc £000	Note Ltd £000	Table Ltd £000
Fixed assets (at cost)	370	200	60
Investments:			
Note Ltd	280		
Table Ltd	120		
Current assets			
Stocks	110	65	40
Debtors	330	60	120
Bank and cash	800	20	10
	2010	345	230
Capital and reserves			
Ordinary shares of £1 each	400	150	100
Revenue reserves	1040	125	90
	1440	275	190
Current liabilities			
Creditors	370	50	30
Taxation	160	20	10
Dividends	40		
	2010	345	230

Additional information
1. Notable acquired an 80% holding in Note on 1 October when Note's revenue reserves were £30 000, and a 100% holding in Table on 1 October 1991 when Table's revenue reserves were £150 000.
2. During the year to 30 September 1992, Note sold goods costing £30 000 to Notable for £50 000; half of these goods were still in stock at the end of the financial year. Similarly, Table sold goods costing £10 000 to Notable for £16 000, and one third of these goods were still in stock at the year end.
3. Notable's creditors include £18 000 owing to Note and £6 000 owing to Table.
4. Table's creditors include £3 000 owing to Notable.
5. Goodwill is written off immediately on acquisition.

Required

Prepare the consolidated balance sheet for the Notable Group at 30 September 1992.

Author's note: Since no information is given on the fair values of net identifiable assets at acquisition, you will have to assume that they are the same as book values.

AAT Final, December 1992

2.4 Park group

The following balances relate to Park Ltd and Gate Ltd at 31 December 19X4

	Park Ltd £	Gate Ltd £
Issued share capital (£1 ordinary shares)	200 000	80 000
Retained profits at 31 December 19X3	45 100	37 500
Profit for 19X4	17 600	28 500
Unsecured loan repayable 19X8	—	30 000
Current liabilities	53 700	26 000
	316 400	202 000
Freehold property, net of depreciation	—	99 000
Other fixed assets, net of depreciation	182 300	35 000
48 000 shares in Gate Ltd at cost	72 000	
Current assets	62 100	68 000
	316 400	202 000

Notes:
1. Park Ltd acquired its shares in Gate Ltd on 31 December 19X3.
2. Park Ltd carried out a fair value assessment of Gate Ltd's net identifiable assets at the date of acquisition and the following surpluses and deficits arising at that date need to be taken into account:

   Freehold property – a revaluation surplus of £6000
   Other fixed assets – a revaluation deficit of £5000

   As a result of these revaluations, the depreciation charged by Gate Ltd for 19X4 must be adjusted in the consolidated accounts as follows:

   Freehold property – no change
   Other fixed assets – reduce by £1000

   Fair values of current assets and current liabilities were equal to book value.

3. Goodwill arising on consolidation is to be written off immediately against the balance on the consolidated profit and loss account.

Required

The consolidated balance sheet of the group at 31 December 19X4 presented in accordance with Format 1 (Companies Act 1985) so far as the information permits.

CIB Diploma, Accountancy, Modified

Acquisition and equity accounting

3

Objectives

After completing this chapter you should be able to:

- prepare a consolidated profit and loss account and balance sheet in a form suitable for publication by a group with direct subsidiaries and investments in associated undertakings;
- make all appropriate consolidation adjustments such as the elimination of inter-company trading transactions, unrealized profits, inter-company dividends and interest;
- reconcile movements on consolidated reserves and minority interests;
- explain and demonstrate the equity method of accounting.

Introduction

In the previous chapter we ignored the detailed construction of the consolidated profit and loss account and concentrated on the balance of retained profit for the balance sheet. The preparation of a detailed consolidated profit and loss account is relatively straightforward providing you keep in mind the basic concept of a group as discussed in Chapter 1. You will be learning the principles by working through the profit and loss account in easy stages. The subject of associated undertakings and equity accounting is dealt with at the end of the chapter.

In this chapter we will be constructing the two primary financial statements required by statute, namely the consolidated profit and loss account and balance sheet. The primary financial statements required by accounting standards, such as the cash flow statement, are dealt with as separate subjects in Chapter 4 and Chapter 7.

Profit and loss account

The consolidated profit and loss account must take the same form as the profit and loss account for a single company. The results of the group are presented as if the group were a single entity. The actual format will depend on which of the four Companies Act formats is adopted; the most popular is Format 1.

Profit for the financial year

The amount for each item in the consolidated profit and loss account from 'Turnover' to 'Profit after tax' is based on adding the amounts shown in the separate profit and loss accounts of each company in the group. The total amount for each of these items is consolidated even if there are minority interests in the subsidiary. The minority interest share of the profits earned by their company is dealt with as an adjustment to group profit after tax.

But there are a number of adjustments, and other matters to consider, when combining the individual figures for income and expenditure from the separate profit and loss accounts. For example:

- inter-company trading transactions (sales and purchases) must be eliminated because they do not represent transactions with parties external to the group;
- cost of sales must be adjusted to recognize any unrealized profit on stock.

These adjustments are a part of the general memorandum exercise of consolidation; the figures in the individual accounts are not altered in any way.

Activity 3.1

A parent company has a 70% interest in a subsidiary. Items in the profit and loss accounts of each company included the following:

	Parent company	Subsidiary
	£	£
Turnover	800 000	600 000
Cost of sales	480 000	350 000

Sales from the subsidiary to the parent company were £100 000. State how much will be included in the consolidated profit and loss account for the following:

1. Turnover
2. Cost of sales

Ignore any adjustment that might be needed to cost of sales for any unrealized profit on stock.

Notice how the consolidated profit and loss account combines the total figures even though the holding company's interest in the subsidiary is 70% only. You will see how the minority interests' share of the subsidiary's profit is dealt with in a moment. Notice also that the consolidated gross profit is the same amount both before and after the adjustment for inter-company trading, as follows:

	Before adjustment	After adjustment
	£	£
Consolidated turnover	1 400 000	1 300 000
Consolidated cost of sales	830 000	730 000
Consolidated gross profit	570 000	570 000

120 000.

This is what you would expect if none of the internal transfers was left in the closing stock of the parent company. If all of the goods transferred had been sold by the parent company the total profit earned on them will have been realized by the group. This profit will be shared by each company if the goods were transferred to the parent company at a transfer price in excess of cost.

Activity 3.2

You are now informed that some of the goods transferred to the parent company form part of the parent company's closing stock. The unrealized profit on this stock amounts to £20 000. Calculate the amount that will be included in the consolidated profit and loss account for 'cost of sales'.

The unrealized profit must be eliminated in full in order to comply with the regulations in FRS 2, as mentioned in Chapter 2.

From your studies of the profit and loss account for a single company you will recall that there are usually some items between the line described as 'Operating profit' and the line described as 'Profit before tax'. In the majority of cases the items presented in this part of the profit statement are 'Investment income' and 'Interest paid and similar charges'. Quite often companies present these two items as a single net figure on the face of the profit and loss account and provide details in 'Notes to the accounts'.

Activity 3.3

In the profit and loss account of a holding company, there is likely to be an item of investment income that will have to be excluded when preparing the consolidated profit and loss account. You might recall reading about this in Chapter 1. Make a note of the item here.

Although these dividends represent investment income of the holding company (if they were paid out of post-acquisition profits), they do not represent investment income of the group. As far as the group is concerned, inter-company dividends are simply a means of transferring some of the profit earned by the subsidiary to the holding company; they do not create any profit for the group.

inter company dividends

A similar adjustment process is required in respect of inter-company interest. In this case the actual payment of the interest might be from holding company to subsidiary or vice-versa. Although a subsidiary is not allowed to own shares in the holding company, there is nothing to prevent it from owning debentures or loan stock in the holding company. Elimination of inter-company interest is simply a matter of excluding the same amount from both interest received and interest paid when consolidating the results of the individual companies.

Taxation

In a straightforward case the charges for taxation in the individual profit statements of each company are combined in total. This is so even if the holding company does not have a 100% interest in the subsidiary. There can sometimes be a slight complication with regard to the tax credits on franked investment income. You will probably recall from your studies of a single company that SSAP 8 requires dividend income to be presented in the pre-tax profits at an amount found by adding the tax credits to the cash received. The amount added for tax credits is then included as a part of the tax charge. What happens if the dividend income includes dividends from a subsidiary?

In most cases, groups take advantage of what is called a 'group election' for the payment of advance corporation tax (ACT). If this election is in operation it means that dividends can be paid by the subsidiary to the holding company without any requirement to account for ACT following payment of the dividend. If this is the case then there are no tax credits attached to the dividend received. The cash amount received will be presented separately in the holding company's profit and loss account as 'Income from shares in group undertakings' and the taxation charge will not include any amount added for tax credits. If tax credits have been added to the dividends received from a subsidiary, both the dividend income and the appropriate amount included in the tax charge will have to be eliminated in the consolidation.

There can be other complications regarding taxation when consolidating the results of individual companies, particularly over deferred tax. These aspects are outside of the scope of subjects to be covered by this book. Most of the students for whom this book is intended will find that their examination questions on consolidation are not complicated by taxation issues. Readers interested in obtaining more information on the tax problems for group accounts should refer to a standard reference work such as *UK GAAP*.

Proprietary interests in group profit

So far we have been discussing the various items in the profit statement that conclude with the line called 'Profit on ordinary activities after tax'. All items above this line were consolidated by adding the full amounts for each item in the separate profit and loss accounts, subject to adjustments such as:

- elimination of inter-company trading transactions;
- adjustment to cost of sales for unrealized profit;
- elimination of dividends received by the holding company from subsidiaries;
- elimination of any inter-company interest (received and paid).

The figure for profit after tax will, therefore, include the total profit after tax earned by the subsidiary. This profit is a part of the total profit earned by the group when viewed as a separate entity but we now need to move away from the entity viewpoint and consider proprietary interests. (See Chapter 2 for a discussion of the proprietary and entity concepts.) There are likely to be two classes of shareholders with an interest in the group profit after tax, namely:

- minority interests in the subsidiary;
- shareholders in the parent company.

If a subsidiary is not wholly owned, some of the group profit after tax is attributable to the minority shareholders in that subsidiary. The minority shareholders' interest in the group profit is a proportion of the profit after tax earned by the subsidiary. This must be calculated and deducted from the group profit after tax in order to determine the amount of group profit attributable to shareholders of the parent company.

In many cases the calculation of the minority shareholders' interest in group profit after tax is quite straightforward. If we look at the profit and loss account of the subsidiary that has minority interests we will see the profit after tax earned by their company. Since this has been consolidated in full we can simply calculate a percentage of that profit in order to calculate the minority interests' share. The percentage will depend on the proportion of shares owned by the minority shareholders.

In some cases, however, there might be a small adjustment to make in order to find the amount of profit after tax that has been consolidated for a subsidiary. We can see what this adjustment is by continuing with the example from Activities 3.1 and 3.2 and assuming that the following figures apply:

	Parent company	Subsidiary	Consolidated
	£	£	£
Turnover	800 000	600 000	1 300 000 ✗
Cost of sales	480 000	350 000	750 000 ✗
Gross profit	320 000	250 000	550 000
Operating costs	220 000	200 000	440 000
Profit before tax	100 000	50 000	130 000
Taxation	20 000	10 000	30 000
Profit after tax	80 000	40 000	100 000

Notice that the consolidated profit after tax is £20 000 less than the total found by adding the profit after tax for each company. This is because the consolidated profit includes the adjustment of £20 000 for unrealized profit as dealt with in Activity 3.2.

Activity 3.4

We now need to determine the amount to be deducted from group profit after tax for the 30% minority interests in the subsidiary. But the amount is not 30% of £40 000 because we have not consolidated £40 000 in respect of the subsidiary. You will find it helpful to do two things, namely:

1. Describe why the group profit of £100 000 does not include £40 000 for the subsidiary. You might need to recall something that was discussed in Chapter 2, pp. 46–47.

2. Calculate the figure that will be deducted from group profit after tax for minority interests.

The way in which the unrealized profit on stock affects the minority interests will depend on which company recorded the profit when the goods were transferred (see paras 39 and 83 of FRS 2). In the above example, the goods were sold by the subsidiary to the parent company and so the unrealized profit forms a part of the total profit recorded by the subsidiary. If the goods had been sold by the parent company to the subsidiary, the profit would have been recorded by the parent company and there would have been no adjustment to make to the subsidiary's profit when calculating the amount for minority interests.

Dividends

After deducting the amount of profit attributable to minority interests we are left with a sub-total which has no official description but could be described as ordinary profit attributable to shareholders of the parent company. Notice how this description uses the word 'attributable' and not distributable. As mentioned in Chapter 1, a group is an artificial entity and as such it cannot make distributions. Any dividends paid to the parent company's shareholders will be paid by the parent company.

According to the Companies Act formats (and illustrations in FRS 3) this sub-total might be followed by 'extraordinary items' but since FRS 3 has made it almost impossible to treat any item as extraordinary we will continue the discussion on the assumption that extraordinary items do not exist. In these circumstances the sub-total of ordinary profit after tax attributable to shareholders in the parent company is the same as 'Profit for the financial year' as described in line 20 of Format 1.

Since this profit represents the interests of the parent company's shareholders in the group profit, it follows that the consolidated profit statement will show how much profit has been (or will be) distributed to shareholders of the parent company in the form of a dividend. The amount shown in the consolidated profit and loss account for dividends (paid and proposed) will, therefore, be the dividends shown in the parent company's own profit and loss account.

You must, however, keep in mind that at this point in the profit statement we are dealing with a situation that is somewhat fictitious. The dividends paid and payable by the parent company are not distributed from group profits; they are distributed from profits of the parent company.

This form of presentation in the group accounts is in keeping with the idea of treating the group as if it were a separate entity owned by shareholders of the parent company. In this context, dividends paid by the subsidiary are not dividends paid by the group. If a subsidiary is wholly owned the dividends paid by that subsidiary are a transfer of profits from subsidiary to parent company (in other words dividends paid by the subsidiary are set off against dividends received by the holding company). If a subsidiary is not wholly owned, the dividends paid (and proposed) by that subsidiary are partly a transfer of profits to the holding company and partly a distribution of the amount of profit attributable to minority interests.

We can practise dealing with this aspect by adding further information to the previous example.

Activity 3.5

Complete the consolidated profit and loss account in the following table by inserting the proposed dividends and retained profit for the financial year.

	Parent	Subsidiary	Consolidated
	£	£	£
Turnover	800 000	600 000	1 300 000
Cost of sales	480 000	350 000	750 000
Gross profit	320 000	250 000	550 000
Operating costs	220 000	200 000	420 000
Profit before tax	100 000	50 000	130 000
Taxation	20 000	10 000	30 000
Profit after tax	80 000	40 000	100 000
Minority interests	—	—	6 000
Profit for the financial year	80 000	40 000	94 000
Proposed dividends	20 000	10 000	20,000
Retained profit for the financial year	60 000	30 000	74

Notice that the profit and loss account for the parent company in the above example does not include dividends receivable from the subsidiary. Examination questions are often presented in this way but it will be necessary to recognize the dividend receivable in the parent company's profit statement if you are required to do something beyond preparing a simple consolidated profit and loss account for the year. Dividend income from investments in companies outside of the group is normally disclosed on a cash received basis, but dividends from investments in subsidiaries must recognize dividends receivable in order to complete some of the procedures beyond preparation of the consolidated profit and loss account.

We can consider one aspect of this in the next section which deals with additional information that must be disclosed if the parent company does not publish its own profit and loss account. On pp. 73–74 you will see how dividends receivable by the parent company are cancelled against dividends payable by the subsidiary when preparing the consolidated balance sheet.

Omitting parent company's own profit and loss account

Each individual company in a group must prepare and approve its own profit and loss account and balance sheet in accordance with provisions in the Companies Act. But Section 230 of the Companies Act 1985 provides that the parent company's profit and loss account may be omitted from the published annual accounts providing certain information is disclosed in the notes. The full wording of Section 230 is included in the appendix to this chapter (Section A) but the effect of these provisions can be stated as follows:

The parent company may omit its own individual profit and loss account from the published annual accounts providing:

1. The parent company produces group accounts in accordance with the Act.
2. The notes to the accounts state the amount of the parent company's profit for the financial year.
3. The notes state that this exemption applies.

The statutory notes supplementing the parent company's own profit and loss account may be omitted.

It would be quite unusual for a parent company not to take advantage of this provision and so the practical effect is that the published accounts of a group normally include the following:

- a consolidated profit and loss account;
- a consolidated balance sheet;
- the parent company's balance sheet;
- supplementary notes to the parent company's balance sheet and to the consolidated balance sheet.

With regard to the balance sheets, it is a common practice to present a single financial statement with separate figures for the parent company and the group set out in adjacent columns. A similar approach is used for the supplementary notes to the balance sheets.

The statutory note regarding the parent company's profit (point 2 above) is presented in various ways. If you read the provision in Section 230 in the appendix you will see that it requires the note to state the amount of the parent company's 'Profit for the financial year'. Strictly speaking this refers to the profit after extraordinary items but since these have been more-or-less banned by FRS 3, profit for the financial year is likely to be the same figure as group profit after tax less minority interests. Some companies simply disclose the amount in a separate note. For example, the financial statements of Marks & Spencer plc for 1993 included the following note:

9. Profit for the financial year

As permitted by Section 230 of the Companies Act 1985, the profit and loss account of the Company is not presented as part of these financial statements.

The consolidated profit of £495.5m includes £452.3m which is dealt with in the accounts of the Company.

The actual note included figures for the previous year but these have been excluded from the above for the sake of clarity. In this example, the term 'the Company' means the parent company. The consolidated profit of £495.5 million was a reference to group profit after deducting minority interests (profit for the financial year).

The above note is all that is required by statute but some companies disclose more information. This can take various forms such as showing how much of the consolidated profit for the financial year has been dealt with in the parent company's accounts and how much has been retained by the subsidiaries. Sometimes companies take the note even further by analysing the closing balance on the consolidated profit and loss account (as shown in the balance sheet) between how much has been retained in the parent company and how much in the subsidiaries.

We must now return to our example and practise applying this provision. The figures for the final part of the profit and loss accounts were as follows:

	Parent	Subsidiary	Consolidated
	£	£	£
Profit after tax	80 000	40 000	100 000
Minority interests	—	—	6 000
Profit for the financial year	80 000	40 000	94 000
Proposed dividends	20 000	10 000	20 000
Retained profit for the financial year	60 000	30 000	74 000 ✳

Activity 3.6

We need to work out how much of the consolidated profit for the financial year (£94 000) has been dealt with in the accounts of the parent company. In this example it would be wrong to disclose the amount as £80 000 as shown in the above accounts for the parent company. You will find it helpful to do this activity in two stages, as follows:

1. Make a note here of why the amount is not £80 000 (you might have to think back to some of the previous text on dividends). Don't forget that the parent company has a 70% interest in the subsidiary.

2. Calculate the amount of group profit for the financial year that has been dealt with in the accounts of the parent company.

If it were necessary to show how the retained profit for the financial year of £74 000 is divided between parent and subsidiary, we would have to take account of adjustments for the dividend receivable and the unrealized profit on stock. Our workings would be on the following lines:

	£
Retained by the parent company (£60 000 + £7000)	67 000
Retained in the subsidiary 70% × (£30 000 – £20 000)	7 000
	74 000

Movements on the profit and loss reserve

The amount for the reserve item called 'Profit and loss account' in the consolidated balance sheet is calculated in the usual way, namely:

- the consolidated balance brought forward from the previous year, plus
- the retained profit for the current year, giving
- the consolidated balance carried forward at the end of the year.

The retained profit for the current year is found by preparing the consolidated profit and loss account. When preparing a statement showing the movements on the profit and loss reserve, you need to take care when calculating the balance of retained profits brought forward from the previous year.

The underlying approach was developed in Chapter 2 where you identified the balance on the profit and loss account reserve as being:

- the whole of the profit retained by the parent company, plus
- the parent company's share of post-acquisition profits retained in the subsidiary.

We can practise preparing a statement showing movements on the consolidated profit and loss reserve by adding information to the example we have been working. Assume that the movements on each company's profit and loss account reserve were shown in the accounts as follows:

	Parent	Subsidiary
	£	£
Balance at beginning of year	400 000	200 000
Retained profit for the financial year (as above)	60 000	30 000
Balance at end of the year	460 000	230 000

Note that the figure of £60 000 for the parent company is the amount shown in its original accounts and does not yet include the adjustment for dividends receivable from the subsidiary.

The following additional information is relevant to the activity:

The parent company obtained its 70% interest in the subsidiary several years earlier when the balance on the subsidiary's profit and loss account was £120 000

Activity 3.7

Your task is to produce a statement showing movements on the consolidated profit and loss reserve. This information is required for notes to the consolidated balance sheet. You will find it helpful to do this in two stages, as follows:

1. Work out the parent company's interest in the post-acquisition profits brought forward by the subsidiary and make a note of it here:

2. Complete the following statement. When doing this, remember to add the whole of the parent company's balance brought forward to the amount for the subsidiary found in 1 above.

Movements on the consolidated profit and loss reserve

Balance at beginning of year   £

Retained profit for the financial year
   (see figures above Activity 3.6)   £ _____

Balance at end of year

Although there is no statutory requirement to analyse this balance between amounts retained by the parent and amounts retained in the subsidiary, some companies do disclose this information. A request for this analysis also appears in examination questions from time to time. It is not difficult to work out the figures from the separate accounts although you do need to keep thinking back to the way these have been adjusted for the consolidation. In our example the analysis is as follows:

Analysis of balance on profit and loss reserve

	Workings £	Amount £
1. *Retained by parent*		
As stated in the accounts	460 000	
Dividends receivable	7 000	
		467 000
2. *Retained in subsidiary*		
Brought forward (Activity 3.7)	56 000	
For the year 70% × (£30 000 − £20 000)	7 000	
		63 000
		530 000

Completing the example with a balance sheet

It is never very satisfying to study the construction of a consolidated profit and loss account in isolation. When we are working on the financial statements for a single company we usually expect to prepare a profit and loss account and a balance sheet. The agreement of the balance sheet totals helps to persuade us that we have not made any arithmetical errors. In the case of a consolidated balance sheet there are additional matters to sort out such as the cancellation of inter-company balances for dividends receivable and payable.

We can do a consolidated balance sheet for our example by providing information on the balance sheets of each company. We will keep the detail to a minimum in order to concentrate on the additional learning points of this chapter. Consequently, we will not be dealing with the various complications that can arise such as recognizing the fair values of the subsidiary's identifiable assets at acquisition, and cancellation of unsettled inter-company balances. These aspects were studied in Chapter 2.

The abbreviated balance sheets of the two companies in our example are as follows:

	Parent	Subsidiary
Fixed assets		
	£	£
Tangible fixed assets	520 000	260 000
Investment in subsidiary at cost	160 000	
	680 000	260 000
Current assets		
Stock	400 000	100 000
Dividends receivable	not recorded	
Others	100 000	50 000
	500 000	150 000
Creditors falling due within one year		
Proposed dividends	20 000	10 000
Others	300 000	70 000
	320 000	80 000
Net current assets	180 000	70 000
Total assets less current liabilities	860 000	330 000
Capital and reserves		
Share capital (£1 ordinary shares)	400 000	100 000
Profit and loss account	460 000	230 000
	860 000	330 000

Most of the information needed in order to prepare the consolidated balance sheet has been given in the previous text. In order to summarize the position, the information is repeated here as follows:

1. The balance on the profit and loss account of the subsidiary at the date of acquisition was £120 000.

2. The unrealized profit on stock was £20 000 and the profit had been recorded by the subsidiary.
3. The parent company has not recorded the dividend receivable from the subsidiary.
4. The parent company's interest in the subsidiary is 70%.

The following additional information is now available:

1. The fair values of the identifiable assets and liabilities at the date of acquisition were the same as their book values.
2. When the subsidiary was acquired, the group decided to write off goodwill on consolidation against the balance on the consolidated profit and loss reserve.
3. There are no unsettled inter-company balances other than those that relate to dividends.

We have already worked out the balance on the consolidated profit and loss account as £530 000 following Activity 3.7. This must now be reduced by the goodwill write-off as mentioned in note 2 above. The matters that we need to resolve before constructing a consolidated balance sheet are:

- calculating goodwill arising on consolidation;
- calculating the amounts attributable to minority interests;
- dealing with the balances for inter-company dividends.

The calculations for goodwill and minority interests were covered in Chapter 2. The extra learning point in this chapter concerns inter-company dividends and so we will deal with that aspect first.

You need to keep in mind that we have been working with a set of accounts for the parent company that do not include dividends receivable from the subsidiary. For consolidation purposes it is necessary to make an adjustment to the parent company's figures for the dividend receivable as follows:

- increase the parent company's retained profits by £7000;
- include a debtor in the parent company's balance sheet for dividends receivable of £7000.

An enthusiast on double entry book-keeping would say: debit dividends receivable with £7000; credit profit and loss account with £7000.

In our activities for the balance on the consolidated profit and loss account we have included the dividend of £7000 receivable by the parent company. Since we have made an adjustment for the income side of the double entry we must also recognize that we have adjusted the parent company's balance sheet to include a debtor of £7000 for the dividend receivable. There is little point in reproducing the adjusted balance sheet of the parent company here because we can easily imagine what it would look like if it included the debtor of £7000.

Any balances for unsettled inter-company items must be cancelled when preparing the consolidated balance sheet. If we now set off the dividend receivable in the parent company's balance sheet against the proposed dividend in the subsidiary's balance sheet we finish up with a net creditor, as follows:

	£
In the parent company's balance sheet	
Dividend receivable (a debtor)	7 000
In the subsidiary's balance sheet	
Dividend payable (a creditor)	10 000
Net creditor	3 000

Activity 3.8

Identify the nature of this creditor and describe it here:

This is a genuine creditor of the group since it represents an amount payable to parties external to the group. It is normally presented in the same part of the balance sheet as dividends payable (by the parent company) to the parent company's shareholders. It is not good practice to add it to the balance sheet figure for minority interests. The dividend does represent an amount which the group will be paying whereas the figure described as minority interests in the consolidated balance sheet is more in the nature of the minority shareholders' interest in the equity of their company.

We now need to calculate the amount for goodwill and for minority interests. The amount for minority interests is always the easiest and so we will do that first. When doing this there is no need to be concerned with the adjustment made for minority interests in the consolidated profit and loss account. The amount for the balance sheet can be found by simply looking at the subsidiary's balance sheet and calculating a percentage of the equity capital and reserves of that subsidiary.

There is, however, one small snag when doing this in our example. You need to remember that for consolidation purposes we have reduced the subsidiary's profits for the current year by £20 000 in order to recognize the unrealized profit on stock. You will recall from Chapter 2 that FRS 2 requires minority interests to bear their share of this adjustment if the profit had been recorded in their company's accounts.

Activity 3.9

Calculate the amount to be included in the consolidated balance sheet for minority interests.

Goodwill is a relatively straightforward calculation in this example because there are no fair value adjustments at the date of acquisition. Since the company has adopted an immediate write-off policy, the following activity requires you to calculate goodwill and then set this off against the balance on the consolidated profit and loss reserve as calculated for Activity 3.7.

Activity 3.10

1. Calculate the amount for goodwill arising on consolidation.

2. Set this amount against the balance on consolidated profit and loss reserve.

Balance on consolidated profit and loss account (Activity 3.7)	£530 000
Less goodwill written off (1 above)	_____
Revised balance	_____

You have now done all the work needed to prepare a consolidated balance sheet. There is an outline format below the next activity box which you can complete by inserting the relevant figures. Take care with the figure for stock; remember that there has been a consolidation adjustment for unrealized profit.

Activity 3.11

Complete the consolidated balance sheet by inserting the figures in the following outline format.

Consolidated balance sheet

Tangible fixed assets — £

Current assets
Stock — £
Others — £ _____

_____

Creditors falling due within one year
Proposed dividends:
Parent company — £
Minority interests — £
Others — £ _____

_____

Net current assets

£ _____

_____

Capital and reserves
Share capital
Profit and loss account

Minority interests

Reconciliation of minority interests

Some students tend to worry about the apparent lack of linkage between the various items that affect minority interests such as: share of profit, dividends, and changes in the final balance. It is possible to reconcile the movements on the balance for minority interests by linking these items. There is usually no need to do this for examination questions but it provides a useful learning point and it is sometimes necessary to reconcile minority interests when sorting out figures for a group cash flow statement (see Chapter 4).

In our example, we can reconcile movements on minority interests over the current year. At the start of the year, the minority interests would have been 30% of the share capital and reserves in the subsidiary. The subsidiary's profit and loss reserve at the start of the year was £200 000 (see figures above Activity 3.7). The figure for minority interests was, therefore, (30% × (£100 000 + £200 000)) £90 000. The figure for minority interests at the end of the year is £93 000. Movements can be reconciled as follows:

	£
Balance at beginning of year	90 000
Add share of profit for current year	
(see consolidated profit and loss account above Activity 3.6)	6 000
	96 000
Less proposed dividend (included as a current liability)	3 000
Balance at end of year	93 000

Associated undertakings — equity accounting

The equity method of accounting for an investment in another company was outlined in Chapter 1. It was designed originally for investments in associated companies but it is also required by statute (and FRS 2) for certain types of subsidiary which have been excluded from the normal consolidation. The circumstances in which a subsidiary might be (or must be) excluded from consolidation are discussed in Chapter 11.

The primary accounting standard on the subject is SSAP 1, issued in 1971. This has been revised from time to time but the basic principle has not changed to any great extent. The statutory regulations for associated companies are in Schedule 4A of the Companies Act 1985, paragraphs 20 to 23. These provisions were introduced by the Companies Act 1989.

Definitions

We will look at two terms: associated companies (or undertakings) and equity accounting.

Companies or undertakings?

The Companies Act refers to 'associated undertakings' whereas SSAP 1 refers to 'associated companies'. The term 'undertaking' includes non-corporate entities and so strictly speaking the term 'associated company' is out of date. The original terminology in SSAP 1 has never been changed, probably because the definitions make it clear that investments in associated companies include investments in non-corporate organizations (para. 11). In this book we will use the term 'associated undertaking' but confine our study of equity accounting to investments in another limited company.

Associated undertaking

The statutory definition of an associated undertaking is similar to that in SSAP 1 except that it includes a term that is defined in another part of the Act. The relevant provisions from the Companies Act are set out in the appendix to this chapter (Section B) but the definition of an associated undertaking can be paraphrased as follows:

- an undertaking, other than a subsidiary of the parent company, in which a member of the group has a participating interest and over whose operating and financial policy it exercises a significant influence;
- where an undertaking holds 20% or more of the voting rights in another undertaking, it shall be presumed to exercise such an influence over it unless the contrary is shown;
- a participating interest means an investment in the shares of another undertaking that are held on a long-term basis for the purposes of securing a gain through the exercise of control or influence over that undertaking;
- a holding of 20% or more of the shares in another undertaking is presumed to be a participating interest.

There are other aspects to the definition of an associated undertaking but in this book we will assume that a company must be treated as an associated undertaking if the investing company owns from 20% up to 50% of the equity shares.

Equity accounting

Although the Companies Act requires associated undertakings to be dealt with by the equity method of accounting, it does not define or explain the equity method; neither does SSAP 1. There is a definition in FRS 2. It is one of the longest (unpunctuated) sentences that I have ever read in official literature and is as follows:

A method of accounting for an investment that brings into the consolidated profit and loss account the investor's share of the investment undertaking's results and that records the investment in the consolidated balance sheet at the investor's share of the investment undertaking's net assets including any goodwill arising to the extent that it has not previously been written off.

Accounting regulations

There is a distinction between the accounting treatment in:

- the investing company's own accounts; and
- the consolidated accounts for the group.

If the investing company is not part of a group, consolidated accounts are not prepared. In this case a supplementary statement must be prepared to incorporate the results of associated undertakings on a basis similar to that required for consolidated accounts. This statement (a supplement to the investing company's own accounts) is not studied in this book since it is assumed that you will always be dealing with associated companies in the context of a group. The effect of the various regulations is as follows:

The investing company's own accounts

Balance sheet

The investment will be shown at cost, less any amounts written off (e.g. for permanent diminution in value). The amount must be presented as a fixed asset investment under 'Participating interests', i.e. item B. III. 3. in Format 1.

Profit and loss account

Include dividends received and dividends receivable. (Note how dividends receivable must be included.) The amount must be presented as a part of 'Income from participating interests', i.e. item 8 in Format 1.

The consolidated accounts

Both SSAP 1 and the Companies Act require that an associated undertaking is dealt with by the **equity method** of accounting. In broad terms, the equity method of accounting requires the following amounts to be reported.

Consolidated balance sheet

The amount of the investment is measured on the basis of a share of the associated undertaking's net assets, including any goodwill arising on the acquisition to the extent that it has not previously been written off. Goodwill is calculated in the same way as for a subsidiary and involves the recognition of fair values.

For presentation purposes, the item described as 'Participating interests' in the official formats (item B. III. 3. in Format 1) is replaced by two items, namely:

- interests in associated undertakings; and
- other participating interests.

Consolidated profit and loss account

Dividends received and receivable are replaced by the investor's share of the associated undertaking's profit (or loss) for the year. This is dealt with on two lines, namely:

- share of associated undertaking's profits before tax; and
- share of associated undertaking's tax charge.

For presentation purposes, the share of profits before tax is described as: 'Income from interests in associated undertakings' and is included as a part of item 8 in Format 1. The group's share of the associated company's tax charge is described as 'Share of tax in associated undertakings' and included with the total tax charge for the group.

Equity accounting is sometimes described as a single line consolidation. Note the following differences between equity accounting and a full consolidation.

Consolidated profit and loss account

In a full consolidation, 100% of each item in the subsidiary's profit and loss account is consolidated on a line by line basis. The minority interests' share of profits in the subsidiary (if any) is deducted from group profit after tax.

Equity accounting consolidates a single amount for a share of the associated undertaking's profits. This is reported on two lines; share of profits before tax, and share of tax charge.

Consolidated balance sheet

In a full consolidation, 100% of each class of asset and liability in the subsidiary is added to the corresponding class of asset and liability in the holding company's balance sheet. The minority shareholders' interests in the net assets of their company is then shown separately (either as a deduction from group net assets, or as part of the capital and reserves).

In equity accounting, a single figure for a share of the associated undertaking's net assets is shown under investments. To the extent that goodwill arising on the acquisition has not been written off, it is added (as an extra line) to this share of net assets.

The mechanics of equity accounting

We can see the mechanics of equity accounting by working on a simple example. In order to clarify the explanation we will assume that the investing company has had no dealings other than those that relate to its investment in an associated undertaking.

Details

On 1 January 1995, a parent company issued 200 £1 shares at par and used the entire proceeds of £200 to acquire 25% of the share capital of an associated undertaking at a cost of £200. The key figures in the financial statements of the associated undertaking for 1995 were as follows:

	£
Net assets at 1 January 1995	700
Profit and loss account for 1995	
Profits before tax	200
Taxation	60
Profits after tax	140
Dividends paid	40
Profit retained	100
Net assets at 31 December 1995	800

The following assumptions will be made.

1. Fair values of assets are the same as book values.
2. The parent company has had no dealings other than those that relate to its investment in the associated undertaking (this will enable you to see the movement of the relevant figures).
3. Tax credits on dividends received can be ignored.
4. None of the goodwill on acquisition is to be written off.

The separate financial statements of the investing company will record the investment at cost in its balance sheet and record dividends received (and receivable) in the profit and loss account. The investing company's financial statements based on these circumstances will be as follows:

Profit and loss account

	£
Income from participating interests (dividends 25% × £40)	10
Retained profit for the financial year	10

Balance sheet
Investments:
Participating interests, at cost 200

	£
Current assets	
Cash at bank	10
	210

Capital and reserves	
Share capital	200
Profit and loss account	10
	210

We now need to think about equity accounting and how the interest in this associated undertaking will be presented in a consolidated balance. At the date when the investment was made the cost of the investment will be the same as the total of the following:

- share of net assets in the associated undertaking; plus
- any premium (goodwill) on acquisition.

You can prove this by working the following activity:

Activity 3.12

Calculate the following:

1. Investing company's share of net assets in associated undertaking at the date of acquisition.

2. Goodwill on acquisition (calculated in the same way as for a subsidiary).

Notice that the total of these two items (£175 + £25) is the same as the cost of the investment. This will always be the case at the date of acquisition.

In the consolidated profit and loss account for 1995, the dividends received from the associated undertaking are replaced by a share of the profits earned by the undertaking. On this basis the consolidated profit and loss account will be as follows:

Consolidated profit and loss account

Income from investments in associated undertakings (25% × £200)	£50
Taxation:	
Share of tax in associated undertakings (25% × £60)	15
Retained profit for the financial year	35

Activity 3.13

Complete the figures for the consolidated balance sheet as set out below this box.

Balance sheet at 31 December 1995

Investments
    Interests in associated undertakings:
        Share of net assets   £
        Goodwill on acquisition   £ _____

Current assets
    Cash at bank   £ _____

_____

Capital and reserves
    Share capital
    Profit and loss account   _____

_____

The amount shown as goodwill is subject to regulations in SSAP 22 in the same way as goodwill arising on the consolidation of a subsidiary.

Notice how the carrying value of the investment has been increased by the amount of profit retained by the associated undertaking, as follows:

	£
Interest in associated undertakings	
Balance at 1 January 1995	200
Share of retained profit for the year (25% × £100)	25
Balance at 31 December 1995	225

Suggested format for the profit and loss account

The positioning in the profit and loss account for income from associated undertakings is best seen by example. The following is a suggested format for the consolidated profit and loss account based on Format 1 in the Companies Act. It will cover most situations but it might have to be modified to suit individual cases.

	£	£
Turnover		
Cost of sales		_____
Gross profit		
Other operating expenses		_____
Operating profit		
Income from interests in associated undertakings		
Investment income		
Interest payable and similar charges		_____
Profit on ordinary activities before tax		
Taxation:		
Group		
Share of tax in associated undertakings	_____	_____
Profit on ordinary activities after tax		
Minority interests		_____
Extraordinary items (included here to show position only — these items are unlikely to occur)		_____
Profit for the financial year		
Dividends (paid and proposed to members of holding company)		_____
Retained profit for the financial year		======

Summary

The main learning points in this chapter can be summarized as follows:

- the individual items in a subsidiary's profit and loss account from turnover to taxation are added in full to the corresponding items in the parent company's profit and loss account;
- there are likely to be some adjustments to this basic process to eliminate the effect of inter-company trading and unrealized profit on stock;
- dividends received by the parent company from the subsidiary do not represent group income and are not included in the consolidated profit and loss account;
- group profit after tax includes the whole of the subsidiary's profits after tax and so an adjustment is made to show the minority interests' share of this profit;
- dividends paid (and proposed) are included in the consolidated profit and loss account according to the amounts shown in the parent company's accounts;
- an adjustment must be made to the parent company's accounts in order to recognize any dividend receivable from the subsidiary;

- the parent company need not publish its own profit and loss account providing the notes to the parent company's balance sheet disclose how much of the group profit for the financial has been dealt with in the parent company's accounts;
- the amount dealt with in the parent company's accounts will be the profit after tax as reported in the parent company's profit and loss account plus any dividend receivable from the subsidiary if this has not been recorded by the parent company;
- the creditor for proposed dividends payable by the subsidiary is set against the corresponding dividends receivable by the parent company; any remaining balance will represent dividends payable to the minority interests;
- dividends payable to minority interests are a real creditor of the group
- investments in another company representing 20% to 50% of the voting capital are likely to be classed as investments in associated undertakings and must be dealt with under the equity method of accounting;
- equity accounting replaces dividends received and receivable as shown in the investing company's accounts with a share of the associated undertakings profits for the financial year; the balance sheet shows the investment at an amount equal to a share of the associated undertaking's net assets plus any goodwill to the extent that it has not been written off.

Key to activities

Activity 3.1

1. Turnover (£800 000 + £600 000 − £100 000) £1 300 000
2. Cost of sales (£480 000 + £350 000 − £100 000) £730 000

(Sales of the holding company become purchases of the subsidiary)

Activity 3.2

£730 000 + £20 000 = £750 000

Activity 3.3

Dividends received from the subsidiary.

Activity 3.4

1. The £20 000 unrealized profit on stock forms a part of the profit recorded by the subsidiary. This has now been eliminated for the consolidation.
2. 30% × (£40 000 − £20 000) = £6000

Activity 3.5

The appropriation section of the consolidated profit and loss account is as follows:

	£
Profit for the financial year	94 000
Proposed dividends	20 000
Retained profit for the financial year	74 000

Activity 3.6

1. The parent company's profit in the example does not include the dividend receivable from the subsidiary of (70% × £10 000) £7000. This must be included as income (by setting up a debtor) in the working papers even if it is not accrued in the actual books of the parent company.
2. £80 000 + £7000 = £87 000

Activity 3.7

1. 70% × (£200 000 – £120 000) = £56 000

2. *Movements on profit and loss reserve*

	£
Balance at beginning of year (£400 000 + £56 000)	456 000 ✔
Retained profit for the financial year	74 000 ✱
Balance at end of year	530 000

Activity 3.8

The dividend payable by the subsidiary to its minority shareholders (30% × £10 000).

Activity 3.9

30% × (£330 000 – £20 000) = £93 000 ✓

Activity 3.10

1. £160 000 – (70% × (£100 000 + £120 000)) = £6000 ✱

	£
2. Consolidated profit and loss account	530 000
Goodwill written off	6 000
Revised balance	524 000

Activity 3.11

Consolidated balance sheet	£	£
Tangible fixed assets		780 000
Current assets		
Stock	480 000	
Others	150 000	
	630 000	
Creditors falling due within one year		
Proposed dividends:		
Parent company	20 000	
Minority interests	3 000	
Others	370 000	
	393 000	
Net current assets		237 000
		1 017 000
Capital and reserves		
Share capital		400 000
Profit and loss account		524 000
		924 000
Minority interests		93 000
		1 017 000

Activity 3.12

1. $25\% \times £700 = £175$
2. $£200 - £175 = £25$

Activity 3.13

Investments

Interest in associated undertakings:

	£
Share of net assets (25% × £800)	200
Goodwill on acquisition	25
	225

Current assets

	£
Cash at bank	10
	235

Capital and reserves

	£
Share capital	200
Profit and loss account	35
	235

Appendix

Section A: extracts from the Companies Act 1985

SEC. 230 Treatment of individual profit and loss account where group accounts prepared

230(1) [**Application**] The following provisions apply with respect to the individual profit and loss account of a parent company where —
  (a)   the company is required to prepare and does prepare group accounts in accordance with this Act, and
  (b)   the notes to the company's individual balance sheet show the company's profit or loss for the financial year determined in accordance with this Act.

230(2) [**Profit and loss account need not have certain information**] The profit and loss account need not contain the information specified in paragraphs 52 to 57 of Schedule 4 (information supplementing the profit and loss account).

230(3) [**Approval, omission**] The profit and loss account must be approved in accordance with section 233(1) (approval by board of directors) but may be omitted from the company's annual accounts for the purposes of the other provisions below this Chapter.

230(4) [**Disclosure re exemption**] The exemption conferred by this section is conditional upon its being disclosed in the company's annual accounts that the exemption applies.

Section B: extracts from Schedule 4A of the Companies Act 1985

20(1)   An "**associated undertaking**" means an undertaking in which an undertaking included in the consolidation has a participating interest and over whose operating and financial policy it exercises a significant influence, and which is not —

(a)   a subsidiary undertaking of the parent company, or

(b)   a joint venture dealt with in accordance with paragraph 19.

20(2)   Where an undertaking holds 20 per cent or more of the voting rights in another undertaking, it shall be presumed to exercise such an influence over it unless the contrary is shown.

Extracts from section 260 (Participating interests) Companies Act 1985

260(1)   ["Participating interest"] In this Part a "participating interest" means an interest held by an undertaking in the shares of another undertaking which it holds on a long-term basis for the purpose of securing a contribution to its activities by the exercise of control or influence arising from or related to that interest.

260(2)   [Presumption] A holding of 20 per cent or more of the shares of an undertaking shall be presumed to be a participating interest unless the contrary is shown.

Questions

Questions for self assessment

Answers to self-assessment questions are given at the end of the book

3.1 Primer

The following are the balance sheets for Parent Ltd and its subsidiary Sub Ltd and associated undertaking Ass Ltd at 31 December 19X1:

	Parent Ltd		Sub Ltd		Ass Ltd	
Fixed assets		30 000		80 000		62 000
Investments:						
Sub Ltd 30 000 shares		50 000				
Ass Ltd 10 000 shares		12 000				
Current assets	34 000		18 000		15 000	
Current liabilities:						
Proposed dividends	16 000		5 000		4 000	
Creditors	10 000		3 000		3 000	
	26 000		8 000		7 000	
Net current assets		8 000		10 000		8 000
		100 000		90 000		70 000
Capital and reserves						
£1 ordinary shares		80 000		50 000		40 000
Share premium account		8 000		2 000		
Profit and loss account		12 000		38 000		30 000
		100 000		90 000		70 000

Parent Ltd's investment in Sub Ltd was made two years earlier when the balance on Sub Ltd's profit and loss account was £20 000. The investment in Ass Ltd was made several years earlier when the balance on Ass Ltd's profit and loss account was £4 000.

At the time of Parent Ltd's acquisition of Sub Ltd, it was considered that the fair values of the fixed assets in Sub Ltd were £3000 in excess of their book value, but the revaluation has never been written into the subsidiary's books. Depreciation charges based on the revalued amounts would exceed the amount provided in the subsidiary's books by £300 for the two years.

The fair values of Ass Ltd's separable net assets at the time of acquisition were considered to be the same as their book value. There have been no new share issues by either Sub Ltd or Ass Ltd since the investments were acquired by Parent Ltd.

Parent Ltd's current assets include stocks purchased from Sub Ltd on which there is an unrealized profit of £500. Parent Ltd has not made any adjustment for dividends receivable from Sub Ltd or Ass Ltd. In the consolidated accounts, goodwill is written off immediately against group reserves.

Required

Prepare a consolidated balance sheet for the group that complies, in so far as the information permits, with all relevant accounting regulations.

Author

3.2 Court group

The following information relates to Court Limited and its subsidiary companies, Trial Limited and Jury Limited, for the year to 31 December 1991:

	Court Ltd £000	Trial Ltd £000	Jury Ltd £000
Profit and loss accounts			
Sales	1000	300	110
Costs	700	100	120
	300	200	(10)
Tax	100	80	10
	200	120	(20)
Dividends	150	—	—
Retained profits/(losses)	50	120	(20)
Balance sheets			
Fixed assets	1500	500	300
Investments in:			
Trial Limited	300		
Jury Limited	200		
Current assets	500	220	100
Creditors	(350)	(200)	(250)
Proposed dividend	(150)		
	2000	520	150
Ordinary share capital (£1 shares)	1500	300	100
Retained profits	500	220	50
	2000	520	150

Additional information

Court Ltd bought a 60% holding in Trial Ltd on 1 January 1985. At that time, Trial's retained profits were £100 000. Court purchased a 100% holding in Jury Ltd on 1 January 1991, Jury's retained profits then being £70 000. Court writes off goodwill arising on consolidation against reserves at the time of acquisition.

Required

Prepare the Court Group of Companies' consolidated profit and loss account for the year to 31 December 1991, and a balance sheet as at that date. The detailed disclosure requirements of the Companies Act 1985 may be ignored, although you should set out your accounts as fully as the information permits.

AAT Final, June 1992

Question without answer

The answer is published separately in the *Teacher's Manual.*

3.3 Alpha group

See author's guidance notes at the end of the question. The question as set out below has been altered slightly from the original in order to bring it into line with the requirements in FRS 2 for unrealized profit on stock.

The following accounts are the consolidated balance sheet and parent company balance sheet for Alpha Ltd as at 30 June 19X2

		Consolidated £		Parent £
Ordinary shares		140 000		140 000
Capital reserves		92 400		92 400
Profit and loss account		79 800		35 280
Minority interests		12 320		
		324 520		267 680
Fixed assets				
Freehold premises		127 400		84 000
Plant and machinery		62 720		50 400
Goodwill arising on consolidation		85 680		
Investment in subsidiary				
(50 400 shares)				151 200
Current assets				
Stock	121 520		71 120	
Debtors	70 420		46 760	
Dividends receivable			5 040	
Cash at bank	24 360			
	216 300		122 920	
Current liabilities				
Creditors	128 660		69 720	
Corporation tax	27 160		20 720	
Bank overdraft			39 200	
Proposed dividend	11 760		11 200	
	167 580		140 840	
Net current assets/(liabilities)		48 720		(17 920)
		324 520		267 680

Notes:
1. There is only one subsidiary called Beta Ltd.
2. There are no capital reserves in the subsidiary.
3. Alpha produced stock for sale to the subsidiary at cost of £3360 in May 19X2. The stock was invoiced to the subsidiary at £4200 and is still on hand at the subsidiary's warehouse on 30 June 19X2. The invoice had not been settled by 30 June 19X2.
4. The profit and loss account of the subsidiary had a credit balance of £16 800 at the date of acquisition.

5. There is no right of set-off between bank overdrafts and bank balances.
6. Alpha Ltd has not yet adopted any accounting policy on goodwill and the amount shown in the group balance sheet is the total amount arising on consolidation. The fair values of Beta Ltd's net identifiable assets at the date of acquisition were the same as book values.

Required

Prepare the balance sheet of the subsidiary, Beta Ltd.

ACCA 2.9 modified

Author's guidance notes on Question 3.3
The proposed dividends in the consolidated balance sheet are £560 greater than the proposed dividends by the parent company. This difference must represent dividends payable by the subsidiary to its minority interests. You will also notice that the parent company has included dividends receivable from the subsidiary of £5040 in its own balance sheet (this must be receivable from the subsidiary because the parent has no investments other than investments in the subsidiary). From these two pieces of information you can calculate the proposed dividends in the subsidiary's balance sheet, as follows:

	£
Payable to parent company	5040
Payable to minority interests	560
Total proposed dividends of Beta Ltd	5600

You will also have to use this information to find the proportion of Beta Ltd's shares owned by Alpha Ltd because this is not stated (directly) in the question.

Group cash flow statements — the basics

Objectives

After completing this chapter you should be able to:

- calculate dividends paid to minority interests and dividends received from associated undertakings by analysing figures in the consolidated accounts;
- prepare a cash flow statement for a group when there have been no changes in the composition of the group during the year, and present this in accordance with the requirements of FRS 1.

Introduction

The introduction of this subject here will help to reinforce your perception of the underlying structure of group accounts, particularly with regard to equity accounting for associated companies and to transactions that affect minority interests. The text has been written on the assumption that you are familiar with the principles and techniques of preparing a cash flow statement for a single company, and with the standard format prescribed by FRS 1

To some extent the cash flow statement required by FRS 1 for a group is much easier to prepare than the former funds flow statement prescribed by SSAP 10. This is certainly the case where there have been no changes in the composition of the group during the year. The cash flow statement is also less confusing to the user. The former funds flow statement included some very peculiar adjustments to deal with minority interests and associated companies and these were almost meaningless to most people outside of the accountancy profession.

The accounting problems that can arise when a new subsidiary is acquired during the year (or a subsidiary is sold) are not covered in this chapter. The treatment of new acquisitions in the cash flow statement of a group is covered by Chapter 7.

Relevant cash flows

Some of the provisions in FRS 1 relating to group cash flow statements are set out in the appendix to this chapter. The effect of these provisions can be summarized as follows:

- cash flow statements presented with group accounts should reflect cash flows of the group (paragraph 9)
- the statement should deal only with cash flows external to the group; internal cash flows should be eliminated (paragraph 38)
- cash flows of an entity that is equity accounted should be included only to the extent of actual cash flows between the group and that entity (paragraph 39).

All inter-company transactions and unsettled inter-company balances will have been eliminated when the consolidated accounts were prepared. Consequently, there should be no need to make adjustments for internal cash flows when preparing the group cash flow statement from the consolidated accounts. Most of the remaining cash flows will be similar to those for a single company. Additional cash flows (to or from external parties) in the case of a group are the result of transactions that affect **minority interests** and **associated companies**.

In most cases the relevant cash flows in respect of these two external parties will be:

- dividends paid to minority interests;
- dividends received from associated companies.

You should note that the above two amounts are not usually shown anywhere in the consolidated accounts, but they can often be derived from related information.

Finding the relevant figures

Consider the following abbreviated consolidated financial statements:

Abbreviated consolidated profit and loss account for year 2

	£
Operating profit	40 000
Income from interests in associated undertaking	4 000
Profit on ordinary activities before tax	44 000

	£	£
Taxation:		
Group	16 000	
Associated undertaking	1 000	
		17 000
Group profit on ordinary activities after tax		27 000
Minority interests (20%)		2 000
Profit for the financial year		25 000
Dividends paid		5 000
Retained profit for the financial year		20 000

Abbreviated consolidated balance sheets

	At end of year 1 £	At end of year 2 £
Tangible fixed assets (net book value)	100 000	102 000
Interests in associated undertaking	60 000	61 000
Net current assets	110 000	128 000
Taxation creditor	(14 000)	(16 000)
Bank balance	4 000	6 000
	260 000	281 000
Share capital	100 000	100 000
Profit and loss account	120 000	140 000
	220 000	240 000
Minority interests	40 000	41 000
	260 000	281 000

The following information was obtained from the notes:

1. Accounting policy

Goodwill arising on consolidation is written off immediately against reserves (there were no acquisitions or disposals of subsidiaries and associated companies during the year).

2. Profit and loss account reserve

	At start of year 2 £	Retained for year £	At end of of year 2 £
Retained by parent company	100 000	15 000	115 000
Retained in subsidiary	16 000	4 000	20 000
Retained in associated undertaking	4 000	1 000	5 000
Group	120 000	20 000	140 000

3. Fixed assets

The schedule of fixed assets shows that there were no sales of fixed assets during the year and that the depreciation charge for the year was £3000.

Notice how the above accounts and related information do not state how much dividend was paid to the minority interests; nor do they disclose the dividend received from the associated company. But it is possible to derive these figures from the information supplied.

In order to find the dividends paid to the minority interests you need to recall how we were able to reconcile movements on the final balance from minority interests in Chapter 3.

Activity 4.1

Calculate the amount for dividends paid to minority interests. Make a note of your computation here:

In the section on associated undertakings in Chapter 3 (p. 82) you saw how the carrying value of the investment was increased by the group's share of the associated company's retained profit for the year. In the above example the carrying value of the investment has increased by £1000 which is a reflection of the group's share of the associated company's retained profit for the year as shown in note 2 of the example.

Notice also how the group's share of the associated company's retained profit for the year is less than the group's share of profit for the year as reported in the consolidated profit and loss account. The difference between these two amounts must be the result of having received a dividend from the associated company.

Activity 4.2

Calculate the amount of dividend received from the associated company and make a note of your calculation here. Take care over profits for the year; the figures are on two lines in the consolidated profit and loss account.

Presentation in the cash flow statement

FRS 1 requires the dividends paid to minority interests, and the dividends received from associated companies, to be reported under the item called 'Returns on investments and servicing of finance'.

Having derived these two cash flows, changes in the balance sheet figures for minority interests and associated undertakings can be ignored when preparing the cash flow statement for this example. All other items for the cash flow statement are calculated and presented in the normal way. From your earlier studies on the cash flow statement you should recall that FRS 1 is quite strict on format.

Activity 4.3

Prepare a cash flow statement for the group. You can assume that all items included in net current assets relate to balances that will affect the calculation of net cash inflow from operating activities. An outline format is provided below this box. In order to refresh your mental image of the format, all main headings are included although there might not be items to report under every heading.

Group cash flow statement for year 2

Net cash inflow from operating activities
Returns on investments and servicing of finance

Taxation paid
Investing activities

Net cash inflow/(outflow) before financing
Financing

Increase in cash and cash equivalents

Notes to the cash flow statement
1. Reconciliation of operating profit to net cash inflow from operating activities.

Variations on the central theme

In the above example, the calculation needed to find dividends received from the associated undertaking was straightforward because the notes gave the group's share of the associated undertaking's retained profit for the year. The dividend received could be found by comparing the share of retained profit with the share of profit for the year as reported in the consolidated profit and loss account.

If we had not been given the information on retained profit we could have found it in this example by examining changes in the carrying value of the investment. This has increased by £1000 and we know from our study of associated undertakings in Chapter 3 that this increase is a reflection of the group's share of the associate's retained profit for the year.

In the group accounts, the following double entry adjustments are made in order to account for items affecting associated undertakings:

	Debit	Credit
1. *Share of associated undertaking's profit for the year*		
Debit carrying value of investment (£4000 – £1000)	£3000	
Credit consolidated profit and loss account		£3000
2. *Dividends received from associated undertaking*		
Debit dividends received (as reported in investor's accounts)	£2000	
Credit carrying value of investment		£2000

Notice that the effect of these entries is as follows:

- in the consolidated profit and loss account, dividends received from the associated undertaking are replaced by a share of its profit for the year, and
- the carrying value of the investment is increased by the group's share of the associated undertaking's retained profit for the year.

Movements on the investment in associated undertaking can be summarized as follows:

	£
Balance at start of year	60 000
Add share of profit for the year	3 000
	63 000
Less dividend received	2 000
Balance at end of year	61 000

In order to use changes in the carrying value of the investment to find dividends received (or share of retained profit) it might be necessary to refer to the detailed disclosure required by SSAP 1. We did not need this information in the above example because of the accounting policy adopted by the company. It will not always be this easy. There are circumstances where a change in the balance sheet value for the investment will result from something other than recording a share of retained profit for the financial year.

Activity 4.4

Make a note of the circumstances where changes in the carrying value of the investment will be for reasons that are in addition to those for recording a share of the associated undertaking's retained profit for the year. When doing this, ignore changes that occur to the carrying value when another associated undertaking is acquired during the year.

Having identified this problem you can practise applying it in the next activity. The details for this activity are as follows:

Extracts from a consolidated balance sheet

	End of year 1	End of year 2
	£	£
Interests in associated undertakings:		
Share of net assets	40 000	50 000
Goodwill arising on acquisition	5 000	4 000
	45 000	54 000

The consolidated profit and loss account shows that the group's share of the associated undertaking's profit after tax for the year was £14 000. There have been no disposals or acquisitions of associated companies during the year.

Activity 4.5

Calculate the amount of dividend that the group received from associated undertakings during the year.

You will also need the information on changes in the carrying value of goodwill in order to make one of the adjustments when calculating net cash inflow from operating activities. In the above example, operating profit will include a charge of £1000 for goodwill written off that will have to be added to operating profit since it does not result from a cash outflow.

Summary

The main learning points in this chapter are as follows:

- the cash flow statement provided with group financial statements should reflect the cash flows of the group;
- a group cash flow statement should deal only with flows of cash external to the group;
- all internal cash flows are effectively eliminated by the adjustments that are made for inter-company transactions and inter-company balances when the consolidated accounts are prepared;
- group cash flows with parties external to the group might include dividends paid to minority interests and dividends received from associated undertakings;

- consolidated accounts do not disclose dividends paid to minority interests and do not disclose dividends received from associated undertakings, but the amounts can be derived by reconciling movements on the balances for minority interests and investment in associated undertakings;
- all dividends paid and received by the group are included in the standard format under 'Returns on investments and servicing of finance'.

Key to activities

Activity 4.1

	£
Opening balance on minority interests	40 000
Add share of profit for the year	2 000
	42 000
Less closing balance	41 000
Difference = dividend paid	1 000

Activity 4.2

	£
Share of profit for the year (£4000 – £1000)	3 000
Share of retained profit for the year	1 000
Difference = dividend received	2 000

Activity 4.3

Group cash flow statement for year 2

	£	£
Net cash inflow from operating activities		25 000
Returns on investments and servicing of finance		
Dividends received from associated undertakings	2 000	
Dividends paid to minority interests	(1 000)	
Dividends paid to parent company's shareholders	(5 000)	
		(4 000)
Taxation paid		(14 000)
Investing activities		
Purchase of tangible fixed assets		(5 000)
Net cash inflow before financing		2 000
Financing		
Nil		
Increase in cash and cash equivalents		2 000

Notes to the cash flow statement
  1. Reconciliation of operating profit to net cash inflow from operating activities:

	£
Operating profit	40 000
Depreciation	3 000
Increase in net current assets	(18 000)
Net cash inflow from operating activities	25 000

Activity 4.4

Where the carrying value includes an amount for goodwill that is being amortized through the profit and loss account.

Activity 4.5

The share of retained profit must be £10 000 (increase in the balance for share of net assets). The dividend received must, therefore, be (£14 000 – £10 000) £4 000.

Appendix

The following paragraphs are included in FRS 1:

  9   The cash flow statement provided with group financial statements should reflect the cash flows of the group.
  38   A group cash flow statement should only deal with flows of cash and cash equivalents external to the group. Accordingly, cash flows that are internal to the group should be eliminated in the preparation of the group cash flow statement. Dividends paid to any minority interests should be reported under the heading returns on investments and servicing of finance, and disclosed separately.
  39   The cash flows of any entity which is equity accounted in consolidated financial statements should only be included in the group cash flow statement to the extent of the actual cash flows between the group and the entity concerned.

Question for self assessment

The answer to this question is given at the end of the book

4.1 Carver plc

The following question is based on one set by ACCA in Paper 13. It has been modified in order to remove certain aspects that are covered by later chapters of this book.

The draft consolidated accounts for the Carver Group are as follows:

Draft consolidated profit and loss account for the year ended 30 September 1994

	£000	£000
Operating profit		1485
Share of profits of associated undertakings		495
Income from fixed asset investment		200
Interest payable		(150)
Profit on ordinary activities before taxation		2030
Tax on profit on ordinary activities		
Corporation tax	391	
Deferred taxation	104	
Tax attributable to income of associated undertakings	145	
Tax attributable to franked investment income	45	
		685
Profit on ordinary activities after taxation		1345
Minority interests		100
Profit for the financial year		1245
Dividends paid and proposed		400
Retained profit for the year		845

Draft consolidated balances sheets at 30 September

	1993		1994	
	£000	£000	£000	£000
Fixed assets				
Tangible assets				
Buildings at net book value		2200		2075
Machinery: Cost	1565		3000	
Aggregate depreciation	1100		1200	
Net book value		465		1800
		2665		3875
Investments in associated undertaking		1000		1100
Fixed asset investments		410		410
		4075		5385

	1993		1994	
	£000	£000	£000	£000
Current assets				
Stocks	1032		1975	
Trade debtors	1303		1850	
Cash	1932		4515	
	4267		8340	
Creditors: amounts falling due within one year				
Trade creditors	280		500	
Corporation tax	167		375	
ACT	135		87	
Dividends	200		300	
Accrued interest	30		40	
	812		1302	
Net current assets		3455		7038
Total assets less current liabilities		7530		12423
Creditors: amounts falling due after more than one year				
Loans		870		2410
Provisions for liabilities and charges				
Deferred taxation		13		30
		6647		9983
Capital and reserves				
Called up share capital in 25p shares		2220		3940
Share premium account		2164		2883
Profit and loss account		2200		3045
Total shareholders' equity		6584		9868
Minority interests		63		115
		6647		9983

Notes

1. There have been no acquisitions or disposals of buildings during the year.
2. Machinery that originally cost £500 000 in a previous year was sold for £500 000 during the year. This resulted in a profit on disposal of £100 000 which has been treated as a part of operating profit.
3. There were no acquisitions of subsidiaries or associated undertakings during the year.
4. The carrying balance for investment in associated undertaking does not include any amount for goodwill; the full amount arising on acquisition was written off against the balance on the profit and loss account at the time of acquisition.
5. No loans were repaid during the year

Required

Prepare a consolidated cash flow statement for the Carver Group for year ended 30 September 1994. The statement should comply with FRS 1 in so far as the information permits.

Question without answer

An answer to this question is published separately in the *Teacher's Manual*.

4.2 XYZ Group plc

You are given the following information relating to the XYZ Group plc:

Consolidated profit and loss account for the year ended 31 December 19X7

		£000
Operating profit		5202
Share of profit of associated undertaking		1240
		6442
Interest payable		721
Profit on ordinary activities before tax		5721
Taxation:		
Corporation tax	1293	
Deferred taxation	252	
Tax attributable to income of associated undertakings	400	
		1945
Profit on ordinary activities after taxation		3776
Minority interests		700
Profit for the financial year		3076
Dividends		600
Retained profit for the financial year		2476

Consolidated balance sheet at 31 December

	19X7 £000	19X7 £000	19X6 £000	19X6 £000
Fixed assets				
Goodwill on consolidation		500		2 000
Tangible assets		21 256		16 214
Investment in associated undertaking		800		600
		22 556		18 814
Current assets				
Stock	28 351		17 243	
Debtors	9 540		6 824	
Bank	642		4 946	
	38 533		29 013	
Creditors: amounts falling due within one year	27 863		20 306	
		10 670		8 707
Total assets less current liabilities		33 226		27 521
Creditors: amounts falling due after more than one year:				
Loans		8 246		7 319
Provision for liabilities and charges				
Deferred taxation		1 483		1 231
		23 497		18 971

	19X7		19X6	
	£000	£000	£000	£000
Capital and reserves				
Ordinary share capital		3 500		3 000
Share premium account		750		200
Revaluation reserve		500		—
Profit and loss account		16 822		14 346
		21 572		17 546
Minority interests		1 925		1 425
		23 497		18 971

Notes

	Land and buildings £000	Equipment £000
1. The schedule of fixed assets includes the following:		
Cost at 1 January 19X7	4 500	25 921
Additions	2 000	6 649
Revaluation	500	
Disposals	—	(2 464)
Cost at 31 December 19X7	7 000	30 106
Aggregate depreciation at 1 January 19X7	1 500	12 707
Charge for the year	500	1 964
On disposals		(821)
Aggregate depreciation at 31 December 19X7	2 000	13 850

The equipment sold during the year realised £350 000

	19X7	19X6
2. Creditors falling due within one year comprised:		
Interest accrued	81	56
Other accruals and trade creditors	26 277	18 760
Proposed dividends	400	300
Corporation Tax (ACT and MCT)	1 105	1 190
	27 863	20 306

3. There were no acquisitions or disposals of subsidiaries and associated undertakings during the year. Goodwill arising on the acquisition of associated undertakings is being amortized over its estimated life. The amount amortized during the year was £400 000.
4. No loans were repaid during the year.

Required

Prepare the group's consolidated cash flow statement for the year.

Modified CIMA Stage 3

The merger method of accounting

Objectives

After completing this chapter you should be able to:

- explain why the acquisition method of consolidation is inequitable in certain circumstances;
- prepare consolidated accounts using the merger method of accounting and contrast the results with the acquisition method;
- analyse business combinations in order to establish whether the consolidated accounts can be prepared by using the merger method.

Introduction

Merger accounting considers the relationship between parent and subsidiary in a way that differs to that in acquisition accounting. The acquisition method is based on the idea that the acquisition of a controlling interest in another company is similar in substance to the acquisition of the business owned by that company. Consequently, the net identifiable assets are brought into the consolidated balance sheet at their fair values on the date of acquisition and any difference between the acquisition cost and the fair values of these net assets is treated as goodwill. Profits earned by the acquired entity are then consolidated as from the date of acquisition. Dividends paid to the parent company out of the subsidiary's pre-acquisition profits must be treated as capital receipts.

Merger accounting is based on the idea that in certain circumstances there has been a merger (or pooling) of interests of the two companies rather than an acquisition. Profits are consolidated as if the combined companies had always been together. Dividends paid to the parent company out of profits that were earned by the subsidiary prior to the date when the two companies came together will be treated as revenue receipts.

The term 'merger of interests' is sometimes misunderstood by students when they first encounter the idea. This is because it seems to suggest that there has been a business combination which results in a single legal entity. This is not so and it is important to keep in mind that we are talking about an alternative method of preparing consolidated accounts for a parent and subsidiary relationship. It might help with your perception of the subject to think of the word 'merger' as relating to the shareholders rather than the companies; two bodies of shareholders merge into one body of shareholders who own shares in the parent company.

There are a substantial number of regulations that affect the legality of merger accounting. Some are in the Companies Act 1985 and some in FRS 6. In this chapter we will consider an outline of the accounting problem and the accounting method before studying the regulations in detail. You will be gratified to learn that the merger method simplifies the mechanical aspects of preparing consolidated accounts; the main difficulty with the subject is in identifying situations where the method must be used.

Background

The acquisition method of consolidation evolved as the accepted practice following a requirement in the Companies Act 1948 for parent companies to produce group accounts. Criticisms of the acquisition method are related to the way that it prevents pre-acquisition profits of the subsidiary from being made available for distribution to members of the parent company. There should be no objection to this when the former shareholders of the subsidiary sell their shares to the parent company for cash. The amount of cash which they receive for their shares has effectively liquidated the profits which their company has created.

But what happens to these shareholders if they accept shares in the parent company instead of cash? They stay in the group (now as members of the parent company) and yet the profits which their company had earned prior to the acquisition are not available for distribution if acquisition accounting is used. Where the objective of the arrangement is to retain the separate existence of each company in a combined organization, this treatment of pre-acquisition reserves is inequitable.

These mergers are usually arranged in one of two ways; either one company acquires a controlling interest (usually 100%) in the other, or a separate parent company is formed which owns the shares of both companies. If the second of these two options is adopted, the earnings of the parent company will consist of dividends received from the subsidiaries. In either case the parent company must prepare consolidated accounts and you will see shortly how the acquisition method of consolidation can be criticized in these circumstances.

Merger accounting was developed as an answer to the criticisms of acquisition accounting. Where it is adopted it will alter the carrying value of the investment in the parent company's books, and will ensure that the pre-acquisition profits of the subsidiary can be made available for distribution to members of the parent company.

Understanding the problem

In trying to understand the criticisms of acquisition accounting you have to think about the shareholders as well as the figures. You will see the problem by working on a contrived situation.

Details for the activities

Company A and Company B are two companies of similar size. They wish to merge their interests into a combined organization but with the separate identity of each company being retained. The combination is to be achieved by Company A offering Company B's shareholders, 1 share in Company A for 1 share in Company B. The market value of shares in Company A is £1.60 each. Assume that the fair value of Company B's fixed assets is £125 000. The two balance sheets immediately prior to the share exchange are as follows:

	Company A	Company B
	£	£
Tangible fixed assets	140 000	120 000
Net current assets	10 000	30 000
	150 000	150 000
Ordinary shares of £1 each	100 000	100 000
Profit and loss account	50 000	50 000
	50 000	150 000

We will use the acquisition method first. Prior to the Companies Act 1981 it would have been necessary for Company A to follow a rule in a case known as *Shearer v. Bercain Ltd* when writing up the share issue in its books. The ruling which affects our example is that when the shares are issued by Company A they must be written into the books at their fair value (market value) and not at their nominal value. Any difference between fair value and nominal value must be credited to the share premium account. The investment in the subsidiary will, therefore, be carried in the parent company's books at the fair value of the shares issued.

Activity 5.1

Write down the double entry that Company A will have to make in its books when the shares are issued, using the rule in *Shearer v. Bercain*:

Debit:

Credit:

Before preparing the consolidated balance sheet of the group (using the acquisition method) you will find it helpful to set out the balance sheet of Company A following the share issue.

Activity 5.2

Prepare the balance sheet of Company A following the share issue. Use the outline format provided below this box.

Balance sheet of Company A after the share issue

	£
Fixed assets	
Tangible	
Investment in subsidiary	_____
Net current assets	_____
	======
Capital and reserves	
Ordinary shares of £1 each	
Share premium account	
Profit and loss account	_____
	======

Now that you have a revised balance sheet of the parent company, you should find it relatively straightforward to produce a consolidated balance sheet for the group. Use the principles of the acquisition method as studied in previous chapters. For the time being we will treat goodwill arising on consolidation as an intangible asset awaiting amortization.

Activity 5.3

Prepare the consolidated balance sheet of Company A and Company B by completing the outline format shown below this box.

Consolidated balance sheet of Company A and Company B

	£
Fixed assets	
Tangible	
Intangible (goodwill arising on consolidation)	_____
Net current assets	_____
	======

Capital and reserves
 Ordinary share capital
 Share premium account
 Profit and loss account

£

_____

=======

We now need to think about the shareholders rather than the figures.

Activity 5.4

For the sake of clarity, imagine that prior to the share exchange there were two shareholders in Company A and two in Company B. All four shareholders will now have something to complain about as a result of the consolidated balance sheet produced by the acquisition method. Make a note here of what these complaints might be.

The shareholders in Company A

The shareholders in Company B

It is not even possible under the acquisition method to make the pre-acquisition profits of Company B available for distribution to the shareholders in Company A by paying a dividend to Company A. As was mentioned in Chapter 2, if Company B does pay such a dividend it must be treated as a capital receipt by Company A and credited to the carrying value of the investment.

Acquisition accounting will make the position worse if the combination is achieved by forming a separate parent company to own the shares in both Company A and Company B. This arrangement is sometimes preferred to that dealt with above because it eliminates the idea that one company (the parent) dominates the other company in the combination. You will see the problem with the figures in a moment but before dealing with those you might find it helpful to have an overview of the new group structure. It can be illustrated by Figure 5.1.

The share capital of the new parent company will be held by the former shareholders of Company A and Company B. The new parent company's assets will consist of an investment in Company A and an investment in Company B.

Activity 5.5

Assume that a new parent company is formed and that its name is P Ltd. It has acquired the entire share capital of Company A and Company B by issuing £1.00 ordinary shares in P Ltd on a 1 for 1 basis. The fair value of the £1 ordinary shares issued by P Ltd is considered to be £1.60 each (this value was based on the terms of the combination). Write up the first balance sheet of P Ltd following the issue of these shares. Use the outline format provided below Figure 5.1.

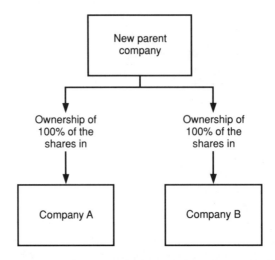

Figure 5.1 Group structure: share capital of new parent company held by former shareholders of Company A and Company B

Balance sheet of P Ltd

£

Fixed assets
Investments in subsidiaries:
Company A Ltd
Company B Ltd

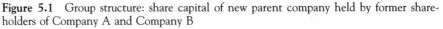

Capital and reserves
Share capital (£1.00 ordinary shares)
Share premium

Now that we have the first balance sheet of P Ltd we can prepare the consolidated balance of the group at the date of acquisition.

Activity 5.6

Set out the first consolidated balance sheet of this group using the acquisition method. Assume that the fair value of Company A's tangible fixed assets is £145 000 and that fair value of Company B's tangible fixed assets is (as before) £125 000. Use the format provided below this box.

Consolidated balance sheet of the P Ltd group

£

Fixed assets
Tangible
Intangible (goodwill arising on consolidation)

	£
Net current assets	————
	═══
Capital and reserves	
Share capital (£1.00 ordinary shares)	
Share premium account	
Profit and loss account	————
	═══

As you can see, the distributable profits of both companies have disappeared down a black hole. Shareholders will have to wait for future profits to be earned by their former companies before they can receive any distributions through the medium of the parent company P Ltd.

Merger accounting — legal background

The judgement given in *Shearer v. Bercain Ltd* was not directly concerned with the accounting treatment in consolidated accounts following an acquisition. It merely gave authority for interpretation of a section in the Companies Act regarding the share premium account when a company issues shares for a consideration other than cash. It was the requirement to write up the share premium account in these circumstances which made it technically impossible to use the merger method of accounting.

Following the court's ruling in that case the government decided that there would be situations (such as a share for share merger) where companies should be relieved from the requirement to write up the share premium account. A relief was introduced by the 1981 Companies Act (now incorporated in the Companies Act 1985) known as 'merger relief'.

If a share issue satisfies the rules on merger relief, the company issuing the shares (as consideration for the shares in another company) is permitted to write the issue into their books at nominal value, thus making it possible to prepare consolidated accounts using the merger method. Note that this is a relieving provision; in a later section of this chapter (p. 121) you will see what happens when a company issues shares in circumstances where merger relief applies but the issuing company is required to use acquisition accounting for the consolidated accounts.

Initially, regulations defining the circumstances in which the merger method could be used were prescribed by SSAP 23. The Companies Act 1981 merely made it possible to comply with these regulations by providing for merger relief. Subsequently, the Companies Act 1989 provided statutory regulations on merger accounting (through Schedule 4A) that were incorporated into the Companies Act 1985. These regulations are similar (but not identical) to those of SSAP 23. Some companies, however, took advantage of the wording in these regulations and devised schemes where merger accounting could be used in circumstances that were not envisaged by the regulators. In order to combat these practices, SSAP 23 was replaced by FRS 6 in September 1994.

Merger accounting — the basic procedure

When a business combination is achieved by a share for share exchange in circumstances where merger relief applies, the issuing company is permitted to write the share issue into its books at the nominal value of the shares issued. Merger relief can be claimed if the arrangement results in the issuing company acquiring at least 90% of the equity shares in the other company.

We will practise at using the merger method for the situation dealt with in Activities 5.1 to 5.3 where the merger is achieved by Company B becoming a subsidiary of Company A. The balance sheets of each company prior to the share exchange are reproduced below.

	Company A	Company B
	£	£
Tangible fixed assets	140 000	120 000
Net current assets	10 000	30 000
	150 000	150 000
Ordinary shares of £1 each	100 000	100 000
Profit and loss account	50 000	50 000
	150 000	150 000

Activity 5.7

First, write down the double entry that will be made when the shares are issued by Company A (the terms were one share in Company A for one in Company B). You can assume that merger relief applies.

Debit:

Credit:

The merger method of accounting is described in both FRS 6 and the Companies Act 1985 (see the appendix to this chapter) but in basic terms it is as follows:

1. Fair values of assets are ignored; assets are combined at book value.
2. The carrying value of the investment in the parent company's balance sheet (being at nominal value of the shares issued) is set off against the nominal value of the issued share capital in the sub-

sidiary's balance sheet, to the extent that these shares are held by the parent company.

3. Everything else is combined, including the whole of the balance on the subsidiary's profit and loss account even if these profits were earned prior to acquisition.

4. Balancing figures will arise only where the nominal value of the shares issued differs from the nominal value acquired. We will look at that situation later.

Activity 5.8

Draft out the balance sheet of Company A following the share issue and then use the above description to produce the first consolidated balance sheet of the group using the merger method.

Balance sheet of Company A following share issue		Consolidated balance sheet using the merger method	
	£		£
Investment in subsidiary			
Tangible fixed assets		Tangible fixed assets	
Net current assets	_____	Net current assets	_____
	======		======
Ordinary shares of £1 each		Ordinary shares of £1 each	
Profit and loss account	_____	Profit and loss account	_____
	======		======

When you compare the above consolidated balance sheet with the balance sheets of the two companies prior to the share exchange (above Activity 5.7) it looks as if you have simply combined the two sets of figures. This is an illusion and you need to keep in mind that the share capital in the consolidated balance sheet is the share capital of Company A. In this case the share capital in the consolidated balance sheet is the same as the sum of two share capitals prior to the combination but only because the nominal value of the shares issued by Company A was the same as the nominal value of the issued share capital in Company B's balance sheet. This will not always be the case.

Differences on consolidation

If the **total** nominal value of shares issued is the same as the **total** nominal value acquired there are no adjustments to deal with on consolidation. The word 'total' in this explanation is important: the nominal value of each share could be different (such as 2 × 50p shares issued in exchange for 1 × £1 share) but if the totals are the same there is no balancing figure. The carrying value of the investment in the parent company's balance sheet is simply eliminated by setting it off against the issued share capital in the subsidiary's balance sheet.

There might be minority shareholders with an interest in the subsidiary's share capital but we will look at that later. The carrying value of the investment might also include a small amount for any cash paid as a part of the consideration. For the time being, however, we will work on the assumption that the parent company owns 100% of the subsidiary's share capital and that the consideration given consisted entirely of equity shares in the parent company.

Where there is a difference between the carrying value of the investment (which will be at the nominal value of the shares issued) and the total nominal value of the shares acquired there will be a balancing figure which must be dealt with somewhere in the consolidated balance sheet. Both FRS 6 and the Companies Act 1985 require these differences to be dealt with in the same way.

The appendix to this chapter includes the relevant paragraphs from FRS 6 and the Companies Act 1985. You will need to refer to these for the next activity. The wording is not difficult to follow although it is slightly cumbersome in places (particularly in the Companies Act) because of the need to recognize that the carrying value of the investment might include some consideration other than shares in the parent company (such as a small amount of cash). In FRS 6 the provisions are in paragraph 18; in Schedule 4A of the Companies Act they are in paragraphs 11(5) and 11(6).

Activity 5.9

Read paragraph 18 in FRS 6 (and paragraphs 11(5) and 11(6) from Schedule 4A of the Companies Act) and make a note here of how these regulations require the differences on consolidation to be disclosed in the consolidated accounts.

The term 'other reserves' is a reference to a specific heading in the official formats. It is identified as item K. IV in Format 1. It falls between the 'Revaluation reserve' and the reserve called 'Profit and loss account'. There are various sub-items under this heading, including the 'capital redemption reserve' (which can arise when a company redeems or purchases its own shares). In the examples that we will be working in this chapter, there will be no 'other reserves' in the balance sheets prior to the combination and so the difference on consolidation will have to be shown as a separate item. It will increase or decrease the total of capital and reserves in the consolidated balance sheet depending on whether the difference is a debit balance or a credit balance.

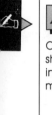

Activity 5.10

Identify whether the following differences on consolidation will increase or decrease the total of capital and reserves in the consolidated balance sheet.

1. The carrying value of investment is less than the nominal value of shares acquired:

2. The carrying value of investment exceeds the nominal value of shares acquired:

Activities 5.11 and 5.12 (below) are two simple problems that will help to illustrate the application of the above rules. These are not difficult providing you remember that the investment in the parent company's balance sheet is a debit balance and the issued share capital in the subsidiary's balance sheet is a credit balance.

Activity 5.11

Company A has acquired the whole of the £200 nominal share capital of Company B by issuing shares which have a nominal value of £190 (i.e. a 19 for 20 share exchange). From the following balance sheets (prepared after the share issue), prepare a consolidated balance sheet using merger accounting. You can do this by completing the right-hand column.

	Parent company A Ltd	Sub B Ltd	Consolidated
Sundry net tangible assets	1500	220	
Investment in subsidiary	190	—	
	1690	220	
Share capital	1190	200	
Consolidation difference			
Profit and loss account	500	20	
	1690	220	

Activity 5.12

The facts are the same as in Activity 5.11 except that the nominal value of the shares issued by Company A Ltd was £250 (a 5 for 4 exchange).

	Parent company A Ltd	Sub B Ltd	Consolidated
Sundry net tangible assets	1500	220	
Investment in subsidiary	250	—	
	1750	220	
Share capital	1250	200	
Consolidation difference			
Profit and loss account	500	20	
	1750	220	

The word 'goodwill' must not be used to describe the difference which arises in Activities 5.10 and 5.11 because no attempt is made to determine either the fair value of the net identifiable assets in the subsidiary, nor the fair value of the consideration given by the parent company.

Regulations

There are three sets of rules that affect this subject:

1. merger relief in Section 131 Companies Act 1985 (introduced in 1981);
2. merger accounting in Schedule 4A Companies Act 1985 (introduced in 1989);
3. FRS 6 which is effective for accounting periods starting on or after 23 December 1994.

Merger relief

The rules on merger relief are quite separate from the rules on merger accounting. Merger accounting is a method of financial reporting whereas merger relief is a legal matter concerned with maintenance of capital in certain types of share issue (although merger accounting would be impossible without it). There could be situations where merger relief can be claimed under a transaction that is accounted for as an acquisition.

A company is relieved from the requirement to write up a share premium account for any issue of equity shares that are part of an arrangement to acquire equity shares in another company. The relief is available only if the arrangement results in the issuing company **acquiring at least 90% of the equity shares in the other company** (Section 131, Companies Act 1985).

Merger accounting: Schedule 4A Companies Act 1985

These rules (which implemented the EC Seventh Directive in 1989) are similar to those that were established by the former SSAP 23, now superseded by FRS 6. All of the rules in both Companies Act 1985 and FRS 6 must be met before merger accounting is permitted. The Companies Act defines the conditions that must apply for an acquisition to be accounted for as a merger. These rules are summarized in the following table.

1.	**Equity shares acquired**	At least 90% of the nominal value of equity is held (note that there can be up to 10% minority interests).
2.	**Equity shares issued**	The shares were acquired under an arrangement that provided for the issue of equity shares by the acquiring group.
3.	**Other consideration**	Fair value of consideration given other than equity shares did not exceed 10% of the nominal value of the equity shares issued.
4.	**GAAP**	Adoption of merger method accords with generally accepted accounting principles or practice.

You should note that merger accounting is an **option** under the Companies Act but mandatory under FRS 6 if the combination qualifies as a merger.

FRS 6

Regulations in the former SSAP 23 were intended to permit the use of merger accounting where a business combination was achieved following a share-for-share exchange. But some companies constructed take-overs in such a way that although the former shareholders in the subsidiary received a cash settlement (rather than shares in the parent company) the arrangement was such that merger accounting could be used. The main device used in these arrangements was a 'vendor placing'. This involved an intermediary (usually a financial institution) purchasing shares from the shareholders in the subsidiary for cash. These shares were then exchanged by the intermediary for shares issued by the parent company. Such an arrangement would have qualified for merger accounting under SSAP 23 because the shares in the parent company have been issued in exchange for shares in the subsidiary.

FRS 6 takes a conceptual approach rather then prescribing a set of measurements (like those in the Companies Act and the former SSAP 23). It does this by defining a merger and then setting out five criteria for determining whether this definition has been met in a particular business combination. The ASB considers that there will be very few business combinations that qualify for merger accounting under these new rules. Some commentators have suggested that since some of the criteria are loose and could easily be met, the number of combinations meeting the criteria could be greater than the ASB expects (for example, see the KPMG review of FRS 6 and 7).

Merger accounting is mandatory (not an option) under FRS 6 if:

1. the use of merger accounting is not prohibited by legislation; and
2. the combination meets the specific criteria that make it fall within the definition of a merger.

The definition of a merger is a bit of a mouthful and you are unlikely to remember it in detail. It is more important to get some idea of the five criteria. The gist of the definition is that **a business combination results in a merger where the shareholders of the combining entities come together in a partnership for a mutual sharing in the risks and rewards of the combined entity**.

The parties to the combination should be seen as equals. You should note that the so called combined entity will consist of at least two companies, one being the parent company and one being the subsidiary. If this were not the case, there would be no need to do merger accounting. Arrangements such as where a new parent company is formed in order to own shares in the two combining entities will also qualify if the various criteria are met. The five criteria contained in FRS 6 are summarized in the following table:

1.	**Portrayal of combination**	No party is portrayed as either acquirer or acquired. Examples that are unlikely to meet this criterion: (a) a hostile takeover (b) consideration given places a premium on the market value of the shares acquired.
2.	**Future management structure**	All parties participate in establishing the management structure.
3.	**Relative sizes of combining entities**	One party does not dominate the other by virtue of size. Dominance is presumed if one party is more than 50% larger than the other party as judged by reference to the relative proportions of equity held in the combined entity by the parties to the combination.
4.	**Consideration given**	Non equity consideration included must be an immaterial proportion of the **fair value** of the total consideration received. This is in addition to the Companies Act 10% rule.
5.	**Retention of an interest in a part of the combined entity**	No equity shareholders retain a material interest in the future performance of only a part of the combined entity. (The Companies Act 1985 permits a minority interest of 10%.)

It will be quite difficult to learn the rules in the Companies Act and FRS 6 by rote. The best way of learning is to try and apply the rules to specific situations. The following activity provides some practice in this respect.

Activity 5.13

Try to identify whether merger accounting would be permitted in the following (mutually exclusive) circumstances. State the reasons for your opinion.

1. Company A acquired the entire equity capital of Company B after a lengthy battle during which Company B sought competitive bids from other interested parties. The consideration consisted entirely of equity shares in Company A.

2. Company A acquired the entire equity capital of Company B in exchange for the following:

	Nominal value £	Fair value £
Equity shares in Company A	100 000	200 000
Cash	12 000	12 000
	112 000	212 000

3. Company A acquired 89% of the equity shares in Company B. The consideration was entirely equity shares in Company A.

4. Company A acquired the entire share capital of Company B. The consideration was settled entirely by an issue of equity shares in Company A. The new body of shareholders in Company A following the merger is analysed as follows:

Former shareholders of Company B	30%
Shareholders of Company A before the merger	70%

5. Following a merger that satisfied all other criteria for merger accounting, the shareholders agreed at a general meeting to replace the board of the subsidiary with directors of the parent company. Think carefully before answering.

Share premium or merger reserve

As stated earlier, the regulations in the Companies Act that provide a relief from the requirement to write up the share premium account on a share issue (merger relief) are quite separate from the rules that permit (or require) merger accounting to be used. This means that there will be many situations where merger relief can be claimed and yet the provisions in FRS 6 will deny use of merger accounting. Situation 4 in Activity 5.13 above is one example of where this applies.

The rules in FRS 6 state that if a combination does not meet the definition of a merger then acquisition accounting must be used. In order to do this it will be necessary to write up the investment in the parent company's books at the fair value of the consideration given. This can then be compared to the fair value of the net identifiable assets acquired in order to calculate goodwill arising on consolidation. The fair value of the shares issued as consideration will be greater than their nominal value and so the question arises: how should we account for the difference between the nominal value and the fair value of the shares issued if it is possible to claim merger relief?

We could credit the difference to a share premium account and thus ignore the relieving provision in Section 131. But this puts the parent company at a disadvantage. There are (as you probably know from previous studies) strict rules in the Companies Act on how the share premium account can be applied. In particular, it is illegal to write off goodwill against the balance on the share premium account. The solution adopted by most companies in these circumstances (based on guidance in the former SSAP 23) is to credit the difference between nominal value and fair value of the shares issued to a separate reserve called a 'merger reserve'.

Activity 5.14

Make a note of why the parent company would prefer to credit the difference between fair value and nominal value of the shares issued to a merger reserve (rather than share premium account) if merger relief applies.

Summary exercises

You will now find it helpful to do a series of consolidated balance sheets for four different situations. Each one is uncomplicated and it will not take you very long to do them. The activity requires you to prepare a consolidated balance sheet using acquisition accounting and merger accounting for each situation. You will find that one of them involves minority interests but the principles in merger accounting are exactly the same as those which you learned for acquisition accounting. The amounts for minority interests will differ as between acquisition accounting and merger accounting. This is because the amount attributed to minority interests is based on the net asset values being consolidated (fair values in acquisition accounting and book values in merger accounting).

The four different situations are all related to two companies (Company A and Company B) whose balance sheets prior to the issue of shares by Company A, stood as follows:

	Company A £	Company B £
Net tangible assets	400 000	300 000
Share capital (£1 equity shares)	300 000	100 000
Profit and loss account	100 000	200 000
	400 000	300 000

The market value of Company A's shares is £3.60 each and the fair value of Company B's net assets is £350 000. You can assume that merger relief applies in each situation and so the balance sheets prepared under the acquisition method will include an item called merger reserve.

Activity 5.15

Prepare consolidated balance sheets under both acquisition accounting and merger accounting for the four situations mentioned in the following table. Treat goodwill (in acquisition accounting) as an asset awaiting amortization. At this stage of your studies you should be able to do the balance sheets without reconstructing Company A's balance sheet for the share issue. Try it; it's a good mental exercise and helps with the skill of throwing ideas and figures around in your head.

Situation 1. All shareholders in B accept 1 share in A for 1 in B

	Acquisition accounting	*Merger accounting*
Net tangible assets		
Goodwill		
Share capital		
Merger reserve		
Profit and loss account		

Situation 2. Only 90% of B's shareholders accept the offer

	Acquisition accounting	*Merger accounting*
Net tangible assets		
Goodwill		
Share capital		
Merger reserve		
Profit and loss account		
Minority interests		

Situation 3. 100% of B's shareholders accept 11 shares in A for 10 in B

	Acquisition accounting	*Merger accounting*
Net tangible assets		
Goodwill		
Share capital		
Merger reserve		
Consolidation difference		
Profit and loss account		

Situation 4. 100% of B's shareholders accept 9 shares in A for 10 in B

	Acquisition accounting	*Merger accounting*
Net tangible assets		
Goodwill (negative)		
Share capital		
Merger reserve		
Consolidation difference		
Profit and loss account		

Although you were asked to treat goodwill as an asset awaiting amortization when using the acquisition method, you should note that it will be possible to set it off immediately against the balance on the merger reserve. This would not be possible if the difference between nominal value and fair value of the shares issued is classified as a share premium.

Profit and loss account and comparatives

In the next chapter you will see how merger accounting produces different figures in the profit and loss account for the year when a subsidiary is acquired during the year. This is because with merger accounting the subsidiary's income and expenditure for the entire year will be consolidated. When acquisition accounting is used the subsidiary's income and expenditure prior to the acquisition are excluded from the consolidation.

There will also be differences in the comparative figures for the previous year (as required in published accounts) if a subsidiary is acquired during the current year. With acquisition accounting the comparatives are not adjusted for the acquisition because the new subsidiary was not a part of the group in the previous year. Merger accounting is based on the idea that the two companies had always been together and so the comparatives must be restated as if the subsidiary were a part of the group in the previous year.

The official wording in the regulations for the above points are included in the appendix to this chapter (see paragraph 17 of FRS 6, and paragraphs 11(3) and 11(4) of Schedule 4A Companies Act 1985).

Summary

The main learning points in this chapter can be summarized as follows:

- the treatment of pre-acquisition profits in acquisition accounting is inequitable when the former shareholders of the subsidiary become shareholders in the parent company as a result of a share exchange;
- except where merger relief applies, a company issuing shares for a consideration other than cash must write the issue into its books at the fair value of the shares issued; any difference between fair value and nominal value must be treated as a share premium;
- merger relief can be claimed if the issue is part of arrangement for acquiring equity shares in another company and at least 90% of the equity shares in that other company are acquired;
- the effect of merger relief is that the issue can be written up in the issuing company's books at nominal value – this enables merger accounting to be used for consolidating the results of the acquired subsidiary;
- merger accounting combines the book value of assets and liabilities of the subsidiary with those of the parent company, and consolidates both pre- and post- acquisition profits of the subsidiary;

- the carrying value of the investment in the parent company's balance sheet is set off against the nominal value of the issued share capital in the subsidiary's balance sheet to the extent that these shares are held by the parent company – any shares not owned by the parent will form part of the minority interests;
- differences between the carrying value of the investment and the nominal value of the shares acquired are dealt with as movement on other reserves;
- if the carrying value of the investment is greater than the nominal value of the shares acquired there will be a deduction from reserves, and if the carrying value of the investment is less than the nominal value of shares acquired there will be an addition to reserves;
- any amount for minority interests under merger accounting is based on book values at the date of acquisition, not fair values;
- the Companies Act specifies conditions that must be met for an acquisition to be treated as a merger, FRS 6 requiring merger accounting to be used if a combination falls within the definition of a merger;
- the definition of a merger in FRS 6 is conceptual and does not specify any particular measurements; five criteria must be satisfied for a combination to be treated as a merger.

Key to activities

Activity 5.1

Debit	Investment in subsidiary	£160 000
Credit	Issued share capital	£100 000
	Share premium account	£60 000

Activity 5.2

	£
Fixed assets	
Tangible	140 000
Investment in subsidiary	160 000
	300 000
Net current assets	10 000
	310 000
Capital and reserves	
Ordinary shares of £1 each	200 000
Share premium account	60 000
Profit and loss account	50 000
	310 000

Activity 5.3

	£
Fixed assets:	
Tangible	265 000
Goodwill (£160 000 – £155 000)	5 000
	270 000
Net current assets	40 000
	310 000
Capital and reserves	
Ordinary share capital	200 000
Share premium account	60 000
Profit and loss account	50 000
	310 000

Activity 5.4

The shareholders in Company A must now share the distributable profits of their company between four people whereas previously there were two. The shareholders in Company B find that the profits earned by their company have not been consolidated.

Activity 5.5

Fixed asset investments	
Investment in Company A Ltd	160 000
Investment in Company B Ltd	160 000
	320 000
Capital and reserves	
Share capital	200 000
Share premium	120 000
	320 000

Activity 5.6

Fixed assets	
Tangible	270 000
Goodwill (£320 000 – £310 000)	10 000
	280 000
Net current assets	40 000
	320 000
Capital and reserves	
Share capital	200 000
Share premium	120 000
Profit and loss account	—
	320 000

Activity 5.7

Debit	Investment in subsidiary	£100 000
Credit	Issued share capital	£100 000

Activity 5.8

Balance sheet of Company A	£	Consolidated balance sheet	£
Investment in subsidiary	100 000		
Tangible fixed assets	140 000	Tangible fixed assets	260 000
Net current assets	10 000	Net current assets	40 000
	250 000		300 000
Ordinary shares of £1 each	200 000	Ordinary shares of £1 each	200 000
Profit and loss account	50 000	Profit and loss account	100 000
	250 000		300 000

Activity 5.9

FRS 6 as a movement on other reserves. Companies Act as an adjustment to the consolidated reserves.

Activity 5.10

1. As an addition to reserves (increase).
2. As a deduction from reserves (decrease).

Activity 5.11

	£
Sundry net tangible assets	1720
Share capital	1190
Consolidation difference	10
Profit and loss account	520
	1720

Activity 5.12

Sundry net tangible assets	1720
Share capital	1250
Consolidation difference	(50)
Profit and loss account	520
	1720

Activity 5.13

1. This appears to have been a hostile take-over rather than a merger. This fails to meet Criterion 1 of FRS 6 and merger accounting is not permitted.
2. The cash consideration exceeds 10% of the nominal value of the shares issued and thus contravenes the conditions for merger accounting in the Companies Act 1985.
3. The Companies Act requires a 90% holding before merger accounting is permitted.
4. The interest of the original shareholders in Company A is more than 50% larger than the interest of the former shareholders of Company B. This fails to meet Criterion 3 in FRS 6 and so the combination cannot be treated as a merger.
5. Since all parties to the combination have participated in the new management structure, there can be no objection to treating the combination as a merger.

Activity 5.14

It creates a reserve that can be applied for writing off goodwill.

Activity 5.15

Situation 1

	Acquisition £	Merger £
Net tangible assets	750 000	700 000
Goodwill	10 000	—
	760 000	700 000
Share capital	400 000	400 000
Merger reserve	260 000	—
Profit and loss account	100 000	300 000
	760 000	700 000

Situation 2

	Acquisition £	Merger £
Net tangible assets	750 000	700 000
Goodwill	9 000	—
	759 000	700 000
Share capital	390 000	390 000
Merger reserve	234 000	—
Profit and loss account	100 000	280 000
Minority interests	35 000	30 000
	759 000	700 000

Situation 3

	Acquisition £	Merger £
Net tangible assets	750 000	700 000
Goodwill	46 000	—
	796 000	700 000
Share capital	410 000	410 000
Merger reserve	286 000	—
Consolidation difference	—	(10 000)
Profit and loss account	100 000	300 000
	796 000	700 000

Situation 4

	Acquisition £	Merger £
Net tangible assets	750 000	700 000
Negative goodwill	(26 000)	—
	724 000	700 000
Share capital	390 000	390 000
Merger reserve	234 000	—
Consolidation difference	—	10 000
Profit and loss account	100 000	300 000
	724 000	700 000

Appendix

Extracts from FRS 6

Merger accounting

16 With merger accounting the carrying values of the assets and liabilities of the parties to the combination are not required to be adjusted to fair value on consolidation, although appropriate adjustments should be made to achieve uniformity of accounting policies in the combining entities.

17 The results and cash flows of all the combining entities should be brought into the financial statements of the combined entity from the beginning of the financial year in which the combination occurred, adjusted so as to achieve uniformity of accounting policies. The corresponding figures should be restated by including the results for all the combining entities for the previous period and their balance sheets for the previous balance sheet date, adjusted as necessary to achieve uniformity of accounting policies.

18 The difference, if any, between the nominal value of the shares issued plus the fair value of any other consideration given, and the nominal value of the shares received in exchange should be shown as a movement on other reserves in the consolidated financial statements. Any existing balance on the share premium account or capital redemption reserve of the new subsidiary undertaking should be brought in by being shown as a movement on other reserves. These movements should be shown in the reconciliation of movements in shareholders' funds.

19 Merger expenses are not to be included as part of this adjustment, but should be charged to the profit and loss account of the combined entity at the effective date of the merger, as reorganisation or restructuring expenses, in accordance with paragraph 20 of FRS 3 "Reporting Financial Performance".

Extracts from Schedule 4A Companies Act 1985

Explanation of merger accounting

11(1) The merger method of accounting is as follows.

11(2) The assets and liabilities of the undertaking acquired shall be brought into the group accounts at the figures at which they stand in the undertaking's accounts, subject to any adjustment authorised or required by this Schedule.

11(3) The income and expenditure of the undertaking acquired shall be included in the group accounts for the entire financial year, including the period before the acquisition.

11(4) The group accounts shall show corresponding amounts relating to the previous financial year as if the undertaking acquired had been included in the consolidation throughout that year.

11(5) There shall be set off against the aggregate of —
   (a) the appropriate amount in respect of qualifying shares issued by the parent company or its subsidiary undertakings in consideration for the acquisition of shares in the undertaking acquired, and
   (b) the fair value of any other consideration for the acquisition of shares in the undertaking acquired, determined as at the date when those shares were acquired,
   the nominal value of the issued share capital of the undertaking acquired held by the parent company and its subsidiary undertakings.

11(6) The resulting amount shall be shown as an adjustment to the consolidated reserves.

Questions

Questions for self assessment

Answers to self-assessment questions are given at the end of the book

5.1 A plc

A plc offers to exchange shares with Z plc on a one-for-one basis and the offer is accepted by all except 4% of the shareholders of Z plc. At the date of the offer the market price of a share in A is £3. Before the offer neither company owned any shares in the other. The summarized balance sheets, before the proposed exchange of shares, are given below:

	A plc £ million	Z plc £ million
Fixed assets		
Land and buildings	1.60	1.15
Plant, fixtures, furniture	2.20	1.35
Vehicles	1.15	0.65
	4.95	3.15
Current assets		
Stocks and WIP	0.80	0.30
Debtors	0.65	0.25
Other assets	0.20	0.45
	1.65	1.00
Creditors	(0.75)	(1.05)
	5.85	3.10
Capital and reserves		
Share capital (£1 ordinary shares)	3.60	1.25
Revaluation reserve	0.60	
Profit and loss account	1.65	1.85
	5.85	3.10

The fair value of the assets of Z plc were:

1. Land and buildings £1.65 million
2. Plant, fixtures and furniture £1.30 million
3. Vehicles £0.62 million
4. Stocks and WIP £0.29 million
5. Debtors £0.24 million

Required

(a) Prepare a consolidated balance sheet using the acquisition method for each of the following situations:
   (i)   Assuming the details given above.
   (ii) Assuming that the offer was three shares in A plc for two shares in Z plc.

(iii) Assuming that the offer was two shares in A plc for three shares in Z plc.

(iv) Assuming that A plc paid cash of 10 pence for each Z share in addition to the one for one share exchange.

(b) Prepare a consolidated balance sheet using the merger method for each of the four situations as in (a) above.

ACCA 2.9

5.2 Dinos and Nivis

The balance sheets of Dinos Ltd and Nivis Ltd at 31 December 19X7 were as follows:

	Dinos £000	Nivis £000
Fixed assets at book value	2465	920
Net current assets	1218	265
	3683	1185
Capital and reserves:		
Share capital (£1 shares)	3000	600
Profit and loss reserve at 1 January 19X7	540	300
Retained profit for 19X7	143	285
	3683	1185

The following additional information is provided:

1. Dinos purchased the entire share capital of Nivis on 1 January 19X7 and issued 400 000 of its own shares in exchange. Dinos shares were valued at £3.50 each at the date of this transaction. The acquisition has not been entered in the books of Dinos, and is not reflected in the balance sheet above.

2. The fair value of Nivis's fixed assets at 1 January 19X7 was £1 200 000 compared with a book value of £930 000 at that date. There were no material differences between the book values and fair values of its current assets.

3. Depreciation charged by Nivis for 19X7 was £87 000. An appropriate charge, based on the fair value of its assets as at 1 January 19X7 and additions during the year, is £116 000.

4. Any goodwill arising on consolidation is to be written off against reserves.

Required

(a) The consolidated balance sheet of Dinos Ltd and its subsidiary at 31 December 19X7. Use the acquisition method described in FRS 2 and Schedule 4A of the Companies Act 1985.

(b) The consolidated balance sheet of Dinos Ltd and its subsidiary at 31 December 19X7. Use the merger method described in FRS 6 and Schedule 4A of the Companies Act 1985.

(c) Outline the conditions which must be satisfied before the merger method may be adopted. Explain the purpose of these conditions.

CIB Accountancy

Question without answer

An answer to this question is published separately in the *Teacher's Manual*.

5.3 Fruit and Vegetables

On 1 January 19X9 Fruit plc acquired all of the issued share capital of Vegetables plc in exchange for shares in Fruit plc. Shares in both companies have a nominal value of £1 each and a market value at 1 January 19X9 of £5 for a £1 Fruit plc share and £2.25 for a £1 Vegetables plc share.

The agreed terms were one ordinary share in Fruit plc for every two ordinary shares in Vegetables plc. At 31 December 19X9 the register of members of Fruit plc was correct but no entries had been made in the books of accounts of either company to record the exchange.

At 1 January 19X9 the balance sheet of Vegetables plc was as follows:

	£	£
Fixed assets		
Freehold premises		573 750
Plant and machinery at cost	316 965	
Less provision for depreciation	127 500	
		189 465
Quoted investments at cost		140 250
Net current assets		309 060
		1 212 525
Capital and reserves		
Ordinary shares of £1 each		765 000
Retained earnings		447 525
		1 212 525

At 1 January 19X9 the quoted investments had a market value of £318 750; the freehold premises a market value of £828 750; the plant and machinery (which had an expected unexpired useful life of four years) a market value of £300 000. Vegetables plc advised that it was their regular practice to invest surplus cash on a short-term basis in quoted investments. Draft accounts prepared for the two companies at the end of their financial year on 31 December 19X9 showed the following:

Profit and loss accounts for the year ended 31 December 19X9

	Fruit plc £	Vegetables plc £
Profit before depreciation	568 310	437 070
Depreciation for the year	91 290	40 035
Trading profit	477 020	397 035
Profit on sale of investments	—	138 465
Profit before tax	477 020	535 500
Taxation	119 255	149 940
Profit after tax	357 765	385 560

Balance sheets at 31 December 19X9

	Fruit plc £	Vegetables plc £
Fixed assets:		
Freehold premises	1 657 500	573 750
Plant and machinery at cost	653 055	316 965
Aggregate depreciation	(276 165)	(167 535)
Net current assets	249 390	874 905
	2 283 780	1 598 085
Capital and reserves		
Ordinary shares of £1 each	1 275 000	765 000
Retained earnings	1 008 780	833 085
	2 283 780	1 598 085

Required

(a) Prepare draft accounts for 19X9 for the consolidation on the basis that:

 (i) The combination satisfies the conditions in FRS 6 for merger accounting and merger accounting is applied.

 (ii) The combination satisfies the conditions for merger relief but that acquisition accounting is applied. Assume a policy of amortization over ten years for any goodwill that arises. Ignore any deferred taxation implications.

(b) Discuss the bases for computing the asset values and reserves in the financial statements that appear under the two alternatives.

ACCA 3.1 (requirement (a) modified)

Additions to the group

Objectives

After completing this chapter you should be able to:

- make appropriate adjustments for dividends received out of the pre-acquisition profits of a subsidiary when acquisition accounting is used;
- produce a complete set of financial statements for a subsidiary acquired during the parent company's accounting period, including cases where a subsidiary produces financial statements that span the acquisition date;
- demonstrate how the consolidated profit and loss account will differ according to whether acquisition accounting or merger accounting is used to consolidate the results of a subsidiary acquired during the parent company's accounting period;
- apply the accounting rules for piecemeal acquisitions and demonstrate how these can sometimes produce misleading figures.

Introduction

The situations covered by this chapter fall under two broad headings, namely

1. acquisition of a subsidiary during the parent company's accounting period;
2. piecemeal acquisitions.

The accounting treatment for the first of these will depend on whether the consolidated accounts are prepared under acquisition accounting or merger accounting. The primary learning material in this chapter is presented in the context of acquisition accounting. Merger accounting is then shown as a variation to this practice.

To some extent the chapter deals with accounting problems for acquisitions during the period that do not arise in practice; they arise mainly in examination questions where the subsidiary produces financial statements that span the acquisition date. In practice, if a subsidiary is acquired during the parent company's accounting period the financial statements of the acquired company are usually prepared for its final period up to the date of acquisition. The balance sheet of the acquired company at the date of acquisition is then used as the basis for determining pre-acquisition reserves and calculating goodwill.

Consolidation of the subsidiary's post-acquisition results is done in the normal way, although it might be necessary to change the accounting date and accounting policies so that they accord with those of the parent company. Both FRS 2 (paragraph 40) and Schedule 4A of the Companies Act 1985 (paragraph 3(1)) require uniform accounting policies be used throughout the group.

The term 'piecemeal acquisitions' is a reference to various situations where the shares held in another company are acquired by a series of separate purchases over a period of time rather than from a single purchase. These situations include an associated company becoming a subsidiary and an increase in the shareholding of an existing subsidiary. There are regulations in FRS 2 to cover these situations but they leave certain aspects open to interpretation.

Dividends received shortly after acquisition

Before studying the accounting implications of an acquisition during the parent company's accounting period, there is a general principle to learn which can apply to the acquisition of any investment where the price paid is quoted as 'cum div'. You might have studied this aspect under a subject heading such as investment accounting. When shares are acquired cum div the new shareholder will receive the whole of the next dividend, even if the shares have been held for only a few weeks. The price paid for the shares recognizes that the purchaser will receive the whole of this dividend. Consequently, when the dividend is received it is effectively a refund of a part of the purchase price.

This aspect often features in exam questions where the acquisition of a subsidiary occurs during the parent company's accounting period. In the context of group accounts the problem is usually known as **dividends received out of pre-acquisition profits**. The accounting treatment of these dividends when the acquisition method of consolidation is used has been mentioned in earlier chapters, although on those occasions you were not required to apply the principle.

Activity 6.1

Imagine that a parent company acquired a 100% interest in a subsidiary at a time when that subsidiary's retained profits were £100 000 after providing for a proposed dividend of £50 000. The price paid was cum div and three weeks later the subsidiary paid the dividend of £50 000. It would be wrong for the parent company to credit this dividend to its own profit and loss account; make a note here of why this is so.

Activity 6.2

If it is wrong for the parent company to credit the dividend to its own profit and loss account, what account should be credited, and why?

A similar principle applies to investment accounting generally. None of this has any bearing on the tax treatment. For tax purposes, the price paid for an investment is all capital; all dividends received are treated as income. Tax is not affected by the way these transactions are dealt with in the accounts.

In the case of groups, there is contention over the extent to which a dividend received following acquisition should be treated as having been paid out of pre- or post-acquisition profits. The normal practice is for dividends paid to be related to a particular accounting period. This period is then used as the frame of reference to establish the extent to which the dividend relates to pre-acquisition profits. For example, if a subsidiary were acquired on 1 July 1995 and some time later the subsidiary pays a dividend for year ending 31 December 1995, it could be argued that half of the dividend has been paid out of pre-acquisition profits and half out of post-acquisition profits.

Details for the next activity

A subsidiary has a 31 December accounting date which is co-terminus with that of the parent company. The parent company acquired a 100% interest in this subsidiary on 1 July 1995 but accounts for the subsidiary were not prepared up to the date of acquisition. The subsidiary's results for year ending 31 December 1995, and its reserve movements, were as follows:

	£
Profits after tax	50 000
Dividend paid 30 September 1995	10 000
Retained profit for the year	40 000
Profit and loss account at 1 January 1995	50 000
Profit and loss account at 31 December 1995	90 000

The subsidiary has no reserves other than the profit and loss account. All transactions accrue evenly throughout the year.

Activity 6.3

Describe how the dividend received should be dealt with in the parent company's accounts.

The information for this activity might have been given to us as part of a problem on preparing consolidated accounts. If this were the case we would need to determine the reserves at the date of acquisition. This would have been required for two purposes, namely:

- to calculate goodwill at the date of acquisition;
- to establish the split between pre- and post-acquisition profits.

Activity 6.4

Calculate the subsidiary's reserves at the date of acquisition on the assumption that profits accrue evenly throughout the year.

Subsidiary acquired during the year

Profit and loss account – acquisition accounting

Most of the procedures discussed in this section assume that the subsidiary produces financial statements that span the acquisition date. As mentioned in the introduction, this happens more in exam questions than it does in practice.

The group profit and loss account is prepared by consolidating the post-acquisition figures for each item in the subsidiary's profit and loss account. In most cases the post-acquisition figures are based on a time-apportioned fraction of the figures for the whole year. This approach makes an assumption that all income and expenditure accrues evenly throughout the year. If this does not apply, there will be other information available to establish a split between the pre- and post-acquisition transactions.

The post-acquisition proportions of the subsidiary's figures are consolidated down to the line called taxation in the same way as when consolidating the results of a subsidiary that was acquired at the beginning of the year. This means that the full post-acquisition figures are consolidated even if the subsidiary has minority interests. The minority shareholders' interest in the profits will then have to be based on a percentage of the amount of profit that has been consolidated for their subsidiary; not on the profits earned by the subsidiary for the year.

We will practise the techniques using the example that follows. In order to see the principle clearly, the example has not been cluttered by the usual adjustments for things like inter-company trading and unrealized profits on stock. The main difficulty will be in the treatment of the dividends and in calculating reserves at the date of acquisition. We will, however, produce a solution (including the balance sheet) in a series of logical steps. You should review the information before starting work on the text and activities that follow.

Details for the activities

Parent Ltd acquired a controlling interest in the ordinary shares of Sub Ltd on 1 April 95 at a cost of £300 000. Both companies have a 31 December accounting date. The following are the abbreviated accounts for both companies in respect of year ended 31 December 1995.

Profit and loss accounts

	Parent Ltd	Sub Ltd
	£	£
Turnover	800 000	200 000
Cost of sales and operating expenses	700 000	120 000
Operating profit	100 000	80 000
Dividends from subsidiary	9 600	—
Profit before tax	109 600	80 000
Taxation	40 000	32 000
Profit after tax	69 600	48 000
Dividends paid 31 July 1995	30 000	12 000
Retained profit for the financial year	39 600	36 000

Movements on profit and loss account reserve	£	£
Balance at 1 January 1995	600 000	100 000
Retained profit for the financial year	39 600	36 000
Balance at 31 December 1995	639 600	136 000

Balance sheets at 31 December 1995		
Sundry net assets	839 600	336 000
Investment in subsidiary	300 000	—
	1 139 600	336 000
Ordinary share capital	500 000	200 000
Profit and loss account	639 600	136 000
	1 139 600	336 000

Sub Ltd's net identifiable assets are considered to have a fair value equal to their book value. It can be assumed that trading items accrue evenly throughout the year. The subsidiary did not account for ACT on dividends paid to the parent company.

If you review the above data again you will notice that it does not state the proportion of shares owned by the parent company. Examination questions are sometimes presented like this, and you might have encountered the problem when working some of the previous end of chapter exercises. It is, however, possible to determine the percentage of shares held by comparing certain items in the profit and loss account of each company. It is a good idea to sort this out before proceeding because it will help you to become familiar with some of the data in the problem.

Activity 6.5

Calculate the proportion of shares in Sub Ltd held by Parent Ltd by comparing information in each company's profit and loss account. Make a note here of the percentage, and how you found it.

The first step will be to produce the consolidated profit and loss account from turnover down to profit after tax. When doing this you must consolidate the full amount of the post-acquisition proportion of the subsidiary's figures. Strictly speaking, we should follow the rules in FRS 3 by disclosing how much of the profit in the consolidated profit and loss account relates to the acquired entity. We will, however, ignore this aspect since it will hold up the learning process.

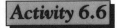

Activity 6.6

Complete the consolidated profit and loss account down to profit after tax by completing the outline format shown below this box. (You could show your workings in the space between the description and the amount.)

Consolidated profit and loss account (part) year ending 31 December 1995

	£
Turnover	
Cost of sales and operating expenses	_____
Profit before tax	
Taxation	_____
Profit after tax	

The next item in the consolidated profit and loss account is minority interests. We need to be a little more careful on this than we have in previous examples. The deduction for minority interests will have to be based on the amount of the subsidiary's profit that has been consolidated, not on the subsidiary's total profit for the year as shown in its own accounts.

Activity 6.7

Calculate the amount for minority interests and then complete the remaining part of the consolidated profit and loss as set out below this box. Remember that dividends paid in the consolidated accounts relate entirely to dividends paid by the parent company.

Minority interests =

Consolidated profit and loss account – continued

	£
Profit after tax	96 000
Minority interests	_____
Profit for the financial year	
Dividends paid	_____
Retained profit for the financial year	=======

All of the remaining figures that are needed to complete this task relate to the balance sheet.

Balance sheet – acquisition accounting

Since we have already prepared a consolidated profit and loss account for the year, the balance on the profit and loss reserve for the consolidated balance sheet is simply the balance brought forward plus the retained profit for the year as shown in the consolidated profit and loss account. The opening balance on the profit and loss reserve in the situation being considered will consist entirely of the opening balance on the parent company's profit and loss account. This is because there was no subsidiary at 1 January 1995.

Activity 6.8

Calculate the closing balance on the consolidated profit and loss account reserve for the consolidated balance sheet, and make a note of your calculations here.

In this new situation, the calculations for goodwill, and the analysis of the balance on the consolidated profit and loss reserve, require a little more thought than they did in earlier chapters. There are no new principles involved, merely the practical problem of dealing with the dividend paid by the subsidiary and in finding the balance on the subsidiary's profit and loss reserve at the date of acquisition. Part of the dividend received by the parent company must be treated as a capital receipt and part will be treated as a revenue item. You will see from the data that the parent company has treated the whole of the dividend received as a revenue item.

Activity 6.9

First, divide the £9600 dividend received between its capital and revenue elements by using the principles established through Activity 6.3. Then, use this information to calculate the revised balance on the cost of the investment and the revised balance on Parent Ltd's profit and loss reserve at 31 December 1995. You can note your calculations in this box.

1. Division of the dividend received between capital and revenue:
    Capital portion   £
    Revenue portion   £
                               £9600

2. Adjusted balances:
    Cost of investment   £
    Profit and loss reserve of Parent Ltd at 31 December 1995   £

You might never be asked to analyse the balance on the consolidated profit and loss reserve but doing so is an excellent learning process. This analysis usually shows how much of the balance on the consolidated profit and loss reserve has been retained by the parent company and how much has been retained in the subsidiary. You can now do the analysis as a result of the information derived from Activities 6.8 and 6.9.

You have already calculated the consolidated profit and loss reserve in Activity 6.8. The revised balance on the profit and loss reserve of Parent Ltd was determined by Activity 6.9. The amount of consolidated profit retained in the subsidiary is based on the parent company's share of the subsidiary's post-acquisition profits less the dividend paid to the parent company that is deemed to have been paid out of these profits.

Analyse the balance on the consolidated profit and loss reserve by completing the figures in the following outline calculation.

Retained by Parent Ltd
   (the adjusted balance from Activity 6.9)   £

Retained in Sub Ltd
   (Parent Ltd's share of post-acquisition profits for
   the year, less dividend received out of these profits)   £ _____

Consolidated profit and loss reserve as in Activity 6.8   =====

We now need to establish the balance on Sub Ltd's profit and loss reserve at 31 March 1995 in order to calculate goodwill. When doing this you will find it helpful to forget about the parent company's share and simply calculate the total balance at 31 March 1995.

Activity 6.11

Determine the total balance on Sub Ltd's profit and loss reserve at 31 March 1995 by completing the outline calculation shown below this box.

Balance at 1 January 1995   £100 000
Add profits from 1 January 1995 to 31 March 1995   £
Less dividend paid out of these profits   £ _____

Retained profit for the three months   £ _____
Balance at 31 March 1995   =====

You can now calculate goodwill because you know what the balance of capital and reserves would have been at 31 March 1995, and you know the adjusted cost of the investment. No adjustment is necessary for the fair values of the subsidiary's net identifiable assets at 31 March 1995.

Activity 6.12

Calculate goodwill on consolidation by completing the outline format shown below this box.

Adjusted cost of the investment (Activity 6.9)   £
Capital and reserves at 31 March 1995:
   Share capital   £
   Profit and loss reserve (Activity 6.11)   £ _____

Less minority interests   £
Parent company's share   £ _____
Goodwill on acquisition   £ _____

Since there are no fair value adjustments, the figure for minority interests to be included in the consolidated balance sheet at 31 December 1995 is simply 20% of the capital and reserves as shown in Sub Ltd's balance sheet at that date.

Activity 6.13

Calculate the figure for minority interests at 31 December 1995 and make a note of the amount here.

You have now calculated all of the figures needed to prepare a consolidated balance sheet at 31 December 1995.

Activity 6.14

Complete the outline balance sheet shown below this box. In this example, goodwill is to be written off immediately against the balance on the consolidated profit and loss reserve.

Consolidated balance sheet at 31 December 1995

Sundry net assets		£
Capital and reserves:		
Ordinary share capital		£
Profit and loss account	£	
Less goodwill written off	£	
Minority interests		

Merger accounting for a new acquisition

In merger accounting an assumption is made that the two companies had always been together. Consequently:

- all dividends received by the parent company can be credited to its own profit and loss account; no adjustment is required to treat dividends paid out of pre-acquisition profits as capital (the concept of pre-acquisition profits does not apply);
- the subsidiary's profits for the whole year are consolidated.

We can practise this on the following example. The details are similar to those in the previous example but in order to make it compatible with merger accounting some of the figures for Parent Ltd have been altered.

Details for the activities

Parent Ltd acquired 100% of Sub Ltd's ordinary shares on 1 April 1995 as a result of a share for share exchange. The terms were one £1 ordinary share in Parent Ltd for one £1 ordinary share in Sub Ltd. The following are the abbreviated accounts of both companies for year ending 31 December 1995.

	Parent Ltd	Sub Ltd	Consolidated
Profit and loss accounts	£	£	
Turnover	800 000	200 000	
Cost of sales and operating expenses	700 000	120 000	
Operating profit	100 000	80 000	
Dividends from subsidiary	12 000	—	
Profit before tax	112 000	80 000	
Taxation	40 000	32 000	
Profit after tax	72 000	48 000	
Dividends paid for the year	30 000	12 000	
Retained profit for the financial year	42 000	36 000	
Movements on profit and loss reserve			
Balance at 1 January 1995	600 000	100 000	
Retained profit for the financial year	42 000	36 000	
Balance at 31 December 1995	642 000	136 000	
Balance sheets at 31 December 1995			
Sundry net assets	1 142 000	336 000	
Investment in subsidiary	200 000	—	
	1 342 000	336 000	
Ordinary share capital	700 000	200 000	
Profit and loss account	642 000	136 000	
	1 342 000	336 000	

The complications that we dealt with under acquisition accounting do not arise with merger accounting. This is because there is no concept of pre- and post-acquisition profits. You can probably recall reading the following paragraph from Schedule 4A of the Companies Act 1985 when studying merger accounting in Chapter 5.

11(3) The income and expenditure of the undertaking acquired shall be included in the group accounts for the entire financial year, including the period before the acquisition.

FRS 2 includes a similar statement. This means that in order to produce consolidated financial statements using merger accounting, the procedure is little more than combining the figures shown in the separate financial statements. This will include combining the balances on the profit and loss reserves at the beginning of the year. It will, however, be necessary to eliminate inter-company dividends and inter-company shareholdings, as follows:

- the consolidated profit and loss account will not show dividends received from the subsidiary and will not show dividends paid to the parent company by the subsidiary; these two items (£12 000 in the example) are set against each other and cancelled;
- the carrying value of the investment in the subsidiary is set off against the nominal value of the issued share capital in the subsidiary held by the parent company. Since both figures are £200 000 in the example, there is no consolidation difference to deal with.

Activity 6.15

In the above example, there is a column to the right of the figures for the individual companies where you can enter the amounts for the consolidated accounts. You should do this now for all three statements. Remember to eliminate the inter-company items.

Dividends paid to former shareholders

A slight complication arises under merger accounting when the subsidiary has paid a dividend to its former shareholders prior to the date that the shares were acquired by the parent company. This dividend will have been paid out of the subsidiary's profit that is now being consolidated and there will be no corresponding dividend received in the parent company's accounts against which it can be eliminated. Since it has been paid to persons outside the group, it will have to be shown in the consolidated profit and loss account as a dividend paid to outsiders. The normal practice is to include this item in the same place as minority interests. It cannot be described as minority interests since it has been paid to the former shareholders of the subsidiary.

We can see the effect of this by modifying the previous example. We will assume that the dividend of £12 000 was paid to the shareholders of the subsidiary prior to the acquisition by Parent Ltd. The revised accounts for each company, including an adjustment to Parent Ltd's sundry net assets to recognize that the £12 000 was not received, are set out below.

	Parent Ltd	Sub Ltd
Profit and loss accounts	£	£
Turnover	800 000	200 000
Cost of sales and operating expenses	700 000	120 000
Profit before tax	100 000	80 000
Taxation	40 000	32 000
Profit after tax	60 000	48 000
Dividends paid for the year	30 000	12 000

	Parent Ltd £	Sub Ltd £
Retained profit for the financial year	30 000	36 000

Movements on profit and loss reserve   Consolidated

	Parent Ltd	Sub Ltd
Balance at 1 January 1995	600 000	100 000
Retained profit for the financial year	30 000	36 000
Balance at 31 December 1995	630 000	136 000

Balance sheets at 31 December 1995

	Parent Ltd	Sub Ltd
Sundry net assets	1 130 000	336 000
Investment in subsidiary	200 000	—
	1 330 000	336 000
Ordinary share capital	700 000	200 000
Profit and loss account	630 000	136 000
	1 330 000	336 000

All of the figures in the consolidated profit and loss account will be the same as in the previous example except that it will be necessary to show dividends of £12 000 being paid to the former shareholders in the subsidiary.

Activity 6.16

Set out the figures for the appropriation section of the consolidated profit and loss account by completing the outline format shown below this box.

Consolidated profit and loss account – appropriation section

	£	£
Profit after tax		108 000
Dividends paid:		
To shareholders of Parent Ltd	30 000	
To former shareholders of Sub Ltd		
Retained profit for the financial year		

You will notice that the consolidated retained profit for the financial year is (as it was in the previous example) the same as the sum of the retained profits in the accounts of the parent company and the subsidiary. The procedures for completing the consolidation are the same as before.

Complete the consolidation by entering the consolidated figures in the column to the right of the individual accounts. It is only necessary to complete the statement showing movements on profit and loss reserve, and the consolidated balance sheet.

Piecemeal acquisitions

This section relates to various situations where the subsidiary is acquired by a series of share purchases at different dates. Some of the earlier purchases will not give control and will be treated in the investing company's books either as fixed asset investments, or as an investment in an associated company, depending on the circumstances. It is also necessary to consider cases where the parent company increases its interest in an existing subsidiary by purchasing shares from the minority interests.

The general problem

At the centre of this problem are the provisions in Schedule 4A of the Companies Act 1985 that define acquisition accounting (para. 9). You have already had an opportunity to read these provisions when working on Chapter 2 (see the appendix to that chapter). The effect of these rules is that goodwill, and pre-acquisition reserves, must be calculated by reference to the facts that apply at the date the undertaking becomes a subsidiary.

These rules must be applied even when the interest is acquired in stages. In these circumstances the acquisition cost will include the cost of earlier purchases and goodwill is calculated by comparing the total acquisition cost with the fair values of the subsidiary's net identifiable assets at the date that it becomes a subsidiary. In other words, goodwill cannot be treated as the sum of the goodwill arising from each purchase and post-acquisition reserves cannot include any amounts attributable to those earlier purchases.

There are not likely to be many objections to this when the earlier purchases of shares in the company that has now become a subsidiary were simply treated as fixed asset investments. But if they resulted in an investment that had to be treated as an investment in an associated undertaking, the Schedule 4A treatment might be inequitable. This can arise because any change in the fair value of the subsidiary's net identifiable assets between the two purchase dates is partly a result of economic factors affecting fair values and partly a result of the profits retained by the investee. If the investment had been dealt with under equity accounting, a share of these retained profits has been included in the consolidated reserves. These profits will, in effect, be capitalized as part of the figure for goodwill if the Schedule 4A treatment is applied.

The prescriptive part of FRS 2 on this matter follows the approach required by Schedule 4A but the explanatory notes recognize that in some cases the calculation of goodwill under these provisions might result in accounts that are misleading. In these circumstances it might be necessary to depart from the regulations in order to show a true and fair view.

Fixed asset investment becomes a subsidiary

If the earlier purchases of shares did not result in an investment being treated as an associated undertaking, the Schedule 4A treatment is less likely to be controversial. There could be problems where a provision has been made for a permanent diminution in the value of an investment that now falls to be treated as a part of the acquisition cost of a subsidiary, but we will not be considering that particular situation.

The way in which the rules apply to a basic problem is best seen by example. We will work on the following situation. All figures are in £000s. The reserves of the investee are represented solely by the balance on the profit and loss reserve at the date of each transaction.

Purchase transaction	% holding purchased	Purchase cost	Fair value of investee	Cumulative cost	Reserves of investee
1	15%	£200	£1200	£200	£500
2	45%	£750	£1500	£950	£800

You should note that it is unlikely that a fair value exercise would have been carried out on the date of the first transaction. The fair values have been included in the tabulation in order to demonstrate a point.

Activity 6.18

Refer to paragraph 50 of FRS 2 as set out in the appendix to this chapter and calculate goodwill arising on consolidation using the principles required by that paragraph.

In the above example, the increase in the fair value of the investee's net assets between transactions 1 and 2 (£300 000) relates solely to the profits retained by the investee during the period that the 15% stake was held. If a stepped approach to the calculation had been allowed, the figures would have been as follows:

(a) *Calculation of goodwill*

Transaction 1: £200 000 − (15% × £1 200 000)	£20 000
Transaction 2: £750 000 − (45% × £1 500 000)	£75 000
Total	£95 000

(b) *Post-acquisition reserves consolidated*

Relating to transaction 1: (15% × £300 000)	£45 000

In this case the goodwill exceeds the amount calculated for Activity 6.18 by £45 000 and this increase would have been represented in the consolidated accounts by post-acquisition reserves of £45 000. The explanatory notes in FRS 2 suggest that there might be special circumstances where goodwill should be calculated for each acquisition; these are mentioned in the next section (where an associated undertaking becomes a subsidiary). In most cases the method required by Schedule 4A and FRS 2 provides a practical way of applying acquisition accounting because it does not require retrospective assessments of fair values for earlier acquisitions (paragraph 89 FRS 2).

Associated undertaking becomes a subsidiary

The principles in Schedule 4A and FRS 2 apply equally to an investment that was previously treated as an associated undertaking. In some cases this could result in misleading figures because we are required to ignore fair values at the date of the earlier purchase and yet the total acquisition cost (at the time when the associate becomes a subsidiary) includes an amount that was paid for that earlier purchase. The effect of this can be that the group's share of profits of its associated undertaking becomes reclassified as goodwill (usually negative goodwill).

We will see what happens by working on the data that follow. As in the previous example, the figures are in £000s and the reserves of the investee are represented solely by the balance on the profit and loss reserve at the date of each acquisition. The increase in fair values over the period is attributed entirely to the retained profits of the investee.

Purchase transaction	% holding purchased	Purchase cost	Fair value of investee	Cumulative cost	Reserves of investee
1	40%	£480	£1200	£480	£500
2	20%	£300	£1500	£780	£800

Notice that the amount paid for each purchase of shares is equal to the percentage interest in the fair value of the investee's net assets. This has been contrived in order to demonstrate that although there can be no goodwill in such circumstances, the Schedule 4A treatment creates a difference that must be classified as goodwill.

The position at various points in time can be illustrated as follows:

1. **On acquiring an associated undertaking**
   The consolidated balance sheet will show a share of the associate's net assets of (40% × £1 200 000) £480 000. Since this is equal to the cost of the investment, there is no goodwill.

2. **Immediately prior to transaction 2**
   In the investing company's balance sheet the investment will still be shown at its original cost of £480 000. In the consolidated balance sheet, however, the application of equity accounting applies and the

carrying value of the investment will have increased to (40% × £1 500 000) £600 000. The difference of (£600 000 – £480 000) £120 000 relates to the investor's share of the associate's post-acquisition profits. A summary of the position is as follows:

In the investor's balance sheet:
Investment at cost   £480 000

In the consolidated balance sheet:
Associated undertaking   £600 000

Share of post-acquisition profits   £120 000

3. **When the associate becomes a subsidiary**
    The Schedule 4A treatment requires us to ignore the investee's fair values at transaction 1 but requires the cost of that transaction to be added to the cost of transaction 2 in order to determine the total cost of acquiring the subsidiary. This total cost is then compared to the parent company's share of the subsidiary's net assets (at fair value) at the date that it became a subsidiary. The result of this requirement is as follows:

    Share of net assets at fair value (60% × £1 500 000)   £900 000
    Cumulative cost of the investment   780 000
    Difference   £120 000

Schedule 4A requires this difference to be classified as goodwill, in this case as negative goodwill. And yet we know that there is no goodwill because the amount paid for each purchase of shares was equal to the percentage interest in the investee's net assets at fair value.

Activity 6.19

This £120 000 is equivalent to something other than negative goodwill. Make a note here of what the difference of £120 000 represents.

The following quotation is from the explanatory notes in paragraph 89 of FRS 2. The paragraphs quoted here follow comments on the treatment required by Schedule 4A.

In special circumstances, however, not using fair values at the dates of earlier purchases, while using an acquisition cost part of which relates to earlier purchases, may result in accounting that is inconsistent with the way the investment has been treated previously and, for that reason, may fail to give a true and fair view. For example, an undertaking that has been treated as an associated undertaking by a group may then be acquired by the group as a subsidiary undertaking. Using the method required by Schedule 4A paragraph 9 to calculate goodwill on such an acquisition has the effect that the group's share of profits or losses [. . .] of its associated undertaking becomes reclassified as goodwill (usually negative goodwill). [. . .]

In the rare cases where the Schedule 4A paragraph 9 calculation of goodwill would be misleading goodwill should be calculated as the sum of goodwill arising from each purchase of an interest in the relevant undertaking [. . .]. Goodwill arising on each purchase should be calculated as the difference between the cost of that purchase and the fair value at the date of that purchase of the identifiable assets and liabilities attributed to the interest purchased. The difference between the goodwill calculated on this method and that calculated on the method provided by the Act is shown in reserves.

In the example we have been using, the amount of goodwill for each purchase would be calculated as nil. The difference between this and the Schedule 4A calculation results in a credit balance of £120 000 which should be included in reserves. The position is then consistent with the way that the former investment in the associated undertaking had been treated.

Parent company purchases shares from minority interests

Prior to the introduction of FRS 2 it was a fairly common practice for companies to compare the amount paid for the additional investment with the carrying value of the minority interest acquired. If you now read paragraph 51 of FRS 2 (in the appendix) you will see that this basis is no longer permitted except where the difference between carrying values and fair values is not material.

FRS 2 requires that the carrying values of the net identifiable assets of the subsidiary should be revalued to fair value and that any goodwill arising as a result of the purchase should be calculated by reference to the revised values. The justification for this treatment is stated in the explanatory notes. If the net assets were not revalued to fair value then the difference between the purchase cost and the relevant proportion of the carrying value of the subsidiary's net assets would relate partly to goodwill and partly to a change in the value of those net assets.

There are, however, no corresponding rules in the Companies Act. The rules in paragraph 9 of Schedule 4A that require fair value adjustments in acquisition accounting apply only when an undertaking becomes a subsidiary undertaking; they do not relate to a parent company increasing its stake by purchasing shares from the minority interests.

Summary

The main learning points in this chapter can be summarized as follows:

- dividends received out of pre-acquisition profits must be treated as capital receipts and credited to the cost of the investment;

- the extent to which a dividend is deemed to have been paid out of pre-acquisition profits is usually based on the accounting period to which the dividend relates;
- when a subsidiary is acquired during the parent company's accounting period, and the subsidiary produces financial statements that span the acquisition date, it is necessary to use time-apportionments to establish the post-acquisition amounts for income and expenditure and to establish the balance on the subsidiary's profit and loss reserve at the acquisition date;
- these apportionments are not necessary if merger accounting can be used because the consolidated financial statements are prepared on the assumption that the two companies had always been together;
- when a subsidiary is acquired by a series of purchases over a period of time, Schedule 4A of the Companies Act 1985, and FRS 2, require goodwill to be calculated by comparing the aggregate acquisition cost with the fair value of the subsidiary's net identifiable assets at the date it became a subsidiary;
- a strict interpretation of these rules might (albeit rarely) produce results that are misleading and in these circumstances goodwill can be calculated as the sum of goodwill attributable to each purchase;
- any difference between goodwill calculated according to Schedule 4A and the sum of goodwill calculated for each purchase should be included in reserves;
- FRS 2 has changed the rules for calculating goodwill when a parent company increases its shareholding in a subsidiary by purchasing shares from the minority interests;
- the former practice of calculating goodwill arising on the acquisition by comparing the purchase cost with the relevant proportion of the carrying value of the net assets in the subsidiary is no longer allowed;
- in such circumstances the purchase cost must be compared to the relevant proportion of the fair value of the subsidiary's net assets except where the difference between fair value and carrying value is not material;
- there are no provisions in the Companies Act regarding fair value adjustments when the interest in a subsidiary is increased.

Key to activities

Activity 6.1

The parent company has paid a price that includes the right to receive the whole of the next dividend. The receipt of this dividend is, therefore, a repayment of a part of the amount paid for the shares.

Activity 6.2

The carrying value of the investment. A part of the purchase cost has now been repaid.

Activity 6.3

In terms of double entry, the dividend received of £10 000 should be recorded as follows:

Debit	bank	£10 000	
	Credit	profit and loss account	£5 000
		cost of investment	£5 000

Activity 6.4

	£	£
Balance at 1 January 1995		50 000
Profits after tax to 30 June 1995	25 000	
Less dividend paid out of these profits	5 000	
		20 000
		70 000

Activity 6.5

Based on dividends received from subsidiary: £9600/£12 000 = 80% (the dividend was paid after acquisition).

Activity 6.6

Turnover (£800 000 + (9/12 × £200 000))	950 000
Cost of sales and operating expenses (£700 000 + (9/12 × £120 000))	790 000
Profit before tax	160 000
Taxation (£40 000 + (9/12 × £32 000))	64 000
Profit after tax	96 000

Activity 6.7

Minority interests (20% × 9/12 × £48 000) = £7200

Profit after tax	96 000
Minority interests	7 200
Profit for the financial year	88 800
Dividends paid	30 000
Retained profit for the financial year	58 800

Activity 6.8

Balance at 1 January 1995 (Parent Ltd)	600 000
Retained profit for the financial year	58 800
Balance at 31 December 1995	658 800

Activity 6.9

		£
1.	Capital portion (3/12 × £9600)	2 400
	Revenue portion (9/12 × £9600)	7 200
		9 600
2.	Cost of investment (£300 000 – £2400)	297 600
	Profit and loss reserve of Parent Ltd at 31 December 1995 (£639 600 – £2400)	637 200

Activity 6.10

	£
Retained by Parent Ltd (as Activity 6.9)	637 200
Retained in Sub Ltd (80% × 9/12 × £48 000) – £7200	21 600
Consolidated balance (as Activity 6.8)	658 800

Note that in this particular case the amount retained in the subsidiary could have been found by taking 80% × 9/12 of the profits retained in Sub Ltd. This will only work, however, when all items (including dividends) are deemed to accrue evenly throughout the year.

Activity 6.11

	£	£
Balance at 1 January 1995		100 000
Profits to 31 March 1995 (3/12 × £48 000)	12 000	
Less dividend paid out of these profits (3/12 × £12 000)	3 000	
		9 000
		109 000

Activity 6.12

	£	£
Adjusted cost of investment		297 600
Capital and reserves at 31 March 1995		
Share capital	200 000	
Profit and loss account	109 000	
	309 000	
Less minority interests	61 800	
		247 200
Goodwill arising on consolidation		50 400

Activity 6.13

20% × £336 000 = £67 200

Activity 6.14

	£	£
Sundry net assets (£839 600 + £336 000)		<u>1 175 600</u>
Capital and reserves		
Share capital		500 000
Profit and loss account	658 800	
Goodwill written off	<u>50 400</u>	
		<u>608 400</u>
		1 108 400
Minority interests		<u>67 200</u>
		<u>1 175 600</u>

Activity 6.15

Consolidated profit and loss account

Turnover	1 000 000
Cost of sales and operating expenses	<u>820 000</u>
Profit before tax	180 000
Taxation	<u>72 000</u>
Profit after tax	108 000
Dividends	<u>30 000</u>
Retained profit for the financial year	<u>78 000</u>

Movements on profit and loss reserve

Balance at 1 January 1995	700 000
Retained profit for financial year	<u>78 000</u>
Balance at 31 December 1995	<u>778 000</u>

Balance sheets at 31 December 1995

Sundry net assets	<u>1 478 000</u>
Ordinary share capital	700 000
Profit and loss account	<u>778 000</u>
	<u>1 478 000</u>

Activity 6.16

Profit after tax		108 000
Dividends paid		
Shareholders of Parent Ltd	30 000	
Former shareholders of Sub Ltd	<u>12 000</u>	
		<u>42 000</u>
Retained profit for the financial year		<u>66 000</u>

Activity 6.17

Movements on profit and loss reserve

	£
Balance at 1 January 1995	700 000
Retained profit for the financial year	66 000
Balance at 31 December 1995	766 000

Balance sheets at 31 December 1995

Sundry net assets	1 466 000

Ordinary share capital	700 000
Profit and loss account	766 000
	1 466 000

Activity 6.18

Share of net assets at fair value (60% × £1 500 000)	900 000
Cumulative cost of investment	950 000
Goodwill arising on consolidation	50 000

Activity 6.19

The investing company's share of the post-acquisition profits earned by its associated undertaking (40% × (£800 000 – £500 000)).

Appendix

Extracts from FRS 2

Changes in stake

Acquiring a subsidiary undertaking in stages

50 Schedule 4A paragraph 9 requires that the identifiable assets and liabilities of a subsidiary undertaking be included in the consolidation at fair value at the date of its acquisition, that is, the date it becomes a subsidiary undertaking. This requirement is also applicable where the group's interest in the undertaking that becomes a subsidiary undertaking is acquired in stages [4A Sch 9].

Increasing an interest held in a subsidiary undertaking

51 When a group increases its interest in an undertaking that is already its subsidiary undertaking, the identifiable assets and liabilities of that subsidiary undertaking should be revalued to fair value and goodwill arising on the increase in interest should be calculated by those fair values. This revaluation is not required if the difference between net fair values and carrying amounts of the assets and liabilities attributable to the increase in stake is not material.

Questions

Question for self assessment

An answer to this question is given at the end of the book.

6.1 Friendly plc

The directors of Friendly plc have decided on a policy of growth by acquisition. On 31 March 19X7 the company acquired a 100% holding in Patience Limited for £400 000 when the retained earnings of that company were £120 000. The goodwill of £230 000 was written off against consolidated reserves in the financial year ending 30 June 1987. No adjustments for fair values were required.

On 31 October 19X7 Friendly plc acquired an 18% holding in Tolerance Limited for £160 000 and on 31 March 19X8 increased its holding to 60% for £373 000. The retained earnings of Tolerance Limited were £200 000 at 31 October 19X7 and £250 000 on 31 March 19X8. The book value of the assets was equal to the fair value of the assets.

The balance sheets of Friendly plc, Patience Limited and Tolerance Limited at 30 June 19X8 showed:

	Friendly plc £000	Patience Ltd £000	Tolerance Ltd £000
Share capital	731.5	50.0	100.0
Share premium	540.0		100.0
Retained earnings	400.0	190.0	360.0
	1671.5	240.0	560.0
Net tangible assets	738.5	240.0	560.0
Investments in			
Patience Ltd	400.0		
Tolerance Ltd	533.0		
	1671.5	240.0	560.0

Required

(a) Prepare the consolidated balance sheet of the group. You must apply the principles in Schedule 4A of the Companies Act 1985 and FRS 2 when dealing with the staged acquisition of Tolerance Ltd. Assume that the immediate write-off policy is adopted for the goodwill arising on the acquisition of Tolerance Ltd.

(b) Demonstrate how the figures in the group balance sheet would differ if a stepped (or proportional) basis for the calculation of goodwill and post-acquisition reserves had been applied, and discuss any arguments that might support adoption of this basis.

(c) Write brief notes on the options for writing off goodwill in the year of acquisition.

ACCA 3.1 requirements modified

Question without answer

An answer to this question is published separately in the *Teacher's Manual*.

6.2 Herne Group
See author's *guidance notes* at the end of the question.

The following are the summarized accounts of four private companies:

Summarised balance sheets at 31 December 19X9

	Herne Ltd £000	Alfred Ltd £000	Ludens Ltd £000	Gildas Ltd £000
Fixed assets				
Tangible	10 978	560	3362	8425
Investments	7 500			
Current assets				
Stock	1 780.8	97.6	590.4	1479.2
Debtors	2 448.6	134.2	811.8	2033.9
Cash	2 893.8	158.6	959.4	2403.7
Creditors falling due within one year:	(4 897.2)	(268.4)	(1623.6)	(4067.8)
Net current assets	2 226	122	738	1849
	20 704	682	4100	10274
Capital and reserves				
£1 Ordinary shares	10 000	100	2000	5000
Profit and loss account	10 704	582	2100	5274
	20 704	682	4100	10274

Summarised Profit and loss accounts year ended 31 December 19X9

	Herne Ltd £000	Alfred Ltd £000	Ludens Ltd £000	Gildas Ltd £000
Turnover	16 613	567	3240	8100
Cost of sales	10 460	357	2040	5100
Gross profit	6 153	210	1200	3000
Distribution costs and administrative expenses	4 102	140	800	2000
Operating profit	2 051	70	400	1000
Investment income	49			
Profit before taxation	2 100	70	400	1000
Taxation	500	20	100	250
Profit after taxation	1 600	50	300	750
Dividends:				
Paid	(400)	(4)	(80)	(200)
Payable	(600)	(6)	(120)	(300)
Retained profit for year	600	40	100	250

	Herne Ltd £000	Alfred Ltd £000	Ludens Ltd £000	Gildas Ltd £000
Retained profit brought forward	10 104	542	2000	5024
Retained profit carried forward	10 704	582	2100	5274

Additional information
1. The investments of Herne Ltd consist of the following

Company	Holding %	Carrying value £000	Date of acquisition	Book value of net assets at acquisition £000	Fair value of net assets at acquisition £000	Consideration
Alfred	25	200	1.4.19X5	614	737	cash
Ludens	15	600	1.1.19X6	3280	3936	cash
Ludens	45	2000	1.1.19X7	3690	4428	cash
Gildas	100	4500	31.12.19X9	10274	12329	shares in Herne Ltd
Franca	10	200	30.9.19X7	1633	1960	cash

The excess of fair values over book values refers to fixed tangible assets. Ignore any additional depreciation which would have resulted from incorporation of fair values into the accounts of the companies concerned.

2. Herne Ltd has not recorded dividends receivable for the current year.

3. Herne Ltd bought stock from Ludens Ltd amounting to £1 500 000 of which 10% was included in closing stock at 31 December 19X9. The profit margin is 20% on selling price for Ludens Ltd.

4. Intra group balances are included in debtors and creditors as follows:

	£000
Herne Ltd creditors include Ludens Ltd	93
Ludens Ltd debtors include Herne Ltd	125

A cheque drawn by Herne Ltd for £32 000 on 28 December 19X9 was received by Ludens Ltd on 5 January 19X0

5. Herne Ltd adopts the following accounting policies on consolidation:

   (i) The merger accounting method is adopted when available. You may assume that the share exchange with Gildas Ltd qualifies as a merger under the terms set out in FRS 6

   (ii) The principles in Schedule 4A of the Companies Act 1985 and FRS 2 are applied to piecemeal acquisitions

   (iii) Goodwill is written off in equal instalments over five years.

Required

(a) The summarized consolidated profit and loss account for the year ended 31 December 19X9.

(b) The summarized consolidated balance sheet as at 31 December 19X9.

ACT has been, and is to be, ignored.

ACCA 2.9 amended

Authors guidance notes on question 6.2
1. This question provides excellent practice on many aspects of group accounts but you must allow yourself something like 3 hours in order to produce a solution.
2. There are several published answers to this question (including the examiner's) that were written prior to changes in regulations. You must ensure that your answer complies with the latest regulations, particularly on aspects such as unrealized profit on stocks and piecemeal acquisitions.
3. The question is quite intricate and the best approach is to start preparing the financial statements in the usual sequence (profit and loss account and then a balance sheet) before starting any workings. By doing this you will find yourself being prompted to go to your working schedules at strategic points in order to calculate the figures needed.

7

Cash flow statements: additions to the group

Objectives

After completing this chapter you should be able to:

- prepare a cash flow statement for a group from the consolidated accounts when there has been an acquisition during the year;
- describe the requirements of FRS 1 for acquisitions and disposals;
- use information in the consolidated accounts to calculate dividends paid to minority interests, and dividends received from associated undertakings, when there have been acquisitions during the year.

Introduction

The basic principles for preparing a cash flow statement of a group were covered in Chapter 4. You will recall that the requirements of FRS 1 made it necessary to calculate dividends paid to minority interests and dividends received from associated companies. In all other respects, we found that the cash flow statement for a group could be prepared by simply treating the consolidated accounts as if they were those of a single company.

A little more work is involved if we use the consolidated accounts to prepare a group cash flow statement when there have been acquisitions or disposals of subsidiaries during the accounting period. FRS 1 requires the cash paid or received on these events to be reported as specific cash flows under 'investing activities'. This by itself does not cause any problem but it does require adjustments to be made to the changes in assets and liabilities between the two balance sheet dates in order to determine cash flows for activities other than the acquisition or disposal. This is because changes to assets and liabilities between the two dates will be the result of two factors, namely:

- normal trading activities by companies in the group, including those by a new subsidiary since it was acquired or by a subsidiary up to the date is was sold; and
- assets and liabilities that have been consolidated for a new subsidiary, or that have been de-consolidated if a subsidiary has left the group.

In order to determine cash flows from the first of these it is necessary to recognize the effect which the second has had on changes to the group's assets and liabilities. In this chapter we will learn how to deal with this for an acquisition; you will be able to see the effect of a disposal after studying Chapter 9.

A problem of double counting

Paragraphs 40 to 42 of FRS 1 state how acquisitions and disposals should be dealt with in a group cash flow statement. These paragraphs are set out in the appendix to this chapter but the basic point to be considered here is that FRS 1 requires the amount of cash paid for an acquisition to be reported as a single cash outflow under 'investing activities'. If we use the consolidated accounts as a basis for preparing the group cash flow statement, the assets and liabilities of the new subsidiary at the date of acquisition must be added to the opening balances for the group when calculating cash flows for activities other than the acquisition.

Failure to make this adjustment will result in an element of double counting. The assets and liabilities of the new subsidiary at the date of acquisition are brought into the consolidated accounts. If we report the cash paid for the acquisition as a single cash outflow, the increases in assets and liabilities that arise through the acquisition do not represent additional cash flows. It is easy to see this by considering two extremes:

Example 7.1
A group acquires a 100% interest in a new subsidiary by paying cash of £100 000. The only asset in the subsidiary at the date of acquisition is a fixed asset with a fair value of £100 000. In the consolidated balance sheet the payment of £100 000 by the parent company is represented by an increase in fixed assets of £100 000. If we report the cash payment as a single cash outflow, the increase in fixed assets of £100 000 does not represent an additional cash outflow.

Example 7.2
The position is the same as in Example 7.1 except that instead of paying cash of £100 000 the parent company issues shares with a market value of £100 000. In this case no cash flow has occurred and so none must be reported by the group. If we did not make an adjustment for the acquisition

when comparing changes between the two balance sheet dates, we would (incorrectly) report the increase in share capital as a cash inflow, and the increase in fixed assets as a cash outflow.

Note that the adjustment relates to the assets and liabilities of the new subsidiary at the date of acquisition. Trading operations by the new subsidiary after acquisition will cause its assets and liabilities to change and, to some extent, these changes will be the result of cash flows that must be reported by the group.

We can see this by using Example 7.1 (above) and assuming that the subsidiary made a post-acquisition cash profit of £20 000, and that the whole of this profit was used to purchase another fixed asset. Changes to fixed assets in the group balance sheet over the year will include an increase of £120 000. If we treat the £100 000 at the date of acquisition as a brought forward item (by adding it to the opening balance in the group balance sheet) we will report a cash outflow of £20 000 for the purchase of fixed assets. We will also include the £20 000 cash profit when reporting the net cash inflow from operating activities.

A slightly different acquisition adjustment is needed to deal with any cash balances that are included in the new subsidiary's assets at the date of acquisition. Since this cash will go to swell the cash balances in the consolidated balance sheet, the amount of cash in the subsidiary at the date of acquisition is effectively a cash inflow. This point is dealt with by paragraph 40 of FRS 1 which you should read before attempting the next activity. It is a slightly awkward paragraph to read because it attempts to cover both acquisitions and disposals, but you should be able see the basic point.

Activity 7.1

A parent company pays £100 000 cash in acquiring a 100% interest in a subsidiary. The fair value of the subsidiary's net identifiable assets at the date of acquisition is as follows:

	£
Tangible fixed assets	60 000
Bank balance	10 000
Other net current assets	25 000
	95 000

After reading paragraph 40 of FRS 1 in the appendix to this chapter, make a note here of the cash flows that will be reported in the group cash flow statement as a result of this acquisition.

The way in which the goodwill of £5000 in Activity 7.1 might affect the calculation of cash flows is discussed in a later section of this chapter. If the group's policy is to write it off immediately against reserves it will not be included in the assets and liabilities of the group and in these cases it can usually be ignored.

Wholly owned subsidiaries

In order to see how the basic principles work for a complete set of accounts we need to use a model with no associated companies and no minority interests. These tend to cloud the learning process and so we will leave them out of the problem for the time being. We will work on the following set of simplified financial statements.

Consolidated balance sheets of a group

	At start of year £	At end of year £
Tangible fixed assets	112 000	190 000
Bank balance	4 000	8 000
Other net current assets	40 000	67 000
Taxation creditor	(6 000)	(15 000)
	150 000	250 000
Capital and reserves:		
Ordinary shares of £1 each	100 000	150 000
Share premium account	10 000	15 000
Profit and loss account	40 000	85 000
	150 000	250 000

Consolidated profit and loss account for the year

Operating profit before tax	82 000
Taxation	15 000
Profit for the financial year	67 000
Dividends paid	20 000
Retained profit for the financial year	47 000

Other information

The group acquired a 100% interest in a new subsidiary during the year. The group's accounting policy on goodwill is to write it off immediately against the balance on the profit and loss reserve. There were no sales of fixed assets during the year. The charge for depreciation in the profit and loss account was £12 000. The balances described as 'other net current assets' in the balance sheets relate entirely to trading items (stocks, debtors and creditors). Review the above information and then deal with the following activity.

Activity 7.2

Before we can prepare a group cash flow statement, more information is needed. This information will fall under two main headings. Make a note here of the two types of information that we need before we can prepare the cash flow statement.

1.

2.

This information is now provided as follows.

1. *Fair value of subsidiary's net identifiable assets at date of acquisition*

	£
Tangible fixed assets	70 000
Bank balance	3 000
Other net current assets	19 000
Taxation creditor	(4 000)
	88 000

2. *Consideration given by parent company*

	£
50 000 £1 ordinary shares with a fair value of £1.10 each	55 000
Cash	35 000
	90 000

We will sort out the figures for the group cash flow statement by working a series of activities.

Capital transactions

Since you have already seen how to deal with acquisition adjustments when calculating cash outflows for the purchase of fixed assets, and how the cash paid for the acquisition must be presented, we will start with those.

When calculating the cash paid for the purchase of fixed assets, the best approach is to add the new subsidiary's fixed assets at the date of acquisition to the fixed assets shown in the opening balance sheet of the group. By doing this, the new subsidiary's fixed assets can be thought of as part of the brought-forward figures rather than as a purchase that occurred during the year. It is not essential to do the calculation this way but it does help to reinforce the basic principle in your mind. This approach can be used for all calculations except the adjustment for cash balances acquired.

Activity 7.3

1. Calculate the amount paid to purchase fixed assets. Remember that there were no sales of fixed assets and that the depreciation charge for the year was £12 000. Make a note of your calculations here.

2. Show how the cash consideration given for the acquisition must be presented in the group cash flow statement.

Since this activity has prompted us to think about the acquisition cost you will find it worthwhile to look at the share capital of the group to see if there has been any cash inflow during the year through an issue of shares.

Activity 7.4

Review the share capital of the group, together with the acquisition information, to see if there has been any cash inflow from the issue of shares during the year. Make a note of your observations here.

You have approached the problem of issued share capital in much the same way as we do for most of the assets and liabilities acquired. The increase in share capital and share premium that arose because of the acquisition is added to the amounts in the opening balance sheet before making a comparison with the closing balances.

Operating transactions

There are only two items that need to be calculated: net cash inflow from operating activities and payment of taxation. With regard to the calculation of net cash inflow from operating activities, you will recall that the indirect method uses the operating profit as a starting point and makes adjustments to this for items such as depreciation and changes in stocks, debtors and creditors. In order to reduce the amount of data in this example the stocks, debtors and creditors have been put together as one single item called net current assets.

We must, however, make an adjustment for the new subsidiary's net current assets at the date of acquisition. The principle is the same as for fixed assets. The net current assets of the new subsidiary at the date of acquisition should be treated as brought forward items and added to corresponding amounts shown in the opening balance sheet of the group. Failure to do this would result in the whole of the subsidiary's closing net current assets being treated as an increase. This cannot be right: the increase over the period that it has been a subsidiary will be its closing balance less the balance at the date of acquisition.

Activity 7.5

Calculate the group's net cash inflow from operating activities and make a note of your calculation here.

In a more complex problem there are likely to be several balances and transactions relating to taxation. When you were learning how to prepare a cash
flow statement for a single company, you probably calculated the amount of
tax actually paid during the year by using a basis similar to the following:

Opening balances on all taxation accounts (including deferred tax)	X
Add total charge in the profit and loss account (but see note below)	X
	X
Less closing balances on all taxation accounts	(X)
Taxation paid in the year	X

Note: Tax credits on franked investment income are not included in this
computation; they are eliminated against the 'grossed-up' dividends so that
the cash amount received can be reported as a cash inflow. The group's share
of tax of associated undertakings is also excluded because it relates to a cash
flow of the associated undertaking rather than the group.

The same kind of computation is used when working out tax paid by a
group. If there has been an acquisition during the period, the taxation balances in the new subsidiary at the date of acquisition are added to the
balances in the group's opening balance sheet. In our example there is only
one type of taxation balance and so the computation will be quite straightforward.

Activity 7.6

Calculate the amount of taxation paid during the year and make a note of your calculations
here.

There is a little more to learn about disclosure of information when there
has been an acquisition during the year but since we have now worked out
all the figures needed to prepare the cash flow statement we will deal with
that first.

Activity 7.7

Prepare the cash flow statement by completing the outline format shown below this box. All FRS
1 headings have been included in the format but there might not be items to report under every
heading. You will see from the balance sheets that the increase in cash balances for the year is
(£8000 – £4000) £4000.

Group cash flow statement for Year 2

	£	£
Net cash inflow from operating activities		
Returns on investments and servicing of finance		
Taxation		
Investing activities		———
Net cash inflow before financing		
Financing		———
Increase in cash and cash equivalents		═══

As you probably know from your previous studies, there are a number of notes that have to be included with the cash flow statement in any event. These include:

1. reconciliation of operating profit to net cash inflow from operating activities;
2. analysis of changes in cash and cash equivalents during the year;
3. analysis of the balances of cash and cash equivalents shown in the balance sheet;
4. analysis of changes in financing during the year.

We will ignore the first three of these since they add nothing to the learning process. Note 1, for example, is usually prepared when working out the figure for the cash flow statement. We will, however, prepare note 4 since our example includes a change in share capital which must be reported. In addition, there are two further notes that will have be given in this case. These are:

5. purchase of subsidiary undertakings;
6. analysis of the net outflow of cash in respect of the purchase of subsidiary undertakings.

Note 5 must set out the various assets and liabilities acquired (including goodwill) and show the consideration given for the acquisition. The following shows how this note could be presented for our example:

5. *Purchase of subsidiary undertakings*

	£
Net assets acquired	
Tangible fixed assets	70 000
Bank balance	3 000
Other net current assets	19 000
Taxation creditor	(4 000)
	88 000
Goodwill	2 000
	90 000

Satisfied by	£
Shares allotted	55 000
Cash	35 000
	90 000

As you can imagine, the item called net current assets in the above illustration should be analysed so as to show the separate items for stocks, debtors and creditors.

Note 6 simply supports the single item shown under investing activities in the cash flow statement. In our example the note would be as follows:

6. *Analysis of the net outflow of cash in respect of the purchase of subsidiary undertakings*

	£
Cash consideration	35 000
Cash at bank acquired	3 000
Net cash outflow	32 000

Although there has been no cash inflow from financing during the year, there has been a change in the share capital which must be explained by a note. In our example the note would be as follows:

4. *Analysis of changes in financing during the year*

	Share capital (including premium) £
Balance at start of year 2	110 000
Shares issued for non-cash consideration	55 000
Balance at end of year 2	165 000

Variations on the central theme

Acquisition of partly owned subsidiaries

The principles discussed in the previous sections of this chapter apply equally to new subsidiaries where less than a 100% interest is acquired. The only reason why the main learning text excluded partly owned subsidiaries was to avoid having too many aspects to handle at the same time. You will recall from Chapter 4 how cash flows between the group and parties external to the group include dividends paid to minority interests. We now need to consider how an acquisition of a partly owned subsidiary during the year affects the calculation of these dividends.

In real life, the amount of dividend paid to minority interests in each subsidiary can be determined from the accounting records. In exams we do not usually have this luxury and have to rely on applying our accounting knowledge to the information supplied by the examiner. In Chapter 4, you calculated the dividend paid to minority interests by using the following approach:

Minority interests at the beginning of the year	X
Add share of profits (from consolidated profit and loss account)	X
	X
Less minority interests at the end of the year	(X)
Dividends paid to minority interests	X

The same idea should be used when a subsidiary is acquired during the period. The computation must be changed slightly in order to recognize that the balance brought forward for minority interests includes the minority interests in the new subsidiary at the date of acquisition. The approach is the same as for most other adjustments: minority interests in the subsidiary at the date of acquisition are added to the opening balance. The computation is, therefore, as follows:

Minority interests at the beginning of the year	X
Add minority interests of new subsidiary at date of acquisition	X
Adjusted balance brought forward	X
Add share of profits as shown in consolidated profit and loss account	X
Minority interests before payment of dividends	X
Less minority interests at the end of the year	(X)
Dividends paid to minority interests during the year	X

You can practise applying this in the next activity.

Details for the activity

During an accounting period a parent company acquired a 75% interest in a subsidiary at a cost of £100 000. The fair value of the net identifiable assets in the subsidiary at the date of acquisition was £112 000. Abbreviated balance sheets for the group were as follows:

	At start of year	At end of year
	£	£
Net assets	600 000	800 000
Capital and reserves		
Issued share capital	400 000	400 000
Profit and loss reserve	150 000	280 000
	550 000	680 000
Minority interests	50 000	120 000
	600 000	800 000

The group's accounting policy is to write off goodwill immediately against the balance on the profit and loss reserve. The abbreviated consolidated profit and loss account for the year was as follows:

Consolidated profit and loss account

	£
Operating profit before tax	358 000
Taxation	90 000
Profit after tax	268 000
Minority interests	52 000
Profit for the financial year	216 000
Dividends paid	70 000
Retained profit for the financial year	146 000

Activity 7.8

Calculate the amount of dividend that was paid to the minority interests. You can assume that there were no transactions affecting minority interests other than those which can be determined from the above information.

Acquisition of associated undertakings

You will recall from Chapter 4 that FRS 1 requires cash flows of an entity that is equity accounted should be included in the group cash flow statement only to the extent of actual cash flows between the group and that entity (para. 39). Since the cash flows that result from trading transactions with an associated undertaking will be included in the calculation of net cash inflow from operating activities they do not require any special treatment.

Dividends received from associated undertakings represent additional cash inflows that are not included in the operating profit and must be included in the cash flow statement under 'Returns on investments and servicing of finance'. These dividends are not reported in the consolidated accounts because equity accounting requires that they are replaced by a share of the associated undertaking's profit.

In real life, the amount for dividends received from associated undertakings is known but in exams you are often expected to calculate it from related data. In Chapter 4, you discovered various ways of doing the calculation according to the information provided. An approach that works in most cases is as follows:

Associated undertakings

Share of net assets at the beginning of the year	X
Add share of profit (net of tax) as reported in the consolidated profit and loss account	X
	X
Deduct share of net assets at the end of the year	(X)
Balance = dividends received	X

When there has been an addition to associated undertakings during the year, the amount of cash paid for the acquisition will be reported as a cash outflow under investing activities. The question of reporting this amount as 'net of cash balances acquired' (as with a new subsidiary) does not arise because the cash balances of the associated undertaking are not brought into the group balance sheet as a specific item; they form part of a single figure called 'share of net assets of associated undertakings'.

The calculation of dividends received can be based on the above format except that it will be necessary to add the share of net assets of the new associated undertaking at the date of acquisition to the opening balance. In this respect, the approach is similar to the way you have calculated cash flows for most other items following an acquisition. You can practise applying this in the next activity.

Details for the activity

The opening and closing balance sheets of a group include the following amounts for investments in associated undertakings:

	At the start of the year	At the end of the year
	£	£
Share of net assets	180 000	250 000

During the year the group acquired a 25% interest in a new associated undertaking at a time when the fair value of the net identifiable assets of that undertaking was estimated at £248 000. The amount paid in cash for the acquisition was £65 000. The group's accounting policy on goodwill is to write it off immediately against the balance on the profit and loss reserve. The consolidated profit and loss account shows the group's share of profits (after tax) of all associated undertakings as £20 000.

Activity 7.9

After making any necessary calculations, make a note here of the cash flows between the group and associated undertakings that will be reported in the cash flow statement.

In cases where the group's accounting policy is to treat goodwill as an asset, it might be necessary to work out the amount of goodwill that has been amortized during the year. You need this information when calculating the net cash inflow from operating activities. If the amount is not given the approach to calculating it is the same as for most items: opening balance plus additions less closing balance.

Details for the activity

The details are the same as for Activity 7.9 except that the group's accounting policy is to treat goodwill as an asset which is amortized over its estimated useful economic life. The opening and closing balance sheets include the following for investments in associated undertakings:

	At the start of the year	At the end of the year
	£	£
Share of net assets	180 000	250 000
Goodwill	20 000	19 000

Activity 7.10

Calculate the amount of goodwill amortized during the year and make a note of your calculation here. You will have to refer back to the details for Activity 7.9 to find the goodwill arising on the new acquisition.

Putting it all together

In this chapter we have worked on the basic principles in a series of gentle steps. In some cases we have looked at particular aspects in an isolated way. It is important that you gain some experience in using all of the principles to solve a single problem where the amount of detail is considerably more than that in the learning models. The exercises at the end of this chapter provide you with an opportunity to gain this kind of experience.

To some extent examiners use the cash flow environment as a means of testing basic accounting skills. The questions nearly always require the use of techniques that students usually learn under subject headings such as 'incomplete records'. Perhaps 'missing information' would be a better way of describing it. You are usually given three pieces of information out of four and are expected to derive the fourth. There is a basic approach that can be used in these problems and it will work no matter whether you are looking for the amount paid for fixed assets, the dividends paid to minority interests, dividends received from associated undertakings, cash received on the issue of shares, or almost any other item of missing information.

The basic approach involves making use of the following outline computation where the information given consists of items 1, 2 and 3:

1. Balance from opening balance sheet	X
2. Factors (as given) that cause this to change over the year	X
	X
3. Balance from closing balance sheet	X
Missing cash flow information derived as a balancing figure	X

Items 1 and 3 do not usually present a problem. The information given for item 2 will vary according to the type of information the examiner expects you to find. For example, in the case of fixed assets there are at least three factors that cause the balance to change: depreciation, sales of fixed assets, purchase of fixed assets. If you are given two of these you can use the above computation to find the third.

In the case of topics covered by this chapter, there is fourth component that causes balance sheet figures to change over the year: the balances (at fair value) for assets and liabilities in the balance sheet of a newly acquired entity at the date of acquisition. This information will be given when you are asked to prepare a group cash flow statement. When this fourth component is brought into the computation it becomes as follows:

1. Balance from opening balance sheet	X
4. Balance in new entity at date of acquisition	X
	X
2. Factors (as given) that cause this total to change over the year	X
	X
3. Balance from closing balance sheet	X
Missing cash flow information derived as a balancing figure	X

In the case of a new associated undertaking, item 4 is a single figure for the net assets; in the case of a new subsidiary the computation has to be worked for various individual balances such as fixed assets, taxation and minority interests. In the case of working capital items (other than cash), item 2 drops out of the equation since the objective is to determine the increase or decrease in stocks, debtors and creditors.

The above explanations have assumed that examiners will provide information from which you are required to prepare a cash flow statement. Since this process creates four financial statements (opening balance sheet, profit and loss account, cash flow statement and closing balance sheet) there is no reason why the examiner should not give you the cash flow statement together with two of the other statements and expect you to construct the fourth. In these cases it will be necessary to rearrange the computation because the cash flow information has been given.

Summary

The key learning points in this chapter can be summarized as follows:

- the amount of cash paid for a new acquisition must be reported as a single cash outflow under investing activities;
- if the net assets of the newly acquired subsidiary include cash balances, there has been an inflow of cash to the group and FRS 1 requires this to be deducted from the cash outflow for the amount of cash paid to acquire the subsidiary;
- all assets and liabilities of the new subsidiary at the date of acquisition (other than cash) must be treated as opening balances and added to those in the consolidated balance sheet at the start of the year in order to calculate cash flows from activities other than the acquisition;
- if the consideration includes an issue of shares by the parent company, the increase in share capital (including the premium) that results from the issue does not represent a cash inflow and is not reported in the cash flow statement;
- FRS 1 requires additional disclosures when a subsidiary has been acquired during the year;
- the calculation of dividends paid to minority interests, and dividends received from associated undertakings, might have to take account of changes to the carrying balances that occurred as a result of an acquisition during the year;
- if goodwill is treated as an asset, and changes in the carrying balance are used to calculate the amount amortized during the year, any goodwill purchased must be added to the opening balance before making a comparison with the closing balance.

Key to activities

Activity 7.1

The bank balance of £10 000 acquired should be set against the cash payment of £100 000. Based on the examples in FRS 1, this item should be described as follows: 'Purchase of subsidiary undertaking (net of cash balances acquired) £90 000'.

Activity 7.2

1. An analysis of the fair value of the subsidiary's identifiable net assets acquired.
2. The consideration given by the parent company in order to acquire the shares.

Activity 7.3

	£
1. Tangible fixed assets in the opening balance sheet of the group	112 000
Add tangible fixed assets of subsidiary at date of acquisition	70 000
	182 000
Less depreciation charge for the year	12 000
	170 000
Tangible fixed assets in the closing balance sheet of the group	190 000
Balance = additions	20 000
2. Purchase of subsidiary undertaking (net of cash balances acquired)	32 000

Activity 7.4

The increase in issued share capital and share premium is equal to the fair value of the shares issued for the acquisition. Consequently, no shares have been issued for cash.

Activity 7.5

Operating profit	82 000
Depreciation	12 000
Increase in net current assets (£67 000 – (£40 000 + £19 000))	(8 000)
	86 000

Activity 7.6

Opening balances (£6000 + £4000)	10 000
Charge for the year	15 000
	25 000
Closing balance	(15 000)
Tax paid	10 000

Activity 7.7

Net cash inflow from operating activities	86 000
Returns on investment and servicing of finance	
Dividends paid	(20 000)
Taxation	
Corporation tax paid	(10 000)

	£	£
Investing activities		
Purchase of subsidiary (net of cash balances acquired)	(32 000)	
Purchase of fixed assets	(20 000)	
		(52 000)
Net cash inflow before financing		4 000
Financing		nil
Increase in cash and cash equivalents		4 000

Activity 7.8

Minority interests in opening balance sheet	50 000
Add minority interests on acquisition (25% × £112 000)	28 000
	78 000
Add minority interests' share of profit for the year	52 000
	130 000
Minority interests in closing balance sheet	120 000
Balance = dividends paid to minority interests	10 000

Activity 7.9

1. Under investing activities: Purchase of shares in associated undertaking £65 000.
2. Under returns on investments and servicing of finance: Dividends received from associated undertakings (£180 000 + £62 000 + £20 000 – £250 000) £12 000.

Activity 7.10

£20 000 + £3 000 – £19 000 = £4000.

Appendix

Extracts from FRS 1

Acquisitions and disposals

40 Where a group acquires or disposes of a subsidiary undertaking, the amounts of cash and cash equivalents paid or received in respect of the consideration should be shown net of any cash and cash equivalent balances transferred as part of the purchase or sale of the subsidiary undertaking. In addition, a note to the cash flow statement

should show a summary of the effects of acquisitions and disposals indicating how much of the consideration comprised cash and cash equivalents and the amounts of cash and cash equivalents transferred as a result of the acquisitions and disposals.

41 Where a subsidiary undertaking joins or leaves a group during a financial year the cash flows of the group should include the cash flows of the subsidiary undertaking concerned for the same period as that for which the group's profit and loss account includes the results of the subsidiary undertaking.

42 Material effects on amounts reported under each of the standard headings reflecting the cash flows of a subsidiary undertaking acquired or disposed of in the period should be disclosed, as far as practicable, as a note to the cash flow statement. This information need only be given in the financial statements for the period in which the acquisition or disposal occurs.

Question

Question without answer

An answer to this question is published separately in the *Teacher's Manual*.

7.1 Unfras group

The following draft financial statements have been prepared for the Unfras group.

Consolidated profit and loss account year ending 31 March 1995

	Continuing operations	Acquisitions	Discontinued operations	Total
	£000	£000	£000	£000
Turnover	4300	800	400	5500
Cost of sales	2580	420	300	3300
Gross profit	1720	380	100	2200
Operating expenses	810	120	70	1000
Operating profit	910	260	30	1200
Loss on disposal			(140)	(140)
	910	260	(110)	1060
Income from interests in associated undertakings				100
Investment income				40
Interest payable and similar charges				(80)
Profit on ordinary activities before tax				1120
Taxation				265
Profit on ordinary activities after tax				855
Minority interests				75
Profit for the financial year				780
Dividends				400
Retained profit for the financial year				380

Balance sheets

	31.3.95 £000	31.3.94 £000
Tangible fixed assets	3765	3450
Investment in associated undertaking	700	650
Other fixed asset investments	500	500
	4965	4600
Current assets:		
Stock	600	200
Debtors	1000	600
Cash and bank balances	210	320
	1810	1120

	31.3.95 £000	31.3.94 £000
Creditors: falling due within one year		
Trade creditors and accruals	375	180
Taxation	192	153
Proposed dividends	200	100
	767	433
Net current assets	1043	687
Total assets less current liabilities	6008	5287
Creditors: falling due after one year		
Debenture loan stock	800	720
	5208	4567
Provision for liabilities and charges		
Deferred tax	8	7
	5200	4560
Capital and reserves:		
Called up share capital (£1 ordinary shares)	2950	2800
Share premium account	115	70
Revaluation reserve	30	20
Profit and loss account	1730	1380
	4825	4270
Minority interests	375	290
	5200	4560

The information given below is also available.

1. Analysis of retained profits:

All figures in £000s	Parent company	Subsidiary undertakings	Associated undertaking	Total for the group
Balance at 1 April 1994	900	400	80	1380
Retained for the year	220	100	60	380
Balance at 31 March 1995	1120	500	140	1760
Goodwill written off				30
Balance in group accounts				1730

2. Movements in capital and reserves:

All figures in £000s	Called up share capital	Share premium	Revaluation reserve	Profit and loss account
Balance at 1 April 1994	2800	70	20	1380
Shares issued during year	150	45		
Revaluation surplus			10	
Retained profit for year				380
Goodwill written off				(30)
Balance at 31 March 1995	2950	115	30	1730

3. Analysis of the taxation charge:

	£000
Share of tax of associated undertaking	30
Tax credits on franked investment income	10
Transfer to deferred tax account	35
Corporation tax on ordinary profits of the group	190
	265

4. Details of the loss on disposal

This arose following the termination of a business segment in a subsidiary. The loss relates to the loss on sale of fixed assets of that segment and was computed as follows:

	£000
Net book value of fixed assets sold	390
Cash received on sale	250
Loss before tax relief	140

The termination did not include the disposal of any stocks, debtors or creditors. There was no material change in the value of these working capital items between the beginning of the period and the date of termination.

5. Details of subsidiary acquired during the year

The parent company acquired a 90% interest in the subsidiary. The following shows the fair values of identifiable assets and liabilities at the date of acquisition together with the consideration given and the amount attributed to goodwill:

Fair values at date of acquisition:	£000	£000
Tangible fixed assets		130
Stocks		50
Debtors		100
Cash and bank balances		10
Trade creditors		(80)
Taxation		(10)
		200
Minority interests' share (10%)		20
Parent company's share		180
Fair value of consideration given:		
50 000 ordinary shares of £1 each	65	
Cash payment	145	
		210
Goodwill arising on consolidation		30

The subsidiary was acquired on the 31 December 1994. The working capital items for operating activities (stocks, debtors and creditors) of this subsidiary had increased by a total of £20 000 between the date of acquisition and 31 March 1995.

6. Details of investment in associated undertakings

	31.3.95 £000	31.3.94 £000
Share of net assets	680	620
Goodwill arising on acquisition	20	30
	700	650

Goodwill arising on acquisition of associated undertakings is amortized and charged against profit on ordinary activities for the year. No associated companies were acquired during the year.

7. Other information

There were no sales of fixed assets during the year other than those which gave rise to the loss on disposal of the business segment (see note 4). Depreciation charged in arriving at operating profit for the year was £125 000. This total included an amount of £5000 charged against operating profit for the acquired subsidiary. No depreciation was charged against operating profit for the discontinued business segment.

The amounts for debtors and trade creditors in the balance sheets relate entirely to operating profit items. The property revaluation does not give rise to any deferred tax adjustment. Proposed dividends in the consolidated balance sheets relate entirely to dividends payable to members of the parent company.

Required

The group cash flow statement based on the data available. You must include all notes required by FRS 1, including a note to show how much of the net cash inflow from operating activities was contributed by the subsidiary acquired and how much by the business segment sold.

Author

8

Indirect holdings

Introduction

The subject of this chapter includes very few additional principles; most of it is concerned with learning a method for dealing with examination data when a group includes indirect subsidiaries. The method that you will learn here is unlikely to be used in practice. This is not a matter of using different principles for examination questions, it is merely a different way of applying the same set of principles. The consolidated accounts will be the same whichever method is used.

To some extent, this distinction between exams and real life applies to many practical ('how to do it') aspects that you are required to learn as a student. For example, imagine you are asked to prepare consolidated accounts for the current year of a parent company with one direct subsidiary acquired several years earlier. The examiner gives you information from which you can determine the adjusted capital and reserves of the subsidiary at the date of acquisition. You then use this to calculate what the goodwill on acquisition would have been. This does not happen in real life. The goodwill is determined as soon as the balance sheet of the subsidiary at the date of acquisition is available. It does not have to be calculated again in a subsequent year.

Consolidation in stages

Parent with no direct interest in the sub-subsidiary

Consolidation techniques are relatively straightforward when the ultimate parent company does not have a direct interest in the sub-subsidiary. Figure 8.1 is a simple structure which we can use to learn the basic principles.

For the group illustrated, both FRS 2 (para. 14) and Section 258(5) of the Companies Act 1985 require Parent Ltd to be treated as the parent of Tail Ltd, even though the immediate parent of Tail Ltd is Sub Ltd. As a result, Tail Ltd becomes a subsidiary of Parent Ltd (in this case an indirect subsidiary) and the accounts of Tail Ltd must be consolidated in the group accounts prepared for the shareholders of Parent Ltd.

The fact that Parent Ltd's indirect interest in Tail Ltd (48%) is less than 50% has no bearing on this requirement. It does, however, have a bearing on the way you will prepare consolidated accounts from information in examination questions. In practice the consolidation is done in stages. We will look at this staged approach first since it will give us a target balance sheet that must be achieved by the examination method.

Accounting practice

In practice, Sub Ltd would produce consolidated accounts incorporating the results of its subsidiary Tail. There is a legal requirement for Sub Ltd to prepare these accounts if its 20% minority interests serve notice on the company requesting it to do so (see Chapter 11). The consolidated accounts

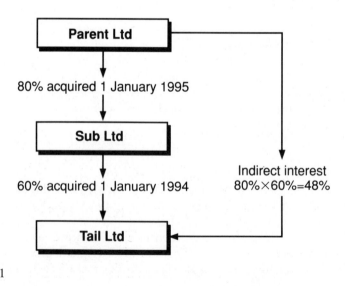

Figure 8.1

prepared by Sub Ltd are then consolidated with those of Parent Ltd. You should note that there would have been no legal requirement for Sub Ltd to produce consolidated accounts if it had been 100% owned by Parent Ltd, but such accounts are usually prepared in practice in order to facilitate the consolidation process. For the sake of convenience we will refer to the group of Sub Ltd and Tail Ltd as the 'sub-group' in the following explanations.

When consolidating the results of Parent Ltd with its subsidiaries, the consolidated accounts of the sub-group are treated as if they were the accounts of a single company. Goodwill is calculated in the normal way by comparing the acquisition cost with Parent Ltd's share of the net identifiable assets in the consolidated accounts of the sub-group at the date of acquisition. Any goodwill shown as an asset in the consolidated balance sheet of the sub-group is not an identifiable asset and will be excluded from this calculation.

The minority shareholders of Sub Ltd will have a 20% interest in the capital and reserves shown in the consolidated balance sheet prepared by Sub Ltd. This amount will be added to the minority interests in Tail Ltd (40%) when preparing the consolidated accounts for the complete group.

You can learn the basis of this two-stage approach by working on a simplified example.

Details for the activities

The abbreviated balance sheets of the above three companies at 31 December 1995 are as follows:

	Parent Ltd	Sub Ltd	Tail Ltd
	£	£	£
Sundry net identifiable assets	129 000	75 000	50 000
Investments in subsidiaries			
In Sub Ltd 80%.	71 000		
In Tail Ltd 60%.		25 000	
	200 000	100 000	50 000
Capital and reserves			
Share capital	150 000	65 000	25 000
Profit and loss account	50 000	35 000	25 000
	200 000	100 000	50 000

The fair values of each subsidiary's net identifiable assets at the date of acquisition are the same as book values. There have been no inter-company trading transactions and no inter-company dividends. The movements on the profit and loss accounts of each subsidiary are:

	Sub Ltd	Tail Ltd
	£	£
Balance at 1 January 1994	14 000	10 000
Retained profits for 1994	6 000	5 000

	£	£
Balance at 1 January 1995	20 000	15 000
Retained profits for 1995	15 000	10 000
Balance at 31 December 1995	35 000	25 000

The accounting policy of the group is to write off goodwill immediately against the balance on the profit and loss reserve. This policy will simplify the learning process because the balance on capital and reserves in the consolidated balance sheet of the sub-group at 1 January 1995 (when it became a subsidiary of Parent Ltd) will be equal to the net identifiable assets in that consolidated balance sheet, less the amount attributable to Tail Ltd's 40% minority interests.

Notice that we have not been given balance sheets at 1 January 1995 of Sub Ltd and Tail Ltd and so the consolidated net assets at that date will have to be determined from the consolidated capital and reserves. To this extent we are mimicking how information is presented in examination questions; in practice the consolidated balance sheet of Sub Ltd and Tail Ltd at 1 January 1995 would be available.

Activity 8.1

Prepare the consolidated balance sheet at 31 December 1995 for the sub-group: Sub Ltd and Tail Ltd. The dates of the acquisition are given in the diagram at the start of this section. Use the outline format shown below this box. In this format, minority interests are being presented in the alternative position allowed by Schedule 4A (a deduction from net assets). You will find that this presentation helps with the visual aspects of learning the subject.

Consolidated balance sheet of Sub Ltd and Tail Ltd at 31 December 1995

		£
Sundry net identifiable assets		£
Less minority interests		£
Capital and reserves		
Share capital		£
Profit and loss account	£	
Less goodwill written off	£	

You now need to think of this consolidated balance sheet as being the balance sheet of a single company. When you come to consolidate this balance sheet with the balance sheet of Parent Ltd, it will be necessary to determine the consolidated capital and reserves of the sub-group at 1 January 1995, the date it was acquired by Parent Ltd. This information is needed for two reasons:

- in order to calculate goodwill we need to know the net identifiable assets of the sub-group at the date it was acquired by Parent Ltd; and
- the post-acquisition profits of the sub-group as far as Parent Ltd is concerned are the profits that have been earned by the sub-group since 1 January 1995.

Note that although Sub Ltd has consolidated the profits earned by Tail Ltd for 1994 and 1995, the 1994 profits are pre-acquisition profits as far as Parent Ltd is concerned. At 1 January 1995 the balance on the profit and loss reserve in the consolidated balance sheet of the sub-group would have been as follows:

Balance on consolidated profit and loss account at 1 January 1995

	£
Sub Ltd	20 000
Sub Ltd's share of Tail Ltd's post-acquisition profits	
(60% × £5000)	3 000
	23 000
Less goodwill written off	4 000
	19 000

The purchase cost of this sub-group is shown in Parent Ltd's accounts as £71 000. Since this represents a 80% interest, the goodwill on acquisition of the sub-group would have been calculated as follows:

		£
Cost of the investment		71 000
Capital and reserves at 1 January 1995		
Share capital (Sub Ltd)	65 000	
Consolidated profit and loss reserve (above)	19 000	
	84 000	
Less minority interests (20%)	16 800	
Parent Ltd's share		67 200
Goodwill on acquisition		3 800

The figure of £84 000 for capital and reserves in the above computation is equal to the sum of the net identifiable assets in the consolidated balance sheet of the sub-group at 1 January 1995, less the amount attributable to Tail Ltd's 40% minority interests. You can see this by adding the net assets of the two companies at 31 December 1995, and deducting the retained profits of both companies for 1995, as follows:

	£
Net identifiable assets at 31 December 1995	
(£75 000 + £50 000)	125 000
Less retained profits for 1995 (£15 000 + £10 000)	25 000
Consolidated net assets at 1 January 1995	100 000
Tail Ltd's minority interests (40% × (£25 000 + £15 000))	16 000
	84 000

If we were producing a consolidated balance sheet at 1 January 1995 for Parent Ltd and its sub-group, the minority interests would be shown in that balance sheet as £32 800, being the total of the minority interests in Tail Ltd (£16 000) and the minority interest in Sub Ltd (£16 800).

Returning to the problem of preparing a consolidated balance sheet at 31 December 1995 for the entire group, we have already calculated the figure for goodwill (£3800) that arises from Parent Ltd's acquisition of the sub-group. We now need to calculate the other two key figures, minority interests and the consolidated profit and loss reserve at 31 December 1995. For the sake of convenience, the two balance sheets at 31 December 1995 are repeated here as follows:

	Parent Ltd (as before)	Sub-group (consolidated)
	£	£
Sundry net identifiable assets	129 000	125 000
Investment in Sub Ltd	71 000	
Less minority interests		20 000
	200 000	105 000
Capital and reserves:		
Share capital	150 000	65 000
Profit and loss account	50 000	40 000
	200 000	105 000

As with most consolidation problems, the figure for minority interests is usually the easiest to calculate. This is certainly the case in the above. The minority shareholders in Sub Ltd have a 20% interest in the capital and reserves of the sub-group.

Activity 8.2

Calculate the amount to be included in the consolidated balance sheet of the entire group for Sub Ltd's minority interests. Make a note of the amount here and then add it to the figure shown in the above balance sheet for Tail Ltd's minority interests.

1. Sub Ltd's 20% minority interests.
2. Minority interests of Sub Ltd and Tail Ltd combined.

With regard to the consolidated profit and loss reserve, this will be based on the same principles as used in previous chapters for a direct subsidiary. The only difference here is that we must use the consolidated balance sheet prepared by the direct subsidiary. The computation to find the balance prior to writing off goodwill takes the following form:

Balance on Parent Ltd's profit and loss account at 31 December 1995	X
Add Parent Ltd's share of post-acquisition profits of the sub-group	X
Consolidated profit and loss reserve at 31 December 1995	X

From the figures calculated previously, it is quite easy to find the post-acquisition profits of the sub-group as far as Parent Ltd is concerned. The balance on the sub-group's consolidated profit and loss reserve at 1 January 1995 was found to be £19 000 when we were working out figures for the goodwill computation. The balance on the sub-group's profit and loss reserve at 31 December 1995 is £40 000, as found from Activity 8.1 and repeated in the balance sheets shown above Activity 8.2.

Activity 8.3

Calculate the balance on the consolidated profit and loss account for the entire group at 31 December 1995 after writing off the goodwill that arises from Parent Ltd's acquisition of the sub-group. Use the following format:

Balance on Parent Ltd's profit and loss account
    at 31 December 1995   £
Parent Ltd's share (80%) of the post-acquisition
    profits of the sub-group   £ _____

Less goodwill (on acquisition of sub-group) written off   _____

                                               =======

We now have all the figures from which to prepare a consolidated balance sheet for the entire group at 31 December 1995.

Activity 8.4

Prepare the consolidated balance sheet for Parent Ltd and its subsidiaries at 31 December 1995. Use the outline format provided below this box.

Consolidated balance sheet at 31 December 1995 for Parent Ltd and its subsidiaries

                                   £

    Net identifiable assets
    Less minority interests (Activity 8.2)   _____

                                      =======

    Capital and reserves
      Share capital
      Profit and loss reserve (Activity 8.3)   _____

                                      =======

No doubt you will agree that the foregoing involved a fair amount of work for what seemed, at the outset, a relatively straightforward problem. This was partly because we used a real life approach to solve a problem where information was presented in the same form as it appears in examination questions. This made it necessary to keep looking backwards to see what the position would have been at an earlier date. This does not arise in practice because accounts are produced each year and consolidation for each successive year is simply a matter of building on the consolidated accounts that were produced for the previous year.

Another problem with using the staged approach for examination type problems is that it is quite easy to lose track of the sequence of what needs to be calculated. This might not have seemed to have been a problem when you were working through the foregoing explanations but you did have the text, activities and formats to guide you along the way. To solve examination type problems you need to learn a method that reduces the amount of work and does not involve too much by way of looking at past positions. The method that has been developed is known by various names, such as the 'one-step method' or the 'proportional interests method'.

Proving the basic principles

Generally speaking, the technique that you will use for examination problems is quite easy to learn but there is one aspect to it that many students find difficult to see and remember. In order to help with this problem we will look at something else first. It might be difficult for you to see the relevance of this at the moment but the idea is to provide a basis for explaining an adjustment that must be made when using the examination method.

If we wanted to be convinced regarding the validity of the consolidated balance sheet produced by Activity 8.4, what we could do is to see what the position of the various shareholders would be if each company in the chain were liquidated in sequence – starting with Tail Ltd. When doing this we can assume that the net identifiable assets of each company at 31 December 1995 are liquidated at their book value.

	Total amount	Paid to parent company	Paid to outside shareholders
	£	£	£
1. Liquidation of Tail Ltd	50 000	(60%) 30 000	(40%) 20 000
2. Total net assets of Sub Ltd			
Net identifiable assets	75 000		
Add cash received on liquidation of investment (as in 1 above)	30 000		
	105 000		
3. Liquidation of Sub Ltd	(105 000)	(80%) 84 000	(20%) 21 000

	£	£	£
4. Total net assets of Parent Ltd			
Net identifiable assets	129 000		
Add cash received on liquidation of investment (as in 3 above)	84 000		
Available for shareholders	213 000	(100%) 213 000	
Paid to outside shareholders		213 000	41 000

As you can see, this exercise provides some kind of proof that the consolidated balance sheet produced from Activity 8.4 is based on valid principles. But the main point of introducing it here is to help with your understanding of an adjustment that must be made when using the examination method.

This adjustment centres around the investment by Sub Ltd in Tail Ltd. You will notice in the above table that when the amount due to the shareholders of Sub Ltd was calculated, we only included the net identifiable assets of Sub Ltd of £75 000. If you look back to the balance sheet of this company you will see that the net assets are £100 000 and so the capital and reserves of that company are £100 000. However, the net assets include the investment in Tail Ltd and since this has been liquidated, this investment has become a worthless piece of paper. It has been replaced by the cash received of £30 000. This £30 000 represents Sub Ltd's 60% share of Tail Ltd's net assets which are substituted for the investment when preparing consolidated accounts.

If we were calculating the amount attributable to the 20% minority interests in Sub Ltd by taking their proportional interests in the capital and reserves of both Sub Ltd and Tail Ltd, we could easily make a mistake. On the surface it looks as if we could calculate the amount as follows:

	£
Minority interests in Sub Ltd	
20% of Sub Ltd's capital and reserves (20% × £100 000)	20 000
20% of 60% of Tail Ltd's capital and reserves (12% × £50 000)	6 000
	26 000

Yet we know that the amount should be £21 000. The reason why the above produces the wrong figure is that the £100 000 for capital and reserves of Sub Ltd is based on net assets that include the investment of £25 000. In the consolidated accounts, this £25 000 is replaced by a share of Tail Ltd's net assets. The figure of £6000 in the above calculation is the proportion of these net assets that are attributable to Sub Ltd's minority interests and so at this stage there has been an element of double counting. The balance of £26 000 includes a share of the investment and a share of Tail Ltd's net assets controlled through that investment. This can be rectified by setting off 20% of the amount shown as an investment in Tail Ltd against the balance of £26 000, as follows:

	£
Balance attributable to Sub Ltd's minority interests (as above)	26 000
Less 20% of the investment in Tail Ltd (20% × £25 000)	5 000
	21 000

This now produces the correct figure and you will have to use an approach similar to this when learning how to use the examination method in the next section. The main point to try and remember is that the set off relates to the investment in the sub-subsidiary (Tail Ltd) but that the fraction is based on the proportion of minority interests in the company that owns the investment (Sub Ltd). It is quite easy to forget this when using techniques in a somewhat mechanical way.

Proportional interests method

In exams, the group balance sheet can be prepared much more quickly (and with less chance of error) by using percentages based on the ultimate parent company's direct and indirect interests in the two subsidiaries; and on the direct and indirect minority interests in each sub-subsidiary.

The first step in the process is to set out a table showing the proportional interests of the two classes of shareholder in each subsidiary. The two classes of shareholder are the ultimate parent company (Parent Ltd in our example) and minority interests. In the case of Tail Ltd there are two groups of minority shareholders with an interest in that company: there is Tail Ltd's own minority shareholders (these are said to have a direct interest) and Sub Ltd's minority shareholders who have an indirect interest. In the next activity you are asked to work out the proportional interests in each subsidiary for Parent Ltd and the minority shareholders. Although this approach has not yet been demonstrated, you should be able to sort out what is required from some of the points in the previous text. For example, you know from Figure 8.1 that Parent Ltd has an indirect interest of (80% × 60%) 48% in Tail Ltd. You also know that Parent Ltd has no direct interest in Tail Ltd. If you have any difficulty with the activity you should complete it by referring to the key.

Activity 8.5

Work out the proportional interests in the two subsidiaries by completing the table set out below this box. This requires you to show Parent Ltd's interest (direct and indirect) in each subsidiary, and the minority interests (direct and indirect) in each subsidiary.

	Sub Ltd	Tail Ltd
Parent Ltd		
Direct interest (%)		
Indirect interest (%)		
Sub-total	_____	_____
	_____	_____

	Sub Ltd	Tail Ltd
Minority shareholders		
Direct interest (%)		
Indirect interest (%)	_____	_____
Sub-total	_____	_____
Total	100%	100%

The distinction between direct and indirect minority interests is not relevant to the workings; we will be using the percentages shown as a sub-total for minority shareholders in the above table. You were asked to calculate both figures as proof of the arithmetic. When you become more confident with the technique, minority interests can be included in the table as a single balancing percentage.

The next stage involves using the percentages shown in this table for allocating the share capital and reserves of each subsidiary between the three key items: goodwill, minority interests, and consolidated profit and loss reserve. There is a working schedule on p. 196 which you will be completing in stages. This method of learning tends to be somewhat mechanical and so you should try to conceptualize as much as you can when allocating the various balances.

The first step is to allocate the amounts shown as investments in subsidiaries to the appropriate columns in the working schedule. If we were dealing with one direct subsidiary, the cost of the investment would be allocated to the column for goodwill where it will be set off against the parent company's share of the subsidiary's capital and reserves at the date of acquisition. In our example there are two investments in subsidiaries and so both of them are included in the goodwill column. We must then remember to transfer a part of the investment in Tail Ltd to the minority interests for the reasons discussed in the previous section.

Activity 8.6

Complete the working schedule on page 196 by following the staged instructions set out below this box. In order to distinguish between debits and credits in this working schedule, we will show the amounts for debits in brackets and the amounts for credits out of brackets. The effect of this convention is that the figures for investments will be in brackets.

Stage 1 Allocate the amounts for investments to the goodwill column and then transfer 20% of the investment in Tail Ltd to the column for minority interests.

Stage 2 Allocate the amounts for share capital in each subsidiary to the columns for goodwill and minority interests. The relevant percentages are given in the appropriate columns.

Stage 3 Allocate the balance on the profit and loss account of each company to the columns for minority interests and profit and loss account according to the percentages shown. At this stage the figures for the profit and loss account are wrong because they include the pre-acquisition profits of the two subsidiaries. This is corrected in stage 4.

Stage 4 Transfer the pre-acquisition profits of each subsidiary from the profit and loss column to the goodwill column. Note that the pre-acquisition profits for this adjustment are the balances on each subsidiary's profit and loss account at 1 January 1995 (the date that the sub-group was acquired by Parent Ltd).

Stage 5 Total the three columns. The three amounts should be the same as the figures derived by the two-stage consolidation on p. 191.

Working schedule

	Total	Goodwill	Minorities	Profit and loss
1. Investments	£			
in Sub Ltd	(71 000)			
in Tail Ltd	(25 000)			
Transfer 20% of investment in Tail Ltd to minorities				
2. Share capital				
Sub Ltd	65 000	80%	20%	
Tail Ltd	25 000	48%	52%	
3. Profit and loss account				
Parent Ltd	50 000		nil	100%
Sub Ltd	35 000		20%	80%
Tail Ltd	25 000		52%	48%
4. Transfer of pre-acquisition profits to goodwill:				
Sub Ltd (80% × £20 000)				
Tail Ltd (48% × £15 000)				
5. Totals	104 000			

Approach check-list

Problems that require you to prepare a set of consolidated accounts when the group includes indirect subsidiaries involve a fair amount of work and it is essential to adopt a methodical approach. The following check-list gives an indication of the approach which you could adopt. In this check-list, it is assumed that the only reserve in each company's balance sheet is the 'profit and loss reserve' whereas some problems might include other types of reserve. These other reserves are allocated in the same way as the profit and loss reserve.

In the problem we have just completed, the indirect subsidiary (Tail Ltd) was acquired by the direct subsidiary (Sub Ltd) prior to the ultimate parent company's acquisition of Sub Ltd. The wording used in the following check-list will also work where an indirect subsidiary comes into the group as a result of an acquisition by an existing direct subsidiary.

1. Identify the group structure (draw a diagram).
2. Identify the date for dividing each subsidiary's profit and loss reserve between pre- and post-acquisition as far as the ultimate parent company is concerned. This will be the date that each subsidiary came under the control of the ultimate parent company.
3. Work out the proportional interests.
4. Set up a working schedule with columns for goodwill, minority interests, and consolidated profit and loss reserve.
5. Transfer the cost of investments as follows:
    (a) the whole cost of investment in the immediate subsidiary to goodwill;
    (b) the cost of investment in a sub-subsidiary to goodwill and minority interests according to the respective interests of the two groups of shareholders in the company that owns the investment.
6. Use the percentages found in the proportional interest table to allocate the share capital of each subsidiary between goodwill and minority interests.
7. Use the percentages found in the proportional interest table to allocate the balance on the profit and loss account of each company between minority interests and consolidated profit and loss reserve.
8. For each subsidiary, pre-acquisition profits must now be transferred from profit and loss reserve to goodwill. The amounts for each subsidiary will be based on the ultimate parent company's share (found from the proportional interest table) of the balance on that subsidiary's profit and loss reserve at the date it became a subsidiary of the ultimate parent company (see stage 2).
9. Total each column and prepare the accounts.

Direct and indirect holdings in a subsidiary

The basic approach to solving a problem where the parent company has both a direct and indirect interest in a subsidiary is the same as that described in the previous section. One slight difference is that these problems often include some aspect of piecemeal acquisition and so it is necessary to apply the regulations in paragraph 9 Schedule 4A Companies Act 1985 as discussed in Chapter 6.

As it happens, these regulations simplify the process because they require the calculation of goodwill (and the split between pre- and post-acquisition profits) to be based on the conditions that existed at the date when the company acquired became a subsidiary of the ultimate parent company. You might recall that FRS 2 supports this treatment, although the explanatory notes suggest that there could be rare circumstances where goodwill should be calculated by reference to each acquisition (para. 89). In this chapter we will apply the Companies Act regulations; you should refer to Chapter 6 for details of the alternative treatment.

We will look at two different scenarios. First consider the group in Figure 8.2.

There is no doubt that Tail Ltd is a subsidiary of Parent Ltd. This is because Parent Ltd has control over 52% of the voting rights in Tail Ltd. Parent Ltd has its own direct interest of 40% and controls another 12% through its control of Sub Ltd. The fact that the combined interest of Parent Ltd in the financial results of Tail Ltd is only 49.6% (40% + (80% ¥ 12%)) is irrelevant. A company becomes a subsidiary as a result of being controlled by another company; the proportion of profits that will be consolidated with those of the parent is irrelevant when establishing if this control exists.

Tail Ltd became a subsidiary of Parent Ltd on 1 November 1995. Prior to this it would have been treated as an investment in the balance sheet of Sub Ltd. If we assume that Parent Ltd has an accounting date of 31 December, then the group accounts for year ending 31 December 1995 will include a proportion of Tail Ltd's profits from 1 November 1995 to 31 December 1995. The balances on Tail Ltd's reserves at 1 November 1995 represent pre-acquistion reserves.

Activity 8.7

Work out the proportional interests in each subsidiary by completing the following:

	Sub Ltd	Tail Ltd
Parent Ltd		
direct interest		
indirect interest		
Minority interests		
direct interest		
indirect interest		
	100%	100%

The working schedule would then follow the same pattern as for an indirect subsidiary with no direct holding.

If the following situation applies, the problem is somewhat different (see Figure 8.3).

In this case, the additional 20% interest acquired by Parent Ltd on 1 November 1995 is in a company that was already a subsidiary at that time. Parent Ltd has simply increased its stake in Tail Ltd by purchasing shares from the minority interests in that company. The regulations regarding the calculation of additional goodwill in these circumstances were discussed in Chapter 6. The purchase cost of the 20% holding should be compared to 20% of the fair value of the net identifiable assets in the balance sheet of Tail Ltd at 1 November 1995.

If we assume that Parent Ltd has an accounting date of 31 December, the consolidated profit and loss account for year ending 31 December 1995 will

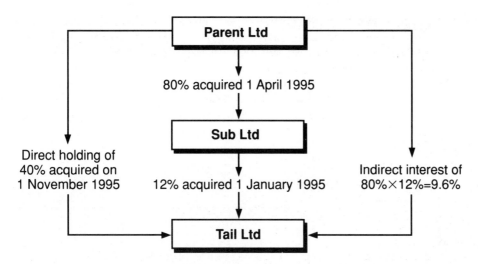

Figure 8.2 Group structure: parent company has direct and indirect holding of sub-subsidiary

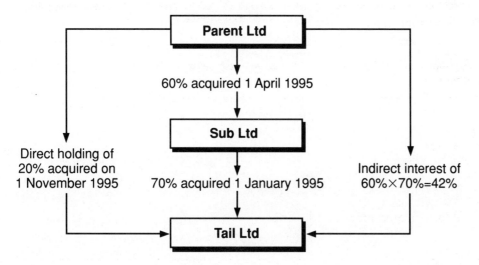

Figure 8.3 Group structure: parent company increases its stake in existing sub-subsidiary

include an additional 20% of Tail Ltd's profits for the last two months of the year.

It is quite easy to make a mistake in these situations when allocating Tail Ltd's reserves between the three working schedules for goodwill, minority interests, and consolidated reserves. Parent Ltd has an indirect interest of (60% × 70%) 42% in Tail Ltd and a direct interest of 20%; but you cannot use the single percentage of 62% to allocate the reserves since each acquisition must be considered separately. For example, the amount of post-acquisition profit that will be consolidated for 1995 will be 42% of Tail Ltd's profits from 1 April 1995 to 31 December 1995, plus 20% of its profits for the last two months of the year.

Details for the next activity

Balances on the profit and loss reserve of the two subsidiaries in this example (Figure 8.3) at various dates:

	Sub Ltd	Tail Ltd
	£	£
1 January 1995	42 000	24 000
1 April 1995	50 000	30 000
1 November 1995	70 000	40 000
31 December 1995	100 000	50 000

Activity 8.8

The balance of £50 000 on Tail Ltd's profit and loss reserve must be allocated to the three working schedules for goodwill, minority interests, and consolidated profit and loss reserve. See if you can carry out this allocation. This is not easy but you should make some attempt before checking with the key. The main point to keep in mind is that the amounts allocated to goodwill and consolidated profit and loss reserve need to recognize that there have been two acquisitions. The total amount to be allocated to minority shareholders with an interest in Tail Ltd is relatively straightforward and will be based on the percentages at the end of the year.

Allocation of Tail Ltd's profit and loss reserve at 31 December 1995

Goodwill

Minority interests

Consolidated profit and loss reserve

$$\underline{\underline{£50\ 000}}$$

Summary

The key learning points in this chapter are as follows:

- the test of whether a company is a subsidiary of another company centres around whether it can be controlled by another company;
- any subsidiary of a company which is a subsidiary of the parent company is a subsidiary of that parent company;

- this relationship arises because the parent company can control the sub-subsidiary by virtue of being able to exercise control over its immediate subsidiary;
- in practice, the accounts of a sub-subsidiary are consolidated with those of its own parent company (in this chapter these accounts were described as the consolidated accounts of the sub-group);
- the consolidated accounts of this sub-group are legally required if the minority interests in the parent company of the sub-group request them;
- even when there are no minority interests in the sub-group, consolidated accounts of the sub-group are usually prepared in order to facilitate the consolidation procedures;
- the solution to exam problems where indirect holdings are concerned is best achieved by using a proportional interests method;
- the proportional interests method looks at each subsidiary and calculates the interests (direct and indirect) of the ultimate parent company, and the interests (direct and indirect) of minority shareholders, in each subsidiary;
- the proportional interests found by this method are then used to apportion the share capital and reserves of each subsidiary between the three working schedules of goodwill, minority interests and consolidated reserves;
- this method requires that the minority interests' share of their company's investment in the sub-subsidiary is charged against their share of the capital and reserves in the sub-subsidiary in order to eliminate an element of double counting;
- problems that include an ultimate parent company with both a direct and indirect interest in a sub-subsidiary are solved in much the same way as when there is no direct interest;
- in most cases the direct and indirect interests in a sub-subsidiary will have been acquired at different dates and so the rules on piecemeal acquisitions (Chapter 6) are relevant.

Key to activities

Activity 8.1

Consolidated balance sheet of Sub Ltd and Tail Ltd at 31 December 1995

	£	£
Identifiable net assets (£75 000 + £50 000)		125 000
Less minority interests (40% × £50 000)		20 000
		105 000

	£	£
Capital and reserves:		
Share capital		65 000
Profit and loss account £35 000 × (60% × £15 000)	44 000	
Less goodwill written off		
£25 000 − (60% × (£25 000 + £10 000))	4 000	
		40 000
		105 000

Activity 8.2

1. Sub Ltd's Minority interests 20% × £105 000 = £21 000
2. Combined £20 000 + £21 000 = £41 000

Activity 8.3

Parent Ltd's profit and loss reserve	50 000
Parent Ltd's share of post-acquisition profits of sub-group	
80% × (£40 000 − £19 000)	16 800
	66 800
Less goodwill written off	3 800
	63 000

Activity 8.4

Identifiable net assets (£129 000 + £125 000)	254 000
Minority interests (Activity 8.2)	41 000
	213 000
Capital and reserves	
Share capital	150 000
Profit and loss account (Activity 8.3)	63 000
	213 000

Activity 8.5

	Sub Ltd	Tail Ltd
Parent Ltd		
direct interest	80%	nil
indirect interest	nil	48%
Parent Ltd sub-total	80%	48%
Minority shareholders		
direct interest	20%	40%
indirect interest	nil	12%
Minorities sub-total	20%	52%
Total	100%	100%

Activity 8.6

After completing the five stages, the working schedule should be as follows.

Working schedule

		Total	Goodwill	Minorities	Profit and loss
		£	£	£	£
1.	Investments				
	in Sub Ltd	(71 000)	(71 000)		
	in Tail Ltd	(25 000)	(25 000)		
	Transfer 20% of investment				
	in Tail Ltd to minorities		5 000	(5 000)	
2.	Share capital				
	Sub Ltd	65 000	52 000	13 000	
	Tail Ltd	25 000	12 000	13 000	
3.	Profit and loss account				
	Parent Ltd	50 000			50 000
	Sub Ltd	35 000		7 000	28 000
	Tail Ltd	25 000		13 000	12 000
4.	Transfer of pre-acquisition profits to goodwill:				
	Sub Ltd (80% × £20 000)		16 000		(16 000)
	Tail Ltd (48% × £15 000)		7 200		(7 200)
5.	Totals	104 000	(3 800)	41 000	66 800

Activity 8.7

	Sub Ltd	Tail Ltd
Parent Ltd		
direct interest	80%	40.0%
indirect interest	—	9.6%
Sub-total	80%	49.6%
Minority interests		
direct	20%	48.0%
indirect	—	2.4%
	20%	50.4%
Total	100%	100%

Activity 8.8

Tail Ltd	£	£
Goodwill:		
60% × 70% (42%) × £30 000	12 600	
plus		
20% × £40 000	8 000	
		20 600

	£	£
Minority interests:		
Direct 10% × £50 000	5 000	
plus		
Indirect 40% × 70% (28%) × £50 000	14 000	
		19 000
Consolidated profit and loss reserve:		
60% × 70% (42%) × (£50 000 − £30 000)	8 400	
plus		
20% × (£50 000 − £40 000)	2 000	
		10 400
Total		50 000

Questions

Questions for self assessment

Answers to self-assessment questions are given at the end of the book.

8.1 Apple, Banana and Cherry

The summarized balance sheets of Apple Ltd, Banana Ltd and Cherry Ltd at 31 December 19X5 are as follows:

	Apple £000	Banana £000	Cherry £000
Fixed assets at book value	800	600	700
Shares in Banana Ltd at cost	1500		—
Shares in Cherry Ltd at cost	—	850	
Net current assets	270	470	310
Total assets less current liabilities	2570	1920	1010
Less: 12% long-term loans	650	500	250
	1920	1420	760
Share capital	1200	1000	600
Retained profit at 1 January 19X5	563	300	100
Profit for 19X5	157	120	60
	1920	1420	760

Apple purchased 60% of the share capital of Banana, and Banana purchased the entire share capital of Cherry, on 1 January 19X5.

At 1 January 19X5 the 'book' value of Banana's fixed assets was £750 000, while their 'fair' value was estimated to be £1 200 000. The amount of depreciation charged in the accounts of Banana for 19X5 was £150 000; an appropriate charge based on the 'fair' valuation would be £240 000. The remaining assets of Banana and all the assets of Cherry were stated in the balance sheets of those companies, at 1 January 19X5, at figures which were approximately equal to their 'fair' values.

Required

Prepare the summarized consolidated balance sheet of Apple Ltd and its subsidiaries at 31 December 19X5.

From an old syllabus of CIB Accountancy

8.2 HRS

The summarized balances extracted from the accounting records of Hale (H) Ltd, Rein (R) Ltd and Snowe (S) Ltd at 30 November 19X7 are given below:

	H Ltd £	R Ltd £	S Ltd £
Land and buildings	447 500	230 950	52 000
Plant and machinery	600 500		61 750
Fixtures and fittings	54 500	41 000	8 800

	H Ltd £	R Ltd £	S Ltd £
Investments at cost:			
420 000 shares in Rein Ltd	367 500		
70 000 shares in Snowe Ltd	49 000		
35 000 shares in Snowe Ltd		24 500	
Stock and work in progress	526 610	163 290	85 700
Debtors	241 920	129 680	29 750
Cash and bank balances	88 200	4 725	8 105
Creditors	(95 480)	(86 645)	(88 605)
	2 280 250	507 500	157 500
Capital and reserves:			
£1 shares	1 750 000		175 000
75p shares		420 000	
Other reserves	350 000	70 000	
Profit and loss account	180 250	17 500	(17 500)
	2 280 250	507 500	157 500

Further information:
1. Hale Ltd purchased its interest in Rein Ltd and Snowe Ltd on 1 December 19X4 at which date there was an adverse balance on Snowe Ltd's profit and loss account of £35 000, and a credit balance of the same amount on the profit and loss account of Rein Ltd.
2. On 30 November 19X7 Hale Ltd dispatched and invoiced goods for £12 500 to Rein Ltd which were not recorded by the latter until 3 December 19X7. A mark-up of 25% is added by Hale Ltd to arrive at selling price. Rein Ltd already had goods in stock which had been invoiced to them by Hale Ltd at £10 400.
3. Since its acquisition Rein Ltd has paid dividends of £70 000 of which half were paid out of pre-acquisition profits. Hale Ltd has credited all dividends received to profit and loss account.
4. Snowe Ltd had an adverse balance of £52 500 on profit and loss account when Rein Ltd purchased 35 000 shares in 19X3.
5. Hale Ltd received a remittance of £8000 on 2 December 19X7 which had been sent by Rein Ltd on 28 November 19X7.
6. Included in Hale's debtors was a balance of £25 500 owed by Rein Ltd.
7. Neither Rein Ltd nor Snowe Ltd had any other reserves when their shares were purchased by Hale Ltd and Rein Ltd.
8. Creditors of Rein Ltd included an amount of £5000 due to Hale Ltd.

Required

Prepare the consolidated balance sheet of Hale Ltd and its subsidiaries at 30 November 19X7. (*Author's note: assume that no fair value adjustments are required.*)

ACCA 2.9

Question without answer

An answer to this question is published separately in the *Teacher's Manual*.

8.3 Sales, Machinery and Components

On 1 April 19X1 Machinery Limited bought 80% of the ordinary share capital of Components Limited and on 1 April 19X3 Machinery Limited was itself taken over by Sales Limited who purchased 75% of the ordinary shares in Machinery Ltd. The balance sheets of the three companies at 31 October 19X5, prepared for internal use, showed the following position:

	Sales £	Machinery £	Components £
Freehold land at cost	89 000	30 000	65 000
Buildings: cost	100 000	120 000	40 000
aggregate depreciation	(36 000	(40 000	(16 400)
Equipment: cost	102 900	170 000	92 000
aggregate depreciation	(69 900	(86 000	(48 200)
	186 000	194 000	132 400
Investments at cost:			
in machinery	135 000		
in components		96 000	
Current assets			
Stocks	108 500	75 500	68 400
Debtors	196 700	124 800	83 500
Cash at bank	25 200	—	25 400
	651 400	490 300	309 700
Current liabilities			
Creditors	160 000	152 700	59 200
Bank overdraft	—	37 400	—
Corporation tax	57 400	47 200	24 500
Proposed dividends	80 000	48 000	12 000
	297 400	285 300	95 700
Total assets less current liabilities	354 000	205 000	214 000
Capital and reserves			
£1 ordinary shares	200 000	120 000	100 000
50p preference shares			40 000
Profit and loss account	154 000	85 000	74 000
	354 000	205 000	214 000

Additional information:
1. Proposed dividends in Components Ltd are £10 000 on the ordinary shares and £2000 on the preference shares.
2. Proposed dividends receivable by Sales Ltd and Machinery Ltd are included in debtors.
3. All creditors are payable within one year.
4. Items purchased by Machinery Ltd from Components Ltd and remaining in stock at 31 October 19X5 amounted to £25 000. The profit element is 20% of selling price for Components Ltd.

5. Included in the equipment of Components Ltd is a machine purchased from Machinery Ltd on 1 January 19X4 for £10 000. The profit recorded by Machinery Ltd on the sale of this machine was £2000. Components Ltd provides depreciation on equipment at the rate of 10% on cost each year, including a full provision in the year of purchase.
6. Intra group balances are included in debtors and creditors respectively and are as follows:

			£
Sales Ltd	Creditors	Machinery Ltd	45 600
		Components Ltd	28 900
Machinery Ltd	Debtors	Sales Ltd	56 900
Components Ltd	Debtors	Sales Ltd	28 900

7. A cheque drawn by Sales Ltd for £11 300 on 28 October 19X5 was received by Machinery Ltd on 3 November 19X5.
8. At 1 April 19X1, the balance on the profit and loss account in Machinery Ltd was £28 000 and in Components Ltd £20 000. At 1 April 19X3 the figures were £40 000 and £60 000 respectively.
9. No fair value adjustments are necessary.

Required

Prepare a group balance sheet at 31 October 19X5 for Sales Ltd and its subsidiaries complying, so far as the information will allow, with the accounting requirements of the Companies Act 1985.

ACCA 2.9 (modified)

Disposal of shares in a subsidiary

9

Objectives

After completing this chapter you should be able to:

- calculate the gain on disposal of shares in a subsidiary for the group accounts;
- demonstrate why this gain differs from the gain in the parent company's accounts;
- explain the requirements of FRS 2 on disposals of investments in subsidiaries;
- devise a method for dealing with examination data that includes disposals of shares in subsidiaries;
- prepare group accounts where the disposal results in various types of retained interest.

Introduction

A disposal of shares in a subsidiary can result in one of four situations, as follows:

1. the parent company retains no interest in the subsidiary (a complete disposal);
2. a small minority interest is retained (the subsidiary becomes an investment);
3. the interest retained must be dealt with as an associated undertaking;
4. the subsidiary remains a subsidiary after some of the shares have been sold.

A common issue in each case is how to calculate the gain or loss on disposal for the group accounts and what effect the disposal has on the way that operating profits are reported in the year of disposal. The regulations in FRS 2 refer to two situations, namely:

1. ceasing to be a subsidiary (situations 1 to 3 above) in paragraphs 46 and 47;
2. reducing an interest in a subsidiary (situation 4 above) in paragraph 52.

The way in which FRS 2 requires the gain or loss on disposal to be calculated for the group accounts is identical in both cases. The principle is discussed in this chapter under the heading of 'A complete disposal'. You will then see how this principle is applied to the remaining three situations mentioned in the opening paragraph. The way that operating profits of the ceased or reduced subsidiary are dealt with will depend on the circumstances.

Overview of the problem

Gain or loss on disposal

The key learning point relates to the gain or loss on disposal of the investment. It is essential to keep in mind that there will be a significant difference between the treatment in the parent company's accounts (where an asset has been sold) and how the matter is dealt with in the group accounts where there will be a full or partial de-consolidation as a result of the disposal.

Parent company's accounts

The cash received on disposal of the investment, and the gain or loss on that disposal, will be recorded in the parent company's own accounts. The gain or loss for a complete disposal is simply the difference between the sale proceeds and the carrying value of the investment. On a partial disposal, the gain or loss will be related to the shares sold by comparing the sale proceeds with the relevant proportion of the carrying value of the investment.

The capital gain or loss will affect the amount of corporation tax payable by the parent company. The group (being an artificial entity) is not a taxable person and so the gain or loss recorded in the consolidated accounts is irrelevant as far as tax is concerned.

Consolidated accounts

The effect of FRS 2 (but not the wording) is that the gain or loss in the group accounts for a complete disposal must be calculated by comparing the sale proceeds with the parent company's share of the carrying amount of the net assets at the date of disposal. On a partial disposal, the comparison is made to a proportion of these net assets based on the number of shares sold. In all cases the net assets compared should include any related goodwill that has not been amortized through the profit and loss account. This will include any goodwill that was previously set against reserves as a result of adopting the immediate write-off policy.

In some cases, the precise wording of FRS 2 will require the gain or loss on a partial disposal to be calculated by reference to the residual interest rather than by reference to the proportion of net assets that are de-consolidated. This matter is discussed on pp. 220–22 below.

Regulations

The treatment of gains or losses in the consolidated profit and loss account was originally regulated by SSAP 14. This was not clear regarding the treatment of goodwill that had been eliminated against reserves on acquisition. This uncertainty was clarified by UITF Abstract 3 and later regulated by FRS 2 (which superseded SSAP 14). The relevant paragraphs in FRS 2 are 47 and 52 and both of these are set out in the appendix to this chapter for reference purposes. This problem is discussed on pp. 211–13 below. Presentation in the profit and loss account is covered by FRS 3.

Operating profits

In the case of a company that ceases to be a subsidiary, FRS 2 requires the subsidiary's results up to the date of disposal to be consolidated in the normal way (para. 46). This includes cases where a small interest has been retained in the company that is no longer a subsidiary. FRS 3 (Reporting Financial Performance) requires the amounts for operating activities in respect of the ceased subsidiary to be presented separately as 'discontinued operations'. Any gain or loss on disposal must be shown separately under this heading as an exceptional item. It can no longer be classed as an extraordinary item as was the case prior to the introduction of FRS 3.

In those cases where a small (non-subsidiary) interest has been retained, the treatment in the group profit and loss account will depend on the circumstances. For example, if the interest retained is such that it represents an associated undertaking, the group results for the year will include the parent company's share of the subsidiary's results up to the date of disposal and a share of the associated company's profits for the period after the date of disposal.

What happened to goodwill?

The regulations in SSAP 14 on the calculation of the gain or loss in the group accounts on disposal of a subsidiary were not clear regarding the treatment of goodwill that had been eliminated against reserves on acquisition. This resulted in different practices depending on how the regulations were interpreted. The example given in UITF Abstract 3 illustrated the problem. It was based on the following data:

Figures on acquisition: Purchase price of shares £500m
Net identifiable assets (at fair value) £150m
Goodwill (eliminated against reserves) £350m

Assume that the subsidiary was sold for £400m in the next period at a time when the fair value of the net identifiable assets was still £150m. The gain or loss on disposal in the group accounts could have been calculated in one of two ways, as follows:

	Method 1		Method 2
	£m		£m
Sale proceeds		400	400
Fair value of net assets	150		150
Add goodwill written off	—		350
		150	500
Gain/(loss) on disposal		250	(100)

Intuitively, the gain under Method 1 does not make sense. The investment was purchased by the parent company at a cost of £500m and was sold for £400m. A loss of £100m would have been recorded in the parent company's accounts. But in the group accounts the investment is represented by the net assets of the subsidiary and so the gain or loss must be calculated by comparing the sale proceeds with the carrying value of the net assets which are about to be de-consolidated. These net assets will not include consolidation goodwill if it had been written off against reserves on acquisition.

The UITF concluded that Method 1 was not acceptable and required (in Abstract 3) that groups should adopt Method 2. The argument put forward in support of this consensus was that Method 1 allows the write-off of goodwill to bypass the profit and loss account.

In order to understand certain aspects of this argument we have to refer to a discussion in Appendix 2 of SSAP 22 dealing with the effect on realized profits of writing off goodwill. The question of whether or not profits and losses are realized is related to the problem of calculating the amount of profit available for distribution. Extracts from paragraphs 71 and 72 of SSAP 22 are included in the appendix to this chapter. If you get an opportunity to study them you will find that the following points emerge:

- the problem is not relevant to group accounts since distributions are made by individual companies (elimination of consolidation goodwill has no effect on the distributable profits of any company);
- writing off goodwill immediately against reserves is an accounting policy, not the recognition of a realized loss;
- SSAP 22 is based on a concept that goodwill has a limited life and, therefore, its elimination must eventually constitute a realized loss;
- if goodwill is eliminated immediately against unrealized reserves, it should be transferred to realized reserves on a systematic basis so as to maintain parity with the amortization method.

These points were not mentioned in the UITF's Abstract 3, presumably because the comments in SSAP 22 make it clear that the question of realized profits is irrelevant in the context of group accounts. However, it is likely that these arguments would have had some influence on the statement that Method 1 allows the write-off to bypass the profit and loss account. There is also a general concept (called the 'all inclusive concept of profit' in the former SSAP 6) which favours the idea that all gains and losses should be reported through the profit and loss account rather than allowing some to be reported through movements on reserves.

The requirement in Abstract 3 is now supported by FRS 2. This makes it clear that the parent company's share of net assets against which the sale proceeds are compared should include any related goodwill that has not previously been written off through the profit and loss account. This will include goodwill eliminated immediately against reserves.

Although this settles the matter of standard accounting practice (at least for the time being) there are still a number of unresolved arguments and practical problems. For example, what happens when the subsidiary is sold in a form that differs to that which applied when it was acquired? This might be the case where there has been some kind of integration or restructuring of the subsidiary's operations. These problems were recognized by the UITF and in cases where it is not possible to ascertain (or estimate) the goodwill associated with the disposal, this fact and the reasons for it should be explained in the notes to the accounts.

A complete disposal

We will study the question of how to calculate the gain or loss on disposal in the context of a complete disposal. The same principles can then be applied to the various sections of this chapter that deal with part disposals.

As stated earlier, the gain or loss on disposal must be treated as an exceptional item, not extraordinary. This means that the gain or loss is reported as a pre-tax figure under ordinary activities. Any tax payable or recoverable will be based on the gain or loss reported in the parent company's own accounts. The taxation implications of the disposal are, therefore, reflected in the provision for corporation tax on ordinary activities made by the parent company. In examination questions it might be necessary to calculate the effect of taxation if an adjustment has not been made in the parent company's accounts. In these cases it is important to remember that the tax adjustment relates to the gain or loss in the parent company's books, not the gain or loss reported in the group accounts.

Working with some simple figures

Apart from practice at applying the regulations, the following activities attempt to illustrate how the figures in the consolidated accounts reconcile to those in the parent company. This reconciliation then leads to a convenient way of dealing with certain types of examination question.

Details for the activities

Cost of investment in subsidiary	£100 000
Percentage holding obtained	80%
Fair value of subsidiary's net identifiable assets on acquisition	£100 000
Profits retained by subsidiary between acquisition and date of sale	£20 000
The entire holding was sold for	£120 000

The group's policy on goodwill is to write it off immediately against reserves.

The change in carrying value of net assets in the subsidiary between the date of acquisition and the date of disposal relates entirely to the effect of retained profits.

Activity 9.1

Work out the gain that will be reported in the parent company's accounts. This is quite simple so don't over-complicate it.

In the group accounts, the effect of the wording in FRS 2 is that the sale proceeds must be compared to the parent company's share of the carrying value of the net assets in the subsidiary at the date of disposal. These net assets must include any goodwill that has not previously been written off through the profit and loss account. In the above details we can work out what the consolidation goodwill would have been but we are not given a figure for the carrying value of the net identifiable assets at the date of disposal. We can, however, work out what these net assets would have been because we know what they were at the date of acquisition and we are told that since then they have increased by the amount of profit retained by the subsidiary.

Activity 9.2

The gain on disposal in the consolidated accounts is £4000. Set out figures showing how this was calculated. Remember that the investment was an 80% interest in the subsidiary.

In the parent company's accounts we have a gain of £20 000 and in the group accounts the gain is £4000. You will find it quite helpful to identify the factor that accounts for this difference.

See if you can identify what accounts for the difference between the gain in Activity 9.1 and the gain in Activity 9.2. Make a note of your observations here.

The parent company does not record a share of the profits earned and retained by the subsidiary in its own accounts and so the pre-tax gain of £20 000 in the parent company's accounts is represented in the group accounts by two types of profit, namely:

		£
•	share of profits retained in the subsidiary (80% × £20 000)	16 000
•	gain on disposal of subsidiary	4 000
		20 000

The gain of £20 000 in the parent company's accounts will be subject to corporation tax payable by the parent company. Yet the above computation suggests that a part of this gain is attributable to the fact that the company in which the investment was made has earned and retained profits on which corporation tax has already been paid. It could be argued that these profits are being taxed twice, but we will not explore the matter any further here.

Examination approach

The main reason for working on the reconciliation between the two gains is that it leads to a convenient way of solving certain types of examination question. In many cases these questions do not state the carrying value of the subsidiary's net assets at the date of disposal. If this is so, the amount has to be determined in the same way as you did for Activity 9.2. In addition, you are unlikely to be given the goodwill arising on acquisition and are often expected to calculate the amount of corporation tax payable on the gain. In these circumstances, it is preferable to approach the calculations as follows.

	£
Sale proceeds	120 000
Original cost	100 000
Gain in parent company's accounts (see note on tax below)	20 000
Less share of post-acquisition profits retained in subsidiary (80% × £20 000)	16 000
Gain in group accounts	4 000

If an adjustment to the tax provision is required, either the amount of tax or the corporation tax rate will be given. If you are given a corporation tax rate of (say) 25%, this is an invitation to make a provision of 25% × £20 000.

Notice how this approach avoids the need to calculate goodwill arising on acquisition, and the proportion of net assets at the date of disposal.

A complete set of consolidated accounts

You should now practise preparing a complete set of consolidated accounts where there has been a complete disposal of a subsidiary during the year. The profit and loss account must comply with FRS 3 (Reporting financial performance). In case you have forgotten (or have never studied) how FRS 3 requires the results of discontinued activities to be presented, there is an outline format following Activity 9.5 based on one of the suggested formats in that standard. The details for the activities are set out below. The text and activities which follow these data are designed to guide you through the problem in stages.

Details for the activities

Parent Ltd owned an 80% holding in Sub Ltd which it sold (cum-div) on 1 July 1995 for £450 000. The accounting date of both companies is 31 December. Parent Ltd had acquired Sub Ltd when the balance on Sub Ltd's profit and loss reserve was £40 000. The fair values of Sub Ltd's net identifiable assets at the date of acquisition were the same as book values. The following are the accounts for year ending 31 December 1995

Profit and loss accounts for year ended 31 December 1995

	Parent Ltd	Sub Ltd
	£	£
Turnover	800 000	200 000
Cost of sales and other expenses	700 000	120 000
Operating profit	100 000	80 000
Profit on sale of investment in subsidiary	150 000	—
Dividends received from subsidiary	4 800	—
Profit before tax	254 800	80 000
Taxation	40 000	32 000
Profit after tax	214 800	48 000
Dividends	30 000	12 000
Retained profit for year	184 800	36 000
Movements on profit and loss reserve		
Retained profits at 1 January 1995	600 000	100 000
Retained profits for the year	184 800	36 000
Retained profits at 31 December 1995	784 800	136 000
Summarized balance sheets at 31 December 1995		
Sundry net assets	1 284 800	336 000
Ordinary share capital	500 000	200 000
Profit and loss account	784 800	136 000
	1 284 800	336 000

Notes

It can be assumed that all trading items accrue evenly throughout the year. In the group accounts, goodwill was eliminated immediately against the balance on the profit and loss account. Corporation tax on the gain has been provided by the parent company. The above accounts of Sub Ltd include a proposed dividend of £6000. Advanced corporation tax is not paid on inter-company dividends.

Guidance text and activities

You will find it helpful to start working on something familiar: the gain or loss on disposal for the group accounts. You could have started work on the top part of the consolidated profit and loss account but the gain or loss on disposal must be presented in the pre-tax section of this account and so you would not have got very far before you had to stop and work it out.

In this example you could calculate the goodwill on consolidation and then calculate the gain on disposal by comparing the sale proceeds to the total of:

- 80% of the subsidiary's net assets at the date of disposal; plus
- goodwill arising on acquisition.

However, this will require you to make a number of calculations that are unnecessary at this stage. For example, notice that neither the goodwill on acquisition nor the sale proceeds are given. Although both of these figures can be determined from the details provided, there is no need to calculate them if you follow the examination approach previously described. The computation for the gain on disposal in the group accounts can commence with the gain reported in the parent company's accounts.

Activity 9.4

Calculate the gain on disposal for the group accounts using the method described previously. Make a note of your computations in the space provided in this box.

Gain on disposal for the group accounts:

We can now construct the consolidated profit and loss account for the year. As is usual with group accounts, the results of the subsidiary are consolidated in total even though the subsidiary is not wholly owned. The minority shareholders' interest in these results is then shown as a separate adjustment. The only difference in this situation is that the various amounts consolidated for the subsidiary will relate to the first six months of the year. The results of the subsidiary in this case must be reported as profits from discontinued activities and the gain on disposal is included as an exceptional item under this heading.

It is important to keep in mind that the minority shareholders do not have any interest in the gain or loss on disposal. The actual gain (or loss) affects the results of the parent company, not the subsidiary.

Activity 9.5

Prepare the consolidated profit and loss account by completing the outline format provided below this box. This format is based on example 2 in FRS 3. Notice that the separation between discontinued and continuing operations is confined to operating profit and the gain (or loss) on disposal. This level of profit is called 'Profit on ordinary activities before interest' in the FRS 3 examples. Interest payable (nil in our example) is then shown next as a single amount under the total column.

Consolidated profit and loss account for 1995

	Discontinued operations	Continuing operations	Total
	£	£	£
Turnover			
Cost of sales and other expenses	___	___	___
Operating profit			
Gain on disposal of discontinued operations	___	___	___
Profit on ordinary activities before interest	══	══	
Interest payable			—
Profit on ordinary activities before tax			
Tax on profit on ordinary activities			___
Profit on ordinary activities after tax			
Minority interests			___
Profit for the financial year			
Dividends			___
Retained profit for the financial year			══

Movements on the consolidated profit and loss reserve

The balance brought forward on the consolidated profit and loss reserve will include the post-acquisition profits retained in the subsidiary at the beginning of the year. We also need to recognize that the total retained profits brought forward in the group accounts will have been reduced by the goodwill written off on acquisition. The reinstatement of this goodwill must then be shown as a movement on the consolidated profit and loss reserve for the current year. It is possible to find the closing balance on the profit and loss reserve by ignoring the goodwill write-off and its reinstatement, but this will not enable you to make a proper disclosure of movements on the reserve

Activity 9.6

Calculate the amount that would have been written off against the balance on the profit and loss reserve for goodwill arising on consolidation. Make a note of the amount here.

For the first six months of the year there was a group that consisted of the parent company and one subsidiary. At the end of the year there is no subsidiary and so if our figures are correct we should find that when we add the retained profit for the year to the adjusted balance brought forward, the balance carried forward is equal to the balance on the profit and loss reserve in the accounts of the parent company.

Activity 9.7

Complete the statement set out below this box to show movements on the profit and loss reserve. Remember that the opening balance will include the parent company's share of the post-acquisition profits retained in the subsidiary, and that the total balance will have been reduced by the goodwill write-off.

Movements on profit and loss reserve

	£
Consolidated balance at 1 January 1995	
Add goodwill previously written off now reinstated	_____
Retained profit for the year	_____
Balance at 31 December 1995 (Parent Ltd)	784 800

In this example, the balance sheet at 31 December 1995 will simply be the balance sheet of Parent Ltd as shown in the details for the activities. This was because the balance sheet of Parent Ltd was drawn up after making appropriate entries for the sale of the investment. In some cases you might be presented with balance sheets where these adjustments have not been made.

Retaining an interest

Apart from the complete disposal as discussed above, there are three other situations to consider, namely:

- the subsidiary remains a subsidiary but the holding is reduced;
- the subsidiary becomes an associated undertaking (an interest of 20% to 50%);
- the retained interest is less than the 20% threshold for an associated company.

As stated earlier, the regulations in FRS 2 are given under the following headings:

- where a subsidiary ceases to be a subsidiary;
- where the interest in a subsidiary is reduced.

Although the gain or loss on disposal must be calculated in the same way in both cases, we will have to look at the precise wording in FRS 2. It was possible to avoid this when dealing with a complete disposal but the words have special significance when an interest is retained.

Retaining an interest but ceasing to be a subsidiary

FRS 2 requires that the consolidated financial statements should include:

- the trading results up to the date of ceasing to be a subsidiary;
- gain or loss arising on disposal.

To this extent, the procedure is the same as for a complete disposal. However, we need to consider how FRS 2 requires the gain or loss on disposal to be calculated for the group accounts. The relevant paragraph (47) is included in the appendix and if you study this you will find that the amount must be found by comparing:

- the parent company's interest in the carrying amount of subsidiary's net assets before the cessation; with
- the parent company's interest in the carrying amount of subsidiary's net assets after the cessation; plus
- the sale proceeds.

The net assets compared should include any related goodwill not previously writing off through the profit and loss account.

Note that the above form of computation is intended to deal with situations where the interest retained by the group should not be valued as a relative percentage of the former interest. This can happen in certain types of management buy-out where the former subsidiary takes on a substantial amount of debt to finance the buy-out. The rule has no significance for a complete disposal because the parent company's interest in the subsidiary's net assets after the disposal is zero: the parent company's interest in the net assets at the time of cessation can simply be compared to the sale proceeds.

Different ways of working

Assume that a parent company previously owned a 100% interest in a subsidiary. It then sells 75% of the investment for £80 000 and retains a 25% interest. At the time of disposal, the carrying value of the subsidiary's net assets is £100 000. After disposal the parent company's interest in these net assets is considered to be (25% of £100 000) £25 000. The goodwill arising on the original acquisition was nil.

Commentary

In this case, the interest of the parent company in the net assets of the subsidiary following the disposal is a direct proportion of its interest prior to the disposal. Consequently, the gain in the consolidated accounts can be calculated in a manner similar to a complete disposal, as follows:

	£
Sale proceeds	80 000
Interest in net assets sold (75% × £100 000)	75 000
Gain	5 000

The same gain will be found by a calculation based on the FRS 2 description, as follows:

	£	£
Interest in carrying value at time of disposal		100 000
Compared with:		
Interest in carrying value after disposal	25 000	
Sale proceeds	80 000	
		105 000
Gain		5 000

The gain (or loss) in the parent company's books is calculated in the normal way except that in this case the sale proceeds will be compared to 75 % of the cost of the investment. When dealing with exam questions for part disposals, you will find it helpful to remember how we calculated the gain in the consolidated accounts for a complete disposal. This was to take the gain in the parent company's books and then deduct the parent company's share of post-acquisition profits retained in the subsidiary. The same approach can be used for the above example. We can see how this works by assuming the following:

	£
The cost of the investment was	60 000
The fair value of the net assets at the time of	
acquisition was	60 000
Goodwill	nil

The increase in net assets between the date of acquisition and the date of disposal is entirely attributable to profits retained by the subsidiary.

In this case the calculation of the gain in the group accounts could be calculated as follows:

Calculation of gain in parent company's books

	£
Sale proceeds	80 000
Less proportion of cost (75% × £60 000)	45 000
Gain (before tax) in parent company's books	35 000
Less post-acquisition profits of subsidiary relating to the 75% interest (75% × (£100 000 − £60 000))	30 000
Gain before tax in the group accounts	5 000

The parent company will have to provide for any corporation tax on the gain of £35 000.

In the above example it was reasonable to assume that the interest of the investing company in the carrying amount of the investee's net assets after the disposal had a value equal to 25% of the former 100% interest. This might not always be the case. If the subsidiary had taken on (say) £24 000 long-term debt as part of a management buy-out arrangement, the carrying value of the net assets immediately after the disposal would be £76 000. A 25% interest in these net assets would then be valued at £19 000, and so the gain on disposal in the group accounts would be as follows:

	£	£
Interest in carrying value at time of disposal		100 000
Compared with:		
Interest in carrying value after disposal	19 000	
Sale proceeds	80 000	
		99 000
Loss		1 000

In this case there is an effective write-down of the residual stake by £6000 which should be recognized in the investing company's own accounts. The investing company will reduce the gain (or increase the loss) on disposal by the amount of this write-down. This type of situation is, however, relatively rare and in most cases the method suggested previously for dealing with examination data can be used.

Reducing an interest in a subsidiary

Paragraph 52 of FRS 2 requires the gain or loss on disposal to be calculated in the same manner as where the subsidiary ceases to be a subsidiary. Some of the words are slightly different to those in paragraph 47 but only because they deal with a 'reduction' of an interest in a subsidiary instead of a cessation. It is more likely in the case of a reduction that the retained interest will be a relative proportion of the previous interest.

Minority interest should be increased by the proportion of carrying value of net assets now being attributed to them as a result of the decrease in the group's interest. The profits of the subsidiary will be consolidated on a line-by-line basis in the normal way. The calculation of minority interests' share of the subsidiary's profit for the year will have to take account of their new holding as from the date that it was increased.

Series of exercises

In the following series of exercises, it will be assumed that the interest following disposal is a direct proportion of the interest prior to the disposal. There are three scenarios, all based on the same primary data, as follows:

1. the subsidiary remains a subsidiary after the disposal;
2. the subsidiary becomes an associated undertaking after the disposal;
3. the subsidiary becomes a trade investment after the disposal.

In all three cases the parent company has not completed any book-keeping entries for the sale of the investment. Consequently, the sale proceeds have been credited to a suspense account pending the adjustments. The details for each case are quite straightforward and most of the usual adjustments associated with group accounts have been excluded so that you can concentrate on the new principles covered by this chapter. Guidance is given in the activity instructions where appropriate. You will find that the key to each activity provides reconciliations that you will not usually have the time to prepare in an examination. A study of them will, however, help with your understanding of the subject.

Exercise 1: subsidiary remains a subsidiary

Parent Ltd received £150 000 for selling 20 000 shares in Sub Ltd on 30 June 1995. The summarized balance sheets at 31 December 1995, prior to accounting for the disposal, are as follows:

	Parent Ltd £	Sub Ltd £
Investment in Sub Ltd		
(75 000 out of 100 000 shares)	112 500	
Sundry net assets	1 120 000	375 000
Suspense account (cash received for sale of shares)	(150 000)	
	1 082 500	375 000
Share capital (£1 ordinary shares)	500 000	100 000
Profit and loss reserve	582 500	275 000
	1 082 500	375 000

Profit and loss accounts year ending 31 December 1995 are as follows:

Operating profit	100 000	60 000
Dividends from subsidiary (cash received)	7 500	
Profit before tax	107 500	
Taxation on operating profit (25%)	25 000	15 000
Profit after tax	82 500	45 000
Dividends paid (31 March 1995)	—	10 000

	Parent Ltd	Sub Ltd
	£	£
Retained profit for financial year	82 500	35 000
Retained profit at 1 January 1995	500 000	240 000
Retained profit at 31 December 1995	582 500	275 000

Parent Ltd's interest in Sub Ltd had been acquired several years earlier when the balance on Sub Ltd's profit and loss account was £90 000. Corporation tax on the gain in the parent company's accounts will be at the rate of 25%.

Activity 9.8

On your own paper, prepare the consolidated accounts for the year. Although the disposal was half-way through the year, Sub Ltd remains a subsidiary and so it will be necessary to consolidate the full amounts for operating profit and taxation in the profit and loss account for the year. The minority interests' share of their company's profit will be based on their relevant interests for each half of the year. Ignore the presentation requirements of FRS 3. Show negative goodwill (as reduced) as a separate item in capital and reserves.

Exercise 2: subsidiary becomes an associate

All figures are the same as before except that Parent Ltd received £300 000 for selling 40 000 shares in Sub Ltd on 30 June 1995. The revised summarized balance sheets at 31 December 1995, prior to accounting for the disposal, are as follows:

	Parent Ltd	Sub Ltd
	£	£
Investment in Sub Ltd		
(75 000 out of 100 000 shares)	112 500	
Sundry net assets	1 270 000	375 000
Suspense account		
(cash received for sale of shares)	(300 000)	
	1 082 500	375 000
Share capital (£1 ordinary shares)	500 000	100 000
Profit and loss reserve	582 500	275 000
	1 082 500	375 000

Profit and loss accounts year ending 31 December 1995 are as follows:

Operating profit	100 000	60 000
Dividends from subsidiary (cash received)	7 500	
Profit before tax	107 500	
Taxation on operating profit (25%)	25 000	15 000

	Parent Ltd	Sub Ltd
	£	£
Profit after tax	82 500	45 000
Dividends paid (31 March 1995)	—	10 000
Retained profit for financial year	82 500	35 000
Retained profit at 1 January 1995	500 000	240 000
Retained profit at 31 December 1995	582 500	275 000

Parent Ltd's interest in Sub Ltd had been acquired several years earlier when the balance on Sub Ltd's profit and loss account was £90 000. Corporation tax on the gain in the parent company's accounts will be at the rate of 25%.

Activity 9.9

On your own paper, prepare the accounts for 1995. In this exercise Sub Ltd was a subsidiary for the first six months of the year, and an associated company thereafter. In the consolidated profit and loss account the profits of the subsidiary for the first six months should be consolidated in full; the minority interests' share of these profits is shown as a deduction in the normal way. Profits of the subsidiary for the last six months should be reported as for an associated undertaking. Strictly speaking, since there is no group at the end of the year the equity accounting figures for the investment in Sub Ltd should be presented as a supplementary statement. We will, however, deal with the exercise as if Parent Ltd were still part of a group. You can ignore the presentation requirements in FRS 3. Show any remaining negative goodwill as a separate item in capital and reserves.

Exercise 3: subsidiary becomes an investment

The figures are the same as before except that Parent Ltd received £450 000 for selling 60 000 shares in Sub Ltd on 30 June 1995. The revised summarized balance sheets at 31 December 1995, prior to accounting for the disposal, are as follows:

	Parent Ltd	Sub Ltd
	£	£
Investment in Sub Ltd		
(75 000 out of 100 000 shares)	112 500	
Sundry net assets	1 420 000	375 000
Suspense account		
(cash received for sale of shares)	(450 000)	
	1 082 500	375 000
Share capital (£1 ordinary shares)	500 000	100 000
Profit and loss reserve	582 500	275 000
	1 082 500	375 000

Profit and loss accounts year ending 31 December 1995 are as follows:

	£	£
Operating profit	100 000	60 000
Dividends from subsidiary (cash received)	7 500	
Profit before tax	107 500	
Taxation on operating profit (25%)	25 000	15 000
Profit after tax	82 500	45 000
Dividends paid (31 March 1995)	—	10 000
Retained profit for financial year	82 500	35 000
Retained profit at 1 January 1995	500 000	240 000
Retained profit at 31 December 1995	582 500	275 000

Parent Ltd's interest in Sub Ltd had been acquired several years earlier when the balance on Sub Ltd's profit and loss account was £90 000. Corporation tax on the gain in the parent company's accounts will be at the rate of 25%.

Activity 9.10

On your own paper, prepare the accounts for 1995. In this exercise Sub Ltd was a subsidiary for the first six months of the year and a fixed asset investment thereafter. The approach will be similar to Activity 9.9 except that there will be no results to report for an associated undertaking. After 30 June 1995, Parent Ltd would simply report any dividends received (none in the example). The effect of the wording in FRS 2 is that the retained investment will be valued at its equity accounting value. You can ignore the presentation requirements of FRS 3. Treat any residual negative goodwill as a separate item in capital and reserves.

Summary

The key learning points in this chapter are as follows:

- where an investment ceases to be a subsidiary, the group accounts should include the results of that subsidiary up to the date of disposal;
- FRS 2 requires the gain or loss on cessation to be calculated by comparing the group's interest in the carrying value of the subsidiary's net assets before the cessation with the group's interest in these net assets after the cessation together with any proceeds received;
- the net assets compared should include any related goodwill not previously written off through the profit and loss account;
- a similar calculation is required by FRS 2 where the disposal relates to a reduction of an interest in a subsidiary;
- in many cases, the interest in the net assets following the cessation or reduction will simply be a percentage of the interest prior to the cessation or reduction;
- treatment of the operating results of a ceased or reduced subsidiary in the profit and loss account is a practical problem that varies according to the status of the retained interest.

Key to activities

Activity 9.1

£120 000 – £100 000 = £20 000

Activity 9.2

	£
Share of net assets at time of disposal (80% × (£100 000 + £20 000))	96 000
Goodwill on acquisition (£100 000 – (80% × £100 000))	20 000
	116 000
Sale proceeds	120 000
Gain	4 000

Activity 9.3

80% of the post-acquisition profits retained by the subsidiary (80% × £20 000).

Activity 9.4

	£	£
Gain in the parent company's accounts		150 000
Less share of post-acquisition profits retained in subsidiary:		
Total at 1 January 1995 (£100 000 – £40 000)	60 000	
Total 1 January 1995 to 30 June 1995 (6/12 × £36 000)	18 000	
Parent Ltd's share 80% × 78 000		62 400
Gain before tax in the group accounts		87 600

Activity 9.5

Consolidated profit and loss account

	Discontinued operations £	Continuing operations £	Total £
Turnover	100 000	800 000	900 000
Cost of sales and other expenses	60 000	700 000	760 000
Operating profit	40 000	100 000	140 000
Gain on disposal of discontinued operations	87 600	—	87 600
Profit on ordinary activities before interest	127 600	100 000	227 600

	Discontinued operations £	Continuing operations £	Total £
Interest payable			—
Profit on ordinary activities before tax			227 600
Tax on profit on ordinary activities (£40 000 + £16 000)			56 000
Profit on ordinary activities after tax			171 600
Minority interests (20% × 6/12 × £48 000)			4 800
Profit for the financial year			166 800
Dividends			30 000
Retained profit for the financial year			136 800

Activity 9.6

£300 000 – (80% × (£200 000 + £40 000)) = £108 000

The purchase cost can be found from details of sale proceeds and profit on disposal.

Activity 9.7

Movements on profit and loss reserve

Consolidated balance at 1 January 1995 (£600 000 + (80% × £60 000)) – £108 000	540 000
Add goodwill previously written off now reinstated	108 000
	648 000
Retained profit for the year	136 800
Balance at 31 December 1995 (Parent Ltd)	784 800

Activity 9.8 (Exercise 1)

Gain on disposal for the group accounts

Sale proceeds		150 000
Less proportion of cost (20/75 × £112 500)		30 000
Gain in parent company's accounts		120 000
(Tax provision required: 25% × £120 000 = £30 000)		
Less share of post-acquisition profits to 30 June 1995:		
Total at 1 January 1995 (£240 000 – £90 000)		150 000
Total 1 January 1995 to 30 June 1995:		
6/12 × £45 000	22 500	
Less dividend paid	10 000	

	£	£
	12 500	
Related to interest sold:	20% × 162 500	32 500
Gain before tax in group accounts		87 500

If the FRS 2 basis had been used, the calculation would have been as follows:

1. *Share of net assets prior to reduction*

	£	£	£
Share capital		100 000	
Profit and loss account			
at 1 January 1995	240 000		
6 months to 30 June 1995 (as above)	12 500		
		252 500	
	75% ×	352 500	264 375
Negative goodwill £112 000 − (75% × (£100 000 + £90 000))			(30 000)
			234 375

2. *Share of net assets after reduction*

Identifiable net assets (55% × £352 500)	193 875	
Negative goodwill (55/75 × £30 000)	(22 000)	
	171 875	
Sale proceeds	150 000	
		321 875
Gain		87 500

Consolidated profit and loss account for 1995

Operating profit (£100 000 + £60 000)		160 000
Gain on disposal of part interest		87 500
Profit before tax		247 500
Taxation (£25 000 + £15 000 + £30 000)		70 000
Group profit after tax		177 500
Minority interests:		
25% × 6/12 × £45 000	5 625	
45% × 6/12 × £45 000	10 125	
		15 750
Profit for the financial year retained		161 750

Profit and loss reserve

Balance at 1 January 1995 (£500 000 + (75% × £150 000))	612 500
Retained profit for the financial year	161 750
Balance at 31 December 1995	774 250

This total does not show how much of the group profit is dealt with in the accounts of Parent Ltd and how much has been retained in Sub Ltd. You will find it helpful to prepare this analysis because it shows the adjustments following the reduction. The figures are as follows:

	£	£	£
Retained in Parent Ltd:			
Balance as per the details		582 500	
Add gain net of tax (£120 000 – £30 000)		90 000	
			672 500
Retained in Sub Ltd			
At 1 January 1995 (75% × £150 000)		112 500	
Profit after tax for year	45 000		
Less minority interests	15 750		
	29 250		
Less dividend received	7 500		
Retained		21 750	
		134 250	
Transferred to minority interests			
(as per calculation of the gain)		32 500	
			101 750
			774 250

Consolidated balance sheet at 31 December 1995

Sundry net assets (£1 120 000 + £375 000 – £30 000)	1 465 000
Capital and reserves	
Share capital	500 000
Negative goodwill (retained interest)	22 000
Profit and loss account	774 250
	1 296 250
Minority interests (45% × £375 000)	168 750
	1 465 000

As an additional learning exercise you will find it quite helpful to reconcile the amount for minority interests. The figures are as follows:

Minority interests:		
Share capital prior to purchase of additional shares		25 000
Shares acquired		20 000
		45 000
Profit and loss reserve:		
Previous holding (25% × £240 000)	60 000	

	£	£
Related to shares acquired:		
Pre-acquisition (20% × £90 000)	18 000	
Post-acquisition transferred (as before)	32 500	
	110 500	
Share of profits for the year	15 750	
	126 250	
Less dividend paid	2 500	
		123 750
		168 750

Activity 9.9 (Exercise 2)

Gain on disposal (before tax) for the group accounts:

Sale proceeds	300 000
Cost of investment (40/75 × £112 500)	60 000
Gain in Parent Ltd's books	240 000
(Tax provision required: 25% × £240 000 = £60 000)	
Less 40% of post-acquisition profits up to date of disposal	
(40% × £162 500) (see Activity 9.8)	65 000
	£175 000

Profit and loss account for 1995

Operating profit (£100 000 + (6/12 × £60 000))		130 000
Gain on disposal of subsidiary		175 000
Share of profits of associated undertaking (35% × £30 000)		10 500
		315 500
Taxation		
Group (£25 000 + £7500 + £60 000)	92 500	
Associated undertaking (35% × £7500)	2 625	
		95 125
		220 375
Minority interests (25% × (6/12 × £45 000))		5 625
Profit for financial year retained		214 750

Profit and loss reserve

Balance at 1 January 1995 (as Activity 9.8)	612 500
Retained for year	214 750
Balance at 31 December 1995	827 250

The statement of adjustments to show where these profits are retained is slightly awkward because some retained profits of the former subsidiary must be attributed to the shares sold and some to the associated company. The statement of retained profits could be as follows:

	£	£
Retained in Parent Ltd (£582 500 + (£240 000 – £60 000))		762 500
Former subsidiary:		
At 1 January 1995 (as before)	112 500	
6 months to 30 June 1995		
(75% × 6/12 × £45 000) – £7500	9 375	
	121 875	
Relinquished on shares sold (40/75)	65 000	
Attributable to associated undertaking	56 875	
Profit for the year (£10 500 – £2625)	7 875	
Retained in associated undertaking		64 750
		827 250

Balance sheet at 31 December 1995

	£
Sundry net assets (Parent Ltd only) (£1 270 000 – £60 000)	1 210 000
Share of net assets of associated undertaking	
35% × £375 000	131 250
	1 341 250
Capital and reserves:	
Share capital	500 000
Negative goodwill (35/75 × £30 000)	14 000
Profit and loss account	827 250
	1 341 250

Activity 9.10 (Exercise 3)

Gain on disposal (before tax) for the group accounts:

	£
Sale proceeds	450 000
Cost of investment (60/75 × £112 500)	90 000
Gain in Parent Ltd's books	360 000
(Tax provision required: 25% × £360 000 = £90 000)	
Less 60% of post-acquisition profits up to date of disposal	
60% × £162 500	97 500
	262 500

Profit and loss account for 1995

	£
Operating profit (£100 000 + (6/12 × £60 000))	130 000
Gain on disposal of subsidiary	262 500
	92 500
Taxation (£25 000 + £7 500 + £90 000)	122 500
	270 000
Minority interests (as Activity 9.9)	5 625
Profit for financial year retained	264 375

Profit and loss reserve

	£	£
Balance at 1 January 1995		612 500
Retained profit for year		264 375
Balance at 31 December 1995		876 875

Reconciliation of retained profits

	£	£
Retained in Parent Ltd (£582 500 + (£360 000 – £90 000))		852 500
Former subsidiary:		
Up to date of disposal (as per Activity 9.9)	121 875	
Relinquished on shares sold (60/75)	97 500	
Added to cost of investment for equity valuation		24 375
		876 875

Equity value of investment at time of disposal

	£
Share capital and reserves of Sub Ltd at 1 January 1995	340 000
Retained profits to 30 June 1995 (6/12 × £45 000) – £10 000	12 500
	352 500

15% × £352 500 = £52 875

Balance sheet at 31 December 1995

	£
Sundry net assets of Parent Ltd (£1 420 000 – £90 000)	1 330 000
Investment at equity value at time of disposal (as above)	52 875
	1 382 875
Capital and reserves:	
Share capital	500 000
Negative goodwill (15/75 × £30 000)	6 000
Profit and loss account	876 875
	1 382 875

Note that the equity value of the investment could have been found as follows:

	£
Cost of investment (15/75 × £112 500)	22 500
Add retained profits as per reconciliation above	24 375
	46 875
Add negative goodwill (shown under reserves)	6 000
	52 875

Appendix

Extracts from FRS 2

Ceasing to be a subsidiary undertaking

46   When an undertaking ceases to be a subsidiary undertaking during a period, the consolidated financial statements for that period should include the results of that subsidiary undertaking up to the date that it ceases to be a subsidiary undertaking and any gain or loss arising on that cessation, to the extent that these have not been already provided for in the consolidated financial statements.

47   The gain or loss directly arising for the group on an undertaking ceasing to be its subsidiary undertaking is calculated by comparing the carrying amount of the net assets of that subsidiary undertaking attributable to the group's interest before the cessation with any remaining carrying amount attributable to the group's interest after the cessation together with any proceeds received. The net assets compared should include any related goodwill not previously written off through the profit and loss account. This calculation of gain or loss applies whether the cause of the undertaking ceasing to be a subsidiary undertaking is a direct disposal, a deemed disposal or other event.

Reducing an interest held in a subsidiary undertaking

52   Where a group reduces its interest in a subsidiary undertaking, it should record any profit or loss arising calculated as the difference between the carrying amount of the net assets of that subsidiary undertaking attributable to the group's interest before the reduction and the carrying amount attributable to the group's interest after the reduction together with any proceeds received. The net assets compared should include any related goodwill not previously written off through the profit and loss account. Where the undertaking remains a subsidiary undertaking after the disposal, the minority interest in that subsidiary undertaking should be increased by the carrying amount of the net identifiable assets that are now attributable to the minority interest because of the decrease in the group's interest. No amount for goodwill that arose on acquisition of the group's interest in that subsidiary undertaking should be attributed to the minority interest.

Extracts from SSAP 22

Effect of elimination of goodwill on realised profits

71   Paragraph 63 of the standard sets out the legal definition of realised profits. This is relevant only in the case of an individual company. In

the case of goodwill arising on consolidation, the distinction between realised and unrealised reserves is not relevant. Distributions are made from the profits of individual companies, not by groups, and hence the elimination of consolidation goodwill has no effect on the distributable profits of any company.

72 Where it is the policy of an individual company to eliminate goodwill against reserves immediately on acquisition, the question arises whether such elimination constitutes a reduction of realised reserves. [. . .], where goodwill is written off on acquisition as a matter of accounting policy, rather than because of an actual diminution in value, realised reserves should not be reduced immediately. However, the standard is based on the concept in the UK Companies Acts that purchased goodwill has a limited useful life so that ultimately its elimination must constitute a realised loss. [. . .] To maintain parity of effect as regards distributable reserves with the amortisation method permitted by paragraph 41 of the standard, the amount written off should then be transferred from unrealised reserves to realised reserves so as to reduce realised reserves on a systematic basis in the same way as if the goodwill had been amortised. In case of doubt on the points in this paragraph, legal advice should be sought.

Questions

Question for self assessment

An answer to this self-assessment question is given at the end of the book.

9.1 Brompton plc

The directors of Brompton plc are considering whether to dispose of a part or the whole of the company's shareholding in Doulidge Limited, one of the company's two subsidiaries.

The draft balance sheets as at 30 June 19X8 of the holding company and the two subsidiaries, Chieftain Limited and Doulidge Limited, are set out below:

	Brompton plc £000	Chieftain Ltd £000	Doulidge Ltd £000
Net tangible assets	3360	2250	2500
Investments at cost:			
1 000 000 £1 ordinary			
shares in Chieftain Ltd	2240		
1 500 000 £1 ordinary			
shares in Doulidge Ltd	2900		
	8500	2250	2500
Share capital			
£1 Ordinary shares	5600	1000	1500
Retained earnings	2900	1250	1000
	8500	2250	2500

Brompton plc acquired its shareholding in Chieftain Ltd on 1 July 19X6 when its retained earnings were £280 000 and in Doulidge Ltd on 1 August 19X6 when its retained earnings were £560 000.

Budgeted profit and loss accounts have been prepared for the three companies for the year ended 30 June 19X9. These show:

Budgeted profit and loss accounts for the year ended 30 June 19X9

	Brompton plc £000	Chieftain Ltd £000	Doulidge Ltd £000
Profit from ordinary activities before tax	2200	820	1344
Tax	1025	402	415
Profit from ordinary activities after tax	1175	418	929

The directors have been considering four proposals, as follows:

1. Dispose of 1 500 000 £1 ordinary shares in Doulidge Ltd on 1 July 19X8 for £3 640 000.

2. Dispose of 1 500 000 £1 ordinary shares in Doulidge Ltd on 1 January 19X9 for £3 640 000. Profits accrue evenly through the year.
3. Dispose of 600 000 £1 ordinary shares in Doulidge Ltd on 1 July 19X8 for £1 300 000.
4. Dispose of 1 350 000 £1 ordinary shares in Doulidge Ltd on 1 July 19X8 for £3 400 000.

A trainee accountant has prepared draft consolidated profit and loss accounts to illustrate the result if the company disposes of its total shareholding of 1 500 000 £1 ordinary shares according to options 1 and 2. His drafts are shown below:

(a) Draft consolidated profit and loss account for year ended 30 June 19X9 on the assumption that the 1 500 000 shares *are sold on 1 July 19X8*.

	Brompton plc £000	Chieftain Ltd £000	Consolidated £000
Profit before tax	2200	820	3020
Tax	1025	402	1427
Profit after tax	1175	418	1593
Extraordinary profit on sale			
of shares Note (1)	740		740
	1915	418	2333
Retained profit brought forward	2900	1250	4150
Retained profit carried forward	4815	1668	6483

Note (1) Profit on sale of shares:	
Sale proceeds	3640
Cost of investment	2900
	740

(b) Draft consolidated profit and loss account for year ended 30 June 19X9 on the assumption that the 1 500 000 shares *are sold on 1 January 19X9*.

	Brompton plc £000	Chieftain Ltd £000	Doulidge Ltd £000	Consolidated £000
Profit before tax	2200	820	1344	4364
Tax	1025	402	415	1842
	1175	418	929	2522
Less post disposal profit				464.5
				2057.5
Extraordinary profit	740	—	—	740
				2797.5
Retained profit brought forward				4150
Retained profit carried forward				6947.5

Required

(a) Review and correct the draft consolidated profit and loss accounts prepared by the trainee accountant. The corporation tax payable on the capital gain that arises from the disposal is £222 000.

(b) Write brief instructions to the trainee accountant so as to advise him on how to prepare the consolidated profit and loss account for:

  (i) the disposal of the 600 000 shares on 1 July 19X8
  (ii) the disposal of the 1 350 000 shares on 1 July 19X8

(c) Critically comment on the above disposals.

ACCA 3.1

Question without answer

An answer to this question is published separately in the *Teacher's Manual*.

9.2 Argent plc

Argent plc acquired the whole of the issued capital of 20 000 000 ordinary shares of £1 each in Plated plc on 1 January 1975 for £64 125 000. At that date the reserves of Plated plc were £38 050 000.

During 1989 Plated plc had been involved in litigation over claims that the company's processing methods were causing serious environmental pollution. Although the company had been successful in its legal action, the management were concerned about the possible adverse effect on the group. Therefore, on 31 December 1989 the directors of Argent plc were considering three alternative courses of action in relation to its investment in Plated plc.

The three alternative courses of action were:

1. Sell the 20 000 000 shares to a competitor, Maple leaf plc, for £90 000 000. At the date of the proposed sale on 31 December 1989 the post-acquisition reserves of Plated plc were £28 350 000.
2. Transfer the business and net assets of Plated plc to Argent Finance plc, which was another company within the Argent group, for £92 475 000 and to liquidate Plated plc.
3. Transfer the business and net assets of Plated plc to Silver Shine plc, a company that was not a member of the group, for £88 525 000 and to liquidate Plated plc.

Required

(a) Evaluate the effect of alternatives 1, 2 and 3 on

  (i) the accounts of Argent plc, and
  (ii) the consolidated accounts.

  Your answer must include a reconciliation of any differences between the amounts reported in the accounts of Argent plc and the amounts reported in the group accounts.

(b) State how the individual items in the consolidated accounts will be affected by the sale to Maple Leaf Ltd if it has been the group policy to amortize the goodwill on consolidation over 20 years.

ACCA 3.1 (requirements modified)

Foreign subsidiaries

10

Objectives

On completing this chapter you should be able to:

- translate unsettled monetary items (short-term and long-term) denominated in foreign currency according to the provisions in SSAP 20;
- apply the principle of the cover/offset policy to foreign currency borrowings when these are obtained as a hedge against exchange losses on foreign equity investments;
- make a judgement on whether the accounts of a foreign subsidiary, branch or associated company should be translated at the closing rate or the temporal rate prior to consolidation with the accounts of the UK company;
- translate the financial statements of an overseas entity and consolidate these translated statements with those of the UK parent company;
- explain the nature of all translation differences, including those at the individual company level, and discuss their impact on the concept of realized profits.

Introduction

The word 'foreign' is used in this chapter to indicate a country other than the UK. This might seem slightly awkward for readers who reside in a country where the UK is foreign to them but the book is intended to be an explanation of UK practices and presumably it is being studied from that viewpoint.

The applicable accounting standard is SSAP 20: *Foreign currency translation*. This standard was issued in April 1983 and although a few minor criticisms of it have been published since then, it was widely accepted when it was introduced and has not been subject to any later amendments. As might be gathered from its title, SSAP 20 deals with matters other than foreign subsidiaries. It covers various aspects of international operations, such as:

- transactions with an overseas entity; and
- translating the financial statements of an overseas branch or subsidiary into sterling so that they can be consolidated with those of the UK entity.

It is helpful to think of the structure of SSAP 20 in terms of two key words: **transactions** and **translation**. This distinction is not made in SSAP 20 because the term 'translation' applies to both transactions of an individual company and the procedures for consolidating the financial statements of an overseas entity. These two words do, however, provide a useful key to how the subject should be studied. In this chapter we deal with transactions first. SSAP 20 describes the rules on transactions as being applicable to the 'individual company stage'. This can be slightly misleading to students because the word 'stage' suggests that something else must be done later. But there will not be any further stage if the individual company does not have a controlling interest in an overseas entity.

The concept of an individual company stage is, however, important when translating the financial statements of an overseas entity for consolidation purposes. This is because the financial statements of an overseas entity (and the UK entity) might include unsettled transactions that are denominated in a currency other than the reporting currency. For example, a French subsidiary might have a creditor denominated in American dollars. This will require translation into French francs at the accounting date before the financial statements of the French subsidiary are translated into sterling for consolidation purposes.

Transactions (individual companies)

The provisions on transactions in SSAP 20 relate to any company, irrespective of whether or not the UK company has a controlling interest in an overseas entity. Many companies import goods from foreign countries where the amount payable is denominated in the currency of the country supplying the goods. A UK company might also borrow from an overseas entity and might invest in the equity capital of an overseas entity. These are all examples of transactions with foreign entities that can result in balances being recorded in the UK books at amounts that might differ from what will ultimately be paid or received when the transactions are settled.

Importing and exporting

If a purchase or sales transaction is conducted on a cash basis, there is no accounting problem. The transaction is simply recorded in the UK books according to the amount of sterling paid or received. Accounting issues arise only when transactions are conducted on a credit basis and the amount payable or receivable is denominated in a currency other than sterling.

Accruals accounting requires the transaction to be recorded at the time it occurs, not when the cash is paid or received. If there is a change in exchange rates between the date of the transaction and the date of settlement, there will be a difference between the amount originally recorded and the amount paid or received.

SSAP 20 requires a **temporal** basis to be used for recording these transactions. Temporal here means 'at the time' and so the transaction must be recorded at the exchange rate ruling on the date of the transaction. For example, if an asset is purchased from an overseas entity on credit terms, the asset must be recorded at the sterling equivalent of the foreign currency amount according to the exchange rate at the time of the transaction. The asset is classified as a 'non-monetary' asset and its cost must not be restated if the exchange rate changes before the transaction is settled. The creditor is, however, a monetary liability denominated in a foreign currency and is subject to the translation provisions in SSAP 20.

If a company has outstanding monetary items (debtors or creditors) at the balance sheet date which are denominated in a foreign currency, they must be restated by using the rate of exchange at that date (this is known as the closing rate). At the time of settlement there could be a further difference between the amount paid or received in sterling and the balance shown in the books for the outstanding item.

Any gains or losses arising on settlement, or on restating the balance at each accounting date, should be reported as part of ordinary profits for the year. This treatment is justified on the grounds that these gains or losses have been (or soon will be) reflected in the cash flows of the UK entity.

Activity 10.1

A UK company purchased some new plant and machinery from France on credit. It was invoiced by the French supplier at FF90 000 when £1.00 = FF9.00. The creditor was outstanding at the accounting date of 31 March when the rate was £1.00 = FF10.00. Payment was made one month later when £1.00 = FF8.00

1. Set out the double entry on purchase of the asset:

    Debit

    Credit

2. Set out the double entry that will be made on 31 March:

    Debit

    Credit

3. Set out the double entry for the final settlement (this can be a composite double entry with two debits):

    Debit

    Debit

    Credit

4. Make a note of how the exchange gains and losses are dealt with in the financial statements:

    Reported as:

Note that the amount recorded for the cost of plant and machinery (£10 000) does not alter even though the monetary liability was restated on two occasions and the amount ultimately paid was £11 250.

Long-term monetary items

Another type of transaction dealt with by SSAP 20 is described as a long-term monetary item denominated in a foreign currency. A long-term monetary item is one that falls due after more than one year from the accounting date. This usually means a loan payable where a UK company has borrowed funds from an overseas entity. The amount received in sterling when the loan was obtained is unlikely to be the same as the amount of sterling needed to fund repayment of the loan when it matures.

For example, a UK entity might raise a loan from France of 90 000 French francs which realizes £10 000 in sterling. If the loan is repayable in French francs (the loan is denominated in French francs) the cost of repaying the loan will depend on the rate of exchange ruling at the time of repayment. This cost is unlikely to be the same as the £10 000 recorded when the loan was obtained. Loans receivable (lending money to an overseas entity) are usually denominated in sterling and if this is the case, the problem of translation does not arise because the amount lent is the same as the amount receivable.

SSAP 20 requires long-term monetary liabilities denominated in foreign currency to be restated at each accounting date to the amount that is likely to be paid on maturity. Since this amount is not known (unless the borrower has made a forward contract to purchase foreign currency at a specified rate on maturity) the SSAP suggests that the rate ruling on each accounting date (the closing rate) gives the best estimate of the amount that will eventually have to be paid. Any gains or losses on restatement of the loan should be reported as part of profit on ordinary activities.

Activity 10.2

A UK company obtains a three year loan from France of FF90 000. The loan realizes £10 000 when converted into sterling. At the end of the UK company's accounting year during which the loan was obtained the exchange rate was £1.00 = FF8.00. Write down the double entry that should be made at the end of the year in order to comply with SSAP 20, and make a note of how the translation difference should be dealt with in the accounts.

Debit

Credit

Treatment of translation difference

The SSAP justifies this periodic translation on the basis of the accruals concept. If these end of period translations are ignored, exchange gains or losses will be recognized only when the amounts are settled. Delaying recognition of these gains and losses until the amounts are settled is inconsistent with the accruals concept.

Forward contracts

Some companies cover their exposure to exchange rate fluctuations by entering into a forward contract for the purchase of foreign currency at a specified rate. The delivery date for the foreign currency is often matched with the date that the liability will be paid. In these circumstances SSAP 20 recognizes that the transaction should not be recorded at the temporal rate, and that the monetary liability (long- or short-term) should not be retranslated to the closing rate at the end of each period. Instead, the asset and liability should be recorded at the rate specified in the forward contract.

Hedging loans

Companies often undertake foreign currency borrowings as a hedge against the risk of losses through investments in a foreign country. If the currency of the country in which an investment has been made should weaken against sterling, the company making the investment will sustain losses when that investment is realized and the proceeds are remitted to the UK. This loss can, to some extent, be offset by a gain on repayment of borrowings from a country whose currency has weakened against sterling.

The reverse of this situation can easily apply. If an equity investment is made in a country whose currency strengthens against sterling, there will be a gain on the ultimate realization of that investment which is partly attributable to movements in the exchange rate. These exchange gains will not be recognized in the UK accounts during the years the investment is owned because non-monetary assets (such as an overseas equity investment) are not retranslated at each accounting date. If the investment had been partly financed by overseas borrowings, and the loan is repayable in a currency that strengthens against sterling, there will be losses to report on retranslating the loan at the end of each year.

SSAP 20 recognizes that this creates an anomalous situation because gains on the investment are being ignored while losses on the loan are being charged to the profit and loss account. In these circumstances, SSAP 20 allows companies to retranslate their foreign equity investments at the closing rate each year. Exchange gains (or losses) on retranslating the investment must be taken to reserves and not treated as part of the profit for the year. Any losses (or gains) that result from retranslating the relevant foreign currency borrowings are then set against the reserve created by the gain on retranslating the investment.

The amount of the set-off is limited to the gain (or loss) from retranslating the investment for the year; any excess must be dealt with in the profit and loss account for the year. If this policy (technically called the cover or offset policy) is adopted, SSAP 20 requires that it must be applied consistently from one year to the next.

Although the cover or offset procedure is often explained in terms of investing and borrowing in the same country, there are no provisions in SSAP 20 that require the borrowings to be from the same country as where the investment is made. The standard recognizes that most companies hedge their foreign investment risks by obtaining finance from a variety of countries.

The French loan of 90 000 francs in Activity 2 was obtained to partly finance the purchase of equity shares in a French company. The cost of these shares was 135 000 French francs and they were purchased on the same date as acquiring the loan. Assuming that the UK company adopts the offset policy, state the amounts that will be included in its financial statements for the following items at the end of the year when the transactions occurred:

1. Equity investment in French company
2. Loan denominated in French francs
3. Net amount taken to reserves

Translation of financial statements

After dealing with the translation of unsettled monetary items for the individual company, it will be necessary to translate the financial statements of a foreign entity into sterling if its results are to be consolidated with those of the UK entity. This applies when the foreign entity is a branch, subsidiary or associated undertaking of the UK company.

Translation methods

SSAP 20 requires either the temporal method or the closing rate method to be used for this translation. The choice will depend on the relationship between the UK company and the foreign entity. This aspect is discussed following an explanation of the two translation methods.

Temporal method

The temporal method is not defined in SSAP 20 although it is explained (in the notes to the standard) as being on the same basis as that used for the individual company stage. Non-monetary assets are translated at the rate ruling when the assets were acquired and outstanding monetary items at the accounting date are translated at the closing rate. The use of the closing rate for these unsettled monetary items is really an application of the temporal basis because the items are being translated to their sterling equivalent at the time of the report (the balance sheet date).

If the temporal method is used, it will normally be much too cumbersome to find the rate ruling at the date of each transaction in the profit and loss account. It is normally assumed that most transactions reported in the profit and loss account occur at an even rate throughout the year. In these circumstances it is reasonable to use an average annual rate for the translation of most income and expenditure items, including the taxation charge. Some exceptions to this are as follows:

- **Depreciation** must be an annual allocation of the translated amount for the fixed assets concerned. The translation rate will, therefore, be the same as the rate used for translation of the relevant fixed asset.

- **Opening and closing stocks** for the cost of sales calculation should be based on the rates ruling when the stocks were acquired. This can normally be estimated by using an average rate for the period over which these stocks were acquired. For example, if the opening stocks were acquired during the last two months of the previous year, opening stock could be translated using an average rate for those two months.
- **Dividends paid** should be translated at the rate ruling on the date they were paid; proposed dividends can be translated at the closing rate.

The closing rate/net investment method

With the closing rate method, all items in the financial statements are translated into sterling at the rate of exchange ruling on the balance sheet date. The closing rate is defined by SSAP 20 as the exchange rate for spot transactions on the balance sheet date based on the mean of buying and selling rates at the close of business on that day.

Under the closing rate method, SSAP 20 allows the profit and loss account to be translated at either the closing rate or the average rate for the year. The arguments for and against using either of these rates for the profit and loss account are somewhat unconvincing and are not discussed any further here. The closing rate is preferable from a pragmatic point of view and the authors of UK GAAP consider that it has more conceptual merit than the average rate.

Which method?

The method chosen must be based on an interpretation of the financial and operational relationship between the UK and the foreign entity. The nature of this relationship will also have a bearing on whether or not changes in exchange rates have an impact on the cash flows of the reporting entity. This aspect is important because if changes in exchange rates have little impact on the cash flows of the UK company, any differences (gains or losses) that arise on translation of the foreign entity's financial statements should not be reported as part of the profit for the year.

Separate and quasi-independent foreign entity

SSAP 20 suggests that in most cases the closing rate (or net investment) method should be used. This is because investments by UK companies are usually in foreign entities whose local trading operations are independent of the UK company. In these cases there is an investment in the net worth of the foreign entity that will remain until it is liquidated or the investment is sold. Movements on exchange rates will cause gains or losses on translation to occur but they will have no impact on the annual cash flows of the UK company.

Foreign entity dependent on UK company

In some cases the overseas entity can be seen as an extension of the UK company rather than a quasi-independent organization. In these circumstances, most transactions of the foreign entity are a continuation of those originated by the UK company. The financial statements of the foreign entity should be translated as if each of its transactions had been undertaken by the UK company. This means that the temporal basis of translation should be used. There will usually be regular and frequent cash flows between the UK company and the overseas entity and so any changes in exchange rates will have an impact on the cash flows of the UK company.

Activity 10.4

A UK tractor manufacturer set up a subsidiary company in Zambalia where the local currency is called the Kwolla. The Zambalian company assembles components supplied by the UK company into complete tractors and then sells these on the local market. By agreement with the central bank of Zambalia, the purchase invoices for components imported can be settled on receipt of the goods, and profits earned by the Zambalian company may be remitted to the UK company on a regular basis. State whether the financial statements of the Zambalian company should be translated into sterling by using the temporal or the closing rate method.

SSAP 20 states that the temporal method is appropriate **where the trade of the foreign entity is more dependent on the economic environment of the investing company's currency than on its own reporting currency.** This raises the question of: **what is the dominant currency?** If the dominant currency is sterling then a temporal basis is appropriate. In order to make a judgement on this, SSAP 20 requires the following points to be considered:

- the extent to which cash flows of the foreign entity affect the investing company (are there regular and frequent cash flows between investing company and foreign entity?);
- the extent to which management of the foreign entity's operations is dependent on the investing company (is management of the foreign entity dominated by UK management?);
- the currency in which the majority of transactions are denominated (are most transactions settled in sterling?);
- the major currency to which the foreign entity is exposed in its financing structure (is the foreign entity financed mainly from the UK?).

The explanatory notes in SSAP 20 give examples of where the temporal basis might be appropriate. These examples are as follows:

- where the foreign entity acts as a selling agency for the UK entity;
- where the foreign entity produces raw materials (or sub-assemblies) for inclusion in the investing company's own products;
- where the foreign entity is located overseas for taxation purposes or, in view of exchange control (or similar) reasons, is located overseas to raise finance for other operations of the group.

Differences on translation

When the financial statements of an overseas entity are translated into sterling it will usually be necessary to insert a balancing figure which is described as a gain or loss on translation. You will see how and why this arises in the next section. These translation gains and losses will have to be reported in the consolidated accounts somewhere and the question arises as to whether or not they should be included as part of the profit for the year.

The treatment required by SSAP 20 is related to the method of translation and the extent to which the gains or losses arising have an impact on the cash flows of the reporting entity. This can be explained as follows:

- **Closing rate method**. In this case the translation difference arises because the net investment at the end of the previous year has been restated by using the exchange rates at the end of the current year. In this case the translation gain or loss has no impact on the cash flows of the UK company and should be reported as a movement on reserves.
- **Temporal method**. Translation differences can arise because transactions (such as purchases from the UK) in the financial statements of the foreign entity are translated at rates that differ from the rates applying at the time of settlement. Even if the transactions have not been settled, closing monetary items (such as cash balances, debtors and creditors) are translated at the closing rate and this is likely to differ from the rates used for translating the transactions that created these monetary items.

  In these circumstances the translation gains and losses have either been reflected in the cash flows of the UK company or they will shortly be so. Consequently, the translation gains or losses under the temporal method should be reported as part of the ordinary profit for the year.

Consolidation of foreign subsidiaries

Types of problem

The accounting issues associated with consolidating foreign subsidiaries vary between two extremes. At one end there is a fairly straightforward situation where the foreign subsidiary was set up by the UK company and where the UK company owns 100% of share capital of that subsidiary. In this case the problems associated with goodwill and minority interests do not arise. At the other extreme the UK company will have acquired a controlling interest of less than 100% in an existing overseas company. This makes it necessary to consider translation principles in relation to goodwill and minority interests.

In all cases there could be the additional matter of translating unsettled monetary items at the individual company level before the financial statements of the foreign entity are translated for consolidation purposes. The method used for translating the financial statements (temporal or closing rate) does not have much impact on the problem although more number crunching is involved when the temporal basis is used.

In this section we will learn the principles by considering two situations, and by applying a different method of translation to each one, as follows:

- **Closing rate method**. This will be used for a case where the parent company acquired a controlling interest of less than 100% in an existing overseas company. Although this is at the more complex end of the spectrum, it does enable most of the basic principles to be covered from one situation. The acquisition of a controlling interest in an existing overseas company suggests that the relationship between the two companies is such that the closing rate method should be used but, as discussed on p. 246, there will be various factors to consider before reaching a conclusion on this.
- **Temporal method**. This will be used for a case where the parent company sets up an overseas company and owns the entire share capital. This will remove the problem of goodwill and minority interests from the problem and enable us to see the effect of the temporal method more clearly. It is often more appropriate to apply the temporal basis to this kind of situation because the overseas company is often set up to act as a selling agency for the UK company.

Closing rate method

We will start by looking at the general effect of translating the balance sheet of a foreign subsidiary.

Details for the activities

A UK company has a controlling interest in a French subsidiary. At the beginning of the year the capital and reserves (net assets) of the subsidiary were FF450 000 and the exchange rate was £1.00 = FF9.00. During the year the French subsidiary made and retained a profit of FF100 000. At the end of the year the exchange rate was £1.00 = FF8.00

Activity 10.5

Without making any calculations, consider whether the change in exchange rate provides the UK company with a gain or a loss on its investment in the French subsidiary. Make a note of your observations here.

We now need to think about the way that this gain is dealt with in accounting terms. To start with, deal with the next activity. Keep in mind that the closing rate method applies.

Activity 10.6

The net assets at the beginning of the year will have been translated into sterling at the end of the previous year according to the exchange rate at that time. The profit for the current year, and the net assets at the end of the year, will both be translated at the closing rate. Calculate the translated amounts and make a note of them here.

Net assets at beginning of year   £

Profit for the year   £

Net assets at end of year   £

In financial accounting, the basic equation is: opening net assets + retained profits = closing net assets. But this will not work in this case because we are not using the same translation factor for all items in the equation. Retained profits and closing net assets have been translated at the same rate but a different rate was used for the opening net assets.

Activity 10.7

The balancing figure in the equation is the difference on translation for the year. This can be calculated by inserting the translated figures in the following computation:

Net assets at the beginning of the year   £

Add retained profit for the year   £

Net assets at end of the year   £

Translation gain for the year

You can now see what happens on the capital and reserves side of the translated balance sheet by working the next activity. This provides an overview of the subsidiary's balance sheet following translation at the closing rate.

Activity 10.8

Complete the following by inserting the translated figures for capital and reserves:

Movements on capital and reserves

Capital and reserves at beginning of year   £

Retained profit for the year   £

Translation gain   £

Capital and reserves at end of year

Represented by

Net assets at end of year   £68 750

These activities were intended to explain the nature of translation gains or losses when the closing rate method is used; they do not represent an approach to solving examination problems. The translation gain arises in this case because the opening net assets which were previously stated at £50 000 have, in effect, been retranslated to £56 250 by using the closing rate. If the profit for the year had been translated at an average rate (an option allowed by SSAP 20), there would have been a further gain on translation.

In examination problems the translation gain or loss will be a figure that is inserted into the financial statements of the foreign subsidiary in order to make the two balance sheet totals agree. In order to see how this works we need a model with more detail.

Details for the activities

The abbreviated balance sheet of a French subsidiary (not connected with the previous activities) is shown below. The column headed 'Revised FF' to the right of the figures will be completed during the activities.

	FF	FF	Revised FF
Sundry net assets		120 000	
Owing to UK parent company	18 000		
German loan	12 000		
		30 000	
		90 000	
Share capital		40 000	
Profit and loss account brought forward	38 000		
Profit retained for year	12 000		
		50 000	
		90 000	

Notes:

1. The closing rate of exchange is £1.00 = FF10.00.
2. The outstanding items on the current account with the UK parent company agree with the parent company's books. These relate to purchases from the parent company and are denominated in sterling. The corresponding debtor in the UK books is £1900. The UK company transfers goods to the French subsidiary at cost price.
3. The German loan was raised when FF24.00 = DM1.00. At the end of the accounting period the rate was FF25.00 = DM1.00. The loan is denominated in German marks. The subsidiary does not have any foreign equity investments.

Approach

There are usually four stages when producing a solution to a problem that involves the consolidation of a foreign subsidiary.

1. translation of unsettled monetary items at the individual company level;
2. translation of the revised financial statements into sterling at the closing rate;

3. inserting a balancing figure representing the gain or loss on translation;
4. consolidating the translated financial statements of the subsidiary with those the parent company.

The product of stages 1 to 3 is a set of financial statements where all amounts are stated in sterling. Consequently, the procedure in stage 4 is the same as if you were consolidating the results of a UK subsidiary. The only difference at this stage is that the translated financial statements of the foreign subsidiary will include an item called 'translation gain or loss'. In cases where the closing rate method is being used, this gain or loss must be dealt with as a movement on reserves.

Activity 10.9

Carry out the individual company stage translation. Do this by writing the revised FF figures in the column provided. The two items that require translation are the German loan and the current account with the parent company. The gains or losses arising from this translation are (as discussed on pp. 242–244) included in the profit for the year. Don't forget that we are not translating the accounts for consolidation at this stage – we are dealing with the translation of unsettled monetary items in the individual company's accounts.

For consolidation purposes, we will need to know the amount for capital and reserves at the date of acquisition (as we do for consolidating the accounts of a UK company). The translated figures at acquisition remain unaltered in subsequent periods; any gains or losses that result from changes in exchange rates following acquisition are dealt with as movements on the **post-acquisition reserves** of the group. It is also necessary to know the exchange rate at the beginning of the year in order to translate post-acquisition reserves brought forward (the figure used in the group accounts for the previous year).

Activity 10.10

The exchange rate on acquisition of the controlling interest was £1.00 = FF8.00. The share capital was the same as it is now, the reserves at acquisition were FF12 000. At the end of the previous year the exchange rate was £1.00 = FF9.00. Produce a translated balance sheet using the closing rate method. The profit for the year is to be translated at the closing rate (not the average rate). An outline format for the translated figures is provided below this box . The format used here for capital and reserves will eventually prove helpful when it comes to consolidating the results of this subsidiary with those of the UK parent company. Take care with the **post-acquisition** profits brought forward – this will not be FF38 000.

Translated balance sheet

£

Sundry net assets
Owing to UK holding company
German loan

Share capital and reserves:
    Capital and reserves at acquisition

Post-acquisition profits brought forward
Retained profit for year
Gain/(loss) on translation

Because of the way the balances for capital and reserves have been presented in this example, the translation loss of £1589 represents the cumulative amount since the subsidiary was acquired. It is possible to analyse this loss between the cumulative amount brought forward from previous years and the amount arising in the current year, as follows:

	FF	Rate	£
Previous years			
Share capital and reserves at acquisition	52 000	8	6 500
Post-acquisition profits brought forward	26 000	9	2 889
	78 000		9 389
Share capital and reserves at end of previous year as translated	78 000	9	8 667
Cumulative translation loss applicable to previous years			722
Current year			
Opening share capital and reserves	78 000	9	8 667
Translated to closing rate	78 000	10	7 800
Translation loss applicable to current year			867
Cumulative translation loss (£722 + £867)			1 589

The financial statements for the foreign subsidiary have now been expressed in sterling and can be consolidated with those of the UK parent company. The abbreviated balance sheet of the UK company (at the same date as the French subsidiary) is set out below. The column headed 'Revised £' will be completed during the activities.

		£	Revised £
Sundry net assets		94 900	
Investment in French subsidiary		7 200	
Owing by French subsidiary		1 900	
		104 000	
French loan		4 000	
		100 000	
Share capital		50 000	
Undistributable reserves		8 000	
Profit and loss account brought forward	30 000		
Retained profit for year	12 000		
		42 000	
		100 000	

The French loan is repayable in francs to a French bank. The loan was for FF32 000. Although the proceeds were used to assist with investment in the French subsidiary, the offset policy will not be adopted (this decision might have been influenced by the fact that there will be a gain on translating the loan).

Activity 10.11

Carry out the individual company stage translation by writing the revised amounts to the right of the figures shown. The only items to be revised are the French loan and the retained profit for the year.

Minority interests

Minority interests (if any) are credited with their share of profits for the year in the normal way. This will include any translation gains or losses which have been taken to their own company's profit and loss account at the individual company stage. The final balance on minority interests will be based on a share of the translated net assets in their company at the accounting date. This effectively attributes to minority interests a share of translation gains or losses at the accounting date. You will recall from previous chapters that the interests of minority shareholders in the net assets of their company should be on the same basis as the parent company's interest.

The main point to keep in mind when preparing the consolidated balance sheet is that the interest of the parent company in the cumulative gains or losses arising on translation of the foreign subsidiary's accounts will be related to the proportion of shares owned by the parent company. This is the same as for the treatment of all post-acquisition gains and losses of the subsidiary.

Goodwill

Some aspects of accounting for goodwill on the acquisition of a foreign subsidiary are open to interpretation. The position is generally less contentious if the immediate write-off policy is adopted. If goodwill is treated as an intangible asset and amortized through the profit and loss account, a question arises as to whether the asset should be restated at each accounting date according to the closing rate. This aspect is not covered by SSAP 20 but it seems that the intention of the standard could have been to leave goodwill at the amount recorded when the acquisition occurred. To some extent this is in keeping with SSAP 22 where revaluations of goodwill are not permitted.

However, some commentators (such as the authors of UK GAAP) have argued that it would be more logical to value goodwill by retranslating the fair value of net assets at acquisition to the closing rate. We will not be considering these arguments in this text book. In our example, goodwill will be based on the conditions applying at the date of acquisition and will be written off against reserves. Students who wish to study further aspects of this problem should refer to the text book mentioned.

Activity 10.12

The group in our example includes 20% minority interests. Translation differences are to be shown as a separate reserve in the capital and reserves section of the balance sheet. Calculate the following amounts and make a note of them here:

1. Goodwill arising on acquisition.

2. Minority interests at the balance sheet date.

3. Consolidated profit and loss reserve (prior to goodwill write-off).

4. Cumulative translation losses for the consolidated balance sheet.

We now have all the figures needed to prepare a consolidated balance sheet.

Activity 10.13

Prepare the consolidated balance sheet by completing the outline format shown below this box. In this format, two items affecting reserves (goodwill write-off and translation losses) are shown as separate items. A discussion of how these could be presented in the consolidated accounts will be covered after the accounts have been prepared.

Consolidated balance sheet

Sundry net assets		£
Loans payable:		
German loan	£	
French loan	£	

Capital and reserves:

Share capital		£
Undistributable reserves	£	
Translation losses	£	
Profit and loss reserve	£	
Goodwill written off	£	
Minority interests		£

When the closing rate method is used, SSAP 20 requires the translation gain or loss to be treated as a movement on reserves. It does not, however, state which reserves should be used to show this movement. Most companies show the movements on the balance for the profit and loss reserve. The impact of translation gains and losses on realized profits is discussed on pp. 261–263.

The treatment of the goodwill write-off is the same as if the subsidiary had been a UK company. In the above example there is no information available on undistributable reserves and so it is not possible to determine whether the goodwill could be written off against this reserve. If undistributable reserves are not available for this purpose, goodwill must be written off against the balance on the profit and loss reserve.

Temporal basis

We will consider the temporal basis in the context of a foreign subsidiary set up by the UK company as an overseas selling agency. In these circumstances we can assume that the share capital of the foreign subsidiary is issued at par and that no goodwill on acquisition arises. It is also reasonable to assume that in these circumstances the UK parent company owns the entire share capital of the subsidiary and if this is so there will be no minority interests to consider.

The situation described above is not by any means specific to use of the temporal basis but it does help to confine the new learning points to the effect of the method. We can also ignore the effect of translation at the individual company level since the principles have been covered under the closing rate method. These principles do not change simply because the financial statements of the foreign subsidiary are being translated for consolidation purposes by using the temporal basis.

Details for the activities

A UK company set up a subsidiary in Zambalia where the local currency is known as the Zambalian Kwolla (ZK). The Zambalian subsidiary was formed at the beginning of the current year when ZK4 = £1 and issued 40 000 shares to the UK company in exchange for £10 000 which realized ZK40 000 in local currency. These funds, together with a short-term loan obtained from a Zambalian bank, enabled the subsidiary to purchase the fixed assets needed to operate the business.

The Zambalian subsidiary acts as a selling agency for the UK company and most of its purchases are supplied by the UK parent. Although the subsidiary earned profits during its first year of operations, none of these profits were remitted to the UK because the funds generated were applied to repayment of the bank loan. The financial statements of the Zambalian subsidiary at the end of its first year of trading are set out below. The columns to the right of the ZK figures will be completed during the activities.

Profit and loss account

	ZK	Rate	Translated £s
Turnover	600 000		
Cost of sales:			
Purchases	203 000		
Less closing stock	23 000		
	180 000		
Gross profit	420 000		
Depreciation	12 180		
Other operating expenses	287 820		
	300 000		
Profit before tax	120 000		
Taxation	20 000		
Profit after tax retained	100 000		

Balance sheet

	ZK	Rate	Translated £s
Fixed assets			
Cost	121 800		
Depreciation	12 180		
	109 620		
Stocks	23 000		
Net monetary assets	7 380		
	140 000		
Capital and reserves:			
Share capital	40 000		
Profit and loss account	100 000		
	140 000		

Difference on translation

Notes:

Income and expenditure accrued at an even rate throughout the year. The closing rate was ZK6 = £1 and the average rate for the year was ZK5 = £1. fixed assets were acquired shortly after formation of the company when the exchange rate was ZK4.20 to the £1. Closing stock was acquired when the rate was ZK5.75 to the £1. Net monetary assets are all local items and do not require translation at the individual company stage.

Activity 10.14

Translate the financial statements of the Zambalian subsidiary by writing the translation rates and the translated amounts to the right of the figures in the accounts shown above. If you have forgotten the basis of the temporal method, refer to the appropriate notes on pp. 246–247. Share capital should be translated at the rate ruling when the shares were issued. The translation gain or loss is a balancing figure.

The translation gain of £2394 will be included as a part of the ordinary profits when the subsidiary's results are consolidated with those of the parent company. We will not be preparing consolidated accounts for this example because nothing will be learned by doing so. The translated share capital of £10 000 is cancelled against the investment in the subsidiary of £10 000 as shown in the parent company's accounts. All other items are simply combined with those of the parent company.

It might seem odd that a translation gain has occurred through an investment in a foreign country where the local currency is weakening against sterling. But the nature of the gain in this case is somewhat different to that when the closing rate method is used. It does not arise because an investment at the beginning of the year is being restated to the closing rate: it arises because profits are translated at a rate that differs from the rate used to translate the net assets created by those profits.

In this example there are differences between the rates used when calculating profit and the rates used to translate closing fixed assets and net monetary assets. There is a loss on translation of net monetary assets because these have been translated at a rate of ZK6 to the £1 whereas the profits that generated the increase in net monetary assets were translated at ZK5 to the £1. In the case of fixed assets, however, the reverse has occurred. To the extent that these were obtained by a local bank loan that was repaid from profits there is a gain. The fixed assets have been translated at ZK4.2 to the £1 whereas the profits that created the funds to repay the loan were translated at ZK5 to the £1. The total gain can be analysed as follows:

	£
Increase in net monetary assets at average rate (ZK7380 ÷ 5)	1 476
Increase in net monetary assets at closing rate (ZK7380 ÷ 6)	1 230
Loss on translation of increase in net monetary items	(246)

	£	£
Translated cost of fixed assets (ZK121 800 ÷ 4.2)		29 000
Funding of fixed assets:		
From translated profits ((ZK121 800 − 40 000) ÷ 5)	16 360	
From initial capital (ZK40 000 ÷ 4)	10 000	
		26 360
Gain on translation of fixed assets		2 640
Gain reported in the consolidated financial statements		2 394

Hedging loans in group accounts

The cover or offset procedure for hedging loans as described on p. 245 for a single company is also available for the group accounts. The provisions for group accounts (para. 57 of the standard) are similar to those for an individual company except that the policy can only be adopted if the relationship between the investing company and the foreign entity is such that it justifies use of the closing rate method of translation for consolidation purposes.

This restricting provision is quite sensible because it is only when the closing rate method is used that the gains or losses on translation will be taken to reserves. There will be a difference between the amount taken to reserves in the investing company's accounts and the amount that arises in the group accounts. The gain or loss in the individual company's accounts is calculated by restating the investment to the closing rate, whereas in the group accounts it is the underlying net assets of the subsidiary that are restated to the closing rate.

When preparing the group accounts, the gain or loss in the parent company's accounts that arises from restating the investment is ignored. This gain or loss is represented in the group accounts by the gain or loss on translating the financial statements of the foreign subsidiary. The revised carrying value of the investment is likewise ignored and the calculation of goodwill on acquisition (if any) is based on the cost of the investment at the date of acquisition. The following example illustrates these points.

Example

A UK company set up a subsidiary in Pololand where the local currency is known as the Polo. At the time when the subsidiary was established the rate of exchange was P5 to the £1. The issued share capital of the subsidiary is P800 and this was all acquired by the UK parent company at a cost of (P800 ÷ 5) £160. As a hedge against exchange losses, the UK parent company acquired a loan from Pololand of P400 at the same time. This loan realized (P400 ÷ 5) £80. The exchange rate at the end of the first year of trading was P4 = £1.

The balance sheets of both companies after the subsidiary's first year of trading are set out below. These include translated figures of the parent company (following adoption of the cover/offset policy) and the translated figures of the subsidiary in preparation for the consolidation.

Balance sheet of UK parent company

	Prior to translation		Translated amounts
	£		£
Investment in subsidiary (P800)	160	(at P4 = £1)	200
Sundry net assets	820		820
	980		1 020
Pololand loan (P400)	80	(at P4 = £1)	100
	900		920
Share capital	600		600
Profit and loss account	300		300
Translation reserve (£40 – £20)			20
	900		920

	Prior to translation		Translated amounts
Balance sheet of subsidiary	P		£
Sundry net assets	1 000	(at P4 = £1)	250
Share capital	800	(at P5 = £1)	160
Profit and loss account	200	(at P4 = £1)	50
Translation gain			40
	1 000		250

Activity 10.15

Prepare the consolidated balance sheet of the group by completing the outline format shown below this box. When doing this ignore the revaluation of the investment in the parent company's accounts (think of these entries as having been reversed). There is no goodwill, no minority interests, and the subsidiary's profits are all post-acquisition.

Consolidated balance sheet

£

Sundry net assets
Less Pololand loan (as restated)
_____
=======

Share capital
Profit and loss account
Translation gain:
   On translation of financial statements
   Less loss on translation of loan
_____

_____
=======

Realized profits

Questions arise with foreign currency translation over whether the various gains and losses should be treated as realized. This is relevant at the individual company level where the problem of calculating realized profits is usually concerned with establishing the amount available for distribution. A group, being an artificial entity, cannot make distributions and so the problem does not apply. The first set of notes in this section deal with exchange gains; the position is less contentious with regard to exchange losses except where the cover policy has been adopted.

Exchange gains

There is no problem on gains that arise when a transaction is settled, or when a short-term monetary item is retranslated at the accounting date. The main difficulty is with long-term monetary items, usually loans repayable in a foreign currency.

Settled transactions and short-term monetary items

Gains on settled transaction have already been reflected in cash flows and are, therefore, realized. Gains arising on retranslation of short-term monetary items at the balance sheet date can be regarded as realized (in accordance with SSAP 2) because their ultimate cash realization is reasonably certain.

Long-term monetary items

This usually relates to gains that arise when loans repayable in a foreign currency are translated to the closing rate. SSAP 20 requires these gains to be included in the profit and loss account, even though it is generally considered that such gains are unrealized. This is justified on two grounds:

- the accruals concept (if gains or losses were recognized only when the loan was settled, the accounting would be on a cash basis);
- symmetry with the way that Section 275 of the Companies Act 1985 would require the difference to be treated as realized if it were a loss (see later). In this context, SSAP 20 states that: 'gains on unsettled transactions can be determined no less objectively than exchange losses; deferring the gains whilst recognizing the losses would [. . .] be illogical'.

In order to understand the conflict and how it is resolved, it is necessary to look at three regulations in the Companies Act 1985, namely:

> **Paragraph 12 of Schedule 4** states that only profits which are realized at the balance sheet date can be included in the profit and loss account.
>
> **Section 262 (3)** defines realized profits in terms of those that 'fall to be treated as realized profits [. . .] in accordance with principles generally accepted'.
>
> **Paragraph 15 of Schedule 4** permits departure from accounting principles where there are special reasons to do so. The departure must be disclosed in notes.

With regard to the exchange gains arising on translation of long-term monetary items, SSAP 20 did not invoke the true and fair override (Section 226) – it invoked paragraph 15 of Schedule 4. The symmetrical treatment of both gains and losses was considered to be a special reason to depart from Paragraph 12. Since this results in an unrealized gain being credited to profit and loss account, details must be disclosed in the notes. This note should include the amount for the year and cumulative amounts to date.

Exchange losses

It is generally recognized that exchange losses on settled transactions, and on unsettled short-term monetary items, should be regarded as realized losses.

Section 275 of the Companies Act 1985 states that a provision of any kind mentioned in Paragraph 89 (Schedule 4) is to be treated as a realized loss. Paragraph 89 deals with provisions for any liability or loss which is likely to arise, even though the amount and timing are uncertain. It is considered that the provision for exchange losses on long-term monetary items should be treated as a realized loss in accordance with the requirements of Section 275.

Distributable profits

Dividends can only be paid out of cumulative realized profits less realized losses. Since the profit and loss account might include unrealized gains in the form of exchange gains arising on the translation of a long-term monetary item, a memorandum adjustment will be required in order to determine the amount of distributable profits. No adjustment is required for exchange losses since these are all treated as realized losses under Section 275 Companies Act 1985.

Cover/offset method

If the cover method is adopted, exchange gains and losses on long-term monetary items will be dealt with as reserve movements. This does not cause a problem with exchange gains because these are considered to be unrealized and not available for distribution. However, the arguments stated above suggest that exchange losses should be treated as realized losses. Yet if the cover method is adopted, these losses will not pass through the profit and loss account.

The ASC considered the position of exchange losses which, if they are provisions under Paragraph 89, should be treated as realized losses. The ASC thought that such treatment would not reflect the economic realities of hedging and that in the context of hedging these so-called losses on the borrowing are neither provisions nor realized losses (Technical Release 504).

Unfortunately, the legal position is not very clear and in Technical Release 504 the ASC suggested that directors should seek legal advice if the matter becomes critical to the determination of distributable profit.

Summary

The main learning points in this chapter can be summarized as follows:

- foreign currency translation is a process whereby amounts denominated in one currency are expressed in terms of another;
- the translation process can apply to transactions by an individual company and to the financial statements of an overseas entity whose results must be consolidated with those of the UK entity;

- the acquisition of non-monetary assets from an overseas entity must be translated at the temporal rate, irrespective of the amount ultimately paid for those assets;
- unsettled monetary items at the balance sheet date that are denominated in a foreign currency (usually creditors) must be retranslated at the closing rate;
- gains or losses on settlement or retranslation of short-term monetary items should be reported as a part of the profit for the year;
- the treatment of these gains or losses is justified on the grounds that they have either been reflected in the cash flows of the reporting entity or they will be reflected in cash flows shortly after the balance sheet date;
- long-term monetary items denominated in a foreign currency (usually loans payable) must be retranslated at each accounting date to the estimated amount that will be payable on maturity; the closing rate normally provides the best estimate of this amount;
- SSAP 20 justifies the treatment of long-term monetary items on the basis of the accruals concept and the symmetry of treatment between losses (which must be provided under paragraph 89 of Schedule 4 Companies Act 1985) and gains;
- gains or losses on retranslation of long-term monetary items should be taken to the profit and loss account unless the cover/offset policy has been adopted;
- the cover/offset policy is available where foreign currency borrowings have been undertaken as a hedge against the risk of exchange losses arising on a foreign equity investment;
- if the policy is adopted, the investment may be translated at the closing rate and any gains or losses taken to reserves; gains or losses on retranslating the loans may then be offset against this reserve instead of being charged to the profit and loss account;
- if the financial statements of a foreign entity are to be consolidated with those of the UK company, they must be translated into sterling by using either the temporal method or the closing rate method;
- the choice of method must be based on the relationship between the UK company and the foreign entity;
- if the operations of the foreign entity are independent (in a trading sense) of the UK company, the closing rate method is appropriate;
- where the foreign entity relies on the UK company for its operations (such as where the UK company supplies most of the goods and finance) the trade of the foreign entity can be seen as an extension of the transactions undertaken by the UK company and the temporal method is appropriate;
- gains or losses arising under the closing rate method of translation should be taken to reserves; those that arise under the temporal method are treated as part of the ordinary profit for the year;
- the justification of how these gains and losses should be reported is based on the impact that they have on the cash flows of the reporting entity;
- the cover/offset policy is available in the consolidated accounts if the foreign entity is such that it justifies the use of the closing rate method;

- gains or losses on translation of short-term monetary items at the individual company stage are considered to be realized gains;
- losses on translation of long-term monetary items at the individual company stage are considered to be realized under the provisions of S.275 Companies Act 1985;
- gains on translation of long-term monetary items at the individual company stage are, however, unrealized and although SSAP 20 requires these to be taken to the profit and loss account (based on symmetry of treatment with losses) it will be necessary to remove them from cumulative realized profits when calculating profits available for distribution;
- the impact on cumulative realized profits when losses on retranslating loans (normally treated as realized losses) have been set against reserves under the cover/offset policy is not clear.

Key to activities

Activity 10.1

1. Debit plant and machinery £10 000
   Credit French supplier £10 000

2. Debit French supplier £1 000
   Credit gain on translation £1 000

3. Debit French supplier £9 000
   Debit translation losses £2 250
   Credit bank £11 250

4. Reported as part of ordinary profit for the year

Activity 10.2

Debit loss on translation £1 250
Credit loan account £1 250

Treatment of loss: include as an item in arriving at ordinary profit or the year.

Activity 10.3

1. FF135 000 ÷ 8 = £16 875
2. £11 250
3. A gain of (£1875 − £1250) £625

Activity 10.4

The temporal basis appears to be appropriate because the Zambalian subsidiary seems to have been established as a conduit for sales by the UK company.

Activity 10.5

There should be a translation gain. The French franc has strengthened against the £1.

Activity 10.6

Net assets at beginning of year (FF450 000 ÷ 9)	£50 000
Profit for the year (FF100 000 ÷ 8)	£12 500
Net assets at end of year (FF550 000 ÷ 8)	£68 750

Activity 10.7

	£
Net assets at beginning of year	50 000
Add retained profit for year	12 500
	62 500
Net assets at end of year	68 750
Translation gain for the year	6 250

Activity 10.8

	£
Capital and reserves at beginning of year	50 000
Retained profit for year	12 500
Translation gain	6 250
	68 750
Net assets at end of year	68 750

Activity 10.9

The adjusted FF figures are as follows:

	FF
Sundry net assets (as existing accounts)	120 000
Owing to UK parent (£1900 × 10)	(19 000)
German loan (DM500 × 25)	(12 500)
	88 500
Share capital (as existing accounts)	40 000
Profit brought forward (as existing accounts)	38 000
Profit retained for year (12 000 − 1000 − 500)	10 500
	88 500

Activity 10.10

The translated balance sheet is as follows:

	£
Sundry net assets (FF120 000 ÷ 10)	12 000
Owing to UK parent (FF19 000 ÷ 10)	(1 900)
German loan (FF12 500 ÷ 10)	(1 250)
	8 850
Capital and reserves:	
At acquisition (FF52 000 ÷ 8)	6 500
Post-acquisition brought forward (FF26 000 ÷ 9)	2 889
Retained for year (FF10 500 ÷ 10)	1 050
Loss on translation	(1 589)
	8 850

Activity 10.11

The French loan will be retranslated to (FF32 000 ÷ 10)	£3 200
Retained profit for the year will be increased to	
(£12 000 + £800)	£12 800

All other items remain the same as in the existing accounts.

Activity 10.12

1.	Goodwill arising on acquisition £7200 – (80% × £6500)	£2 000
2.	Minority interests (20% × £8850)	£1 770
3.	£30 000 + £12 800 + (80% × (£2889 + £1050))	£45 951
4.	80% × £1589	£1 271

Activity 10.13

Consolidated balance sheet

	£	£
Sundry net assets (£94 900 + £12 000)		106 900
German loan	1 250	
French loan	3 200	
		4 450
		102 450
Capital and reserves:		
Share capital		50 000
Undistributable reserves		8 000
Translation losses		(1 271)
Profit and loss reserve		45 951
Goodwill written off		(2 000)
		100 680
Minority interests		1 770
		102 450

Activity 10.14

Profit and loss account

		ZK	Rate	Translated £s
Turnover		600 000	5	120 000
Cost of sales:				
Purchases	203 000		5	40 600
Less closing stock	23 000		5.75	4 000
		180 000		36 600
Gross profit		420 000		83 400
Depreciation	12 180		4.2	(2 900)
Other operating expenses	287 820		5	(57 564)
		300 000		
Profit before tax		120 000		22 936
Taxation		20 000	5	(4 000)
Profit after tax retained		100 000		18 936

Balance sheet

	ZK	Rate	Translated £s
Fixed assets	109 620	4.2	26 100
Stocks	23 000	5.75	4 000
Net monetary assets	7 380	6	1 230
	140 000		31 330
Capital and reserves:			
Share capital	40 000	4	10 000
Profit and loss account	100 000	(as above)	18 936
	140 000		
Difference on translation (gain)			2 394
			31 330

Activity 10.15

Consolidated balance sheet

		£
Sundry net assets (£820 + £250)		1 070
Less Pololand loan		100
		970
Share capital		600
Profit and loss account (£300 + £50)		350
Translation gain:		
On translation of financial statements	40	
Less loss on translation of loan	20	
		20
		970

In this example the gain on translation of the subsidiary's financial statements for consolidation is the same as the gain on the translation of the investment at the individual company stage. This will not apply in every case.

Question for self-assessment

An answer to this question is given at the end of the book.

10.1 Somco plc

Somco plc, whose registered office is in London, conducts operations and transactions both in the United Kingdom and overseas.

During the year ended 31 December 1989, the company was involved in various transactions in foreign currencies. Relevant exchange rates, except where given separately in the individual circumstances, were as scheduled below:

	Rolads (R) R = £.1	Nidars (N) N = £1	Krams (K) K = £1	Sarils (S) S = £1
At				
31 December 1988	1.6	0.52	6.9	2210.0
27 February 1989			7.0	
4 March 1989		0.65		
25 May 1989	1.5		6.7	
25 August 1989		0.50		
2 September 1989				2224.0
11 November 1989	1.8			
31 December 1989	2.0	0.54	7.5	2250.0
Average for 1989	1.7			

The transactions concerned are identified by the letters (A) to (F) and are detailed thus:

(A) Somco plc bought equipment (as a fixed asset) for 130 000 nidars on 4 March 1989 and paid for it on 25 August 1989 in sterling.

(B) On 27 February 1989 Somco plc sold goods which had cost £46 000 for £68 000 to a company whose currency was krams. The proceeds were received in krams on 25 May 1989.

(C) On 2 September 1989 Somco plc sold goods which had cost £17 000 for £24 000 to a company whose currency was sarils. The amount was outstanding at 31 December 1989 but the proceeds were received in sarils on 7 February 1990 when the exchange rate was S2306.0 = £1. The directors of Somco plc approved the final accounts on 28 March 1990.

(D) Somco plc borrowed 426 000 rolads on 25 May 1989 and repaid it in sterling on 11 November 1989.

(E) On 9 November 1988 Somco plc had acquired an equity investment at a cost of 196 000 krams when the rate of exchange was K7.3 = £1. This investment was hedged by a loan of 15 000 nidars, at an exchange rate of N0.56 = £1, obtained on the same day.

(F) Somco plc has an overseas wholesale warehouse which is financed locally in rolads and is treated as an independent branch for accounting purposes. The net investment in the branch was R638 600 on 1 January 1989 and R854 700 on 31 December 1989. During the year 1989 the branch had made a net profit of R423 400, of which R207 300 had been remitted to the UK parent company; these had realized £116 727. In accounting for the branch, Somco plc uses the average annual rate in translating profit and loss account items.

Required

For each of the above independent transactions:

(a) Calculate the gross profit or loss (if any) and the foreign currency gain or loss which would be included in the company's final accounts for year ended 31 December 1989.

(b) State how each of the gains or losses in (a) would be accounted for by Somco plc to comply with the requirements of SSAP 20 and SSAP 17, as appropriate. Give brief reasons to justify the treatment which you have adopted.

(c) Additionally, in respect of (F) only, prepare the branch current account in the UK head office ledger, in both foreign currency and sterling and, as a separate calculation, show the composition of the foreign currency retranslation difference.

All calculations should be to the nearest £1.

ACCA 2.9

Question without answer

An answer to this question is published separately in the *Teacher's Manual*.

10.2 Peach plc

Peach plc has a wholly owned German subsidiary company, Bremen GmbH, that it set up to manufacture machine tools that would satisfy European safety regulations. The directors of Peach plc look forward to a steady stream of dividends during the 1990s.

The balance sheets of Peach plc and Bremen GmbH as at 1 December 1991 and 30 November 1992 were as follows:

		Peach plc		Bremen GmbH	
		1991	1992	1991	1992
		£000	£000	000DM	000DM
Fixed assets					
Plant at cost		42 000	42 000	28 000	28 000
Aggregate depreciation		11 200	14 000	4 900	7 560
Net book value		30 800	28 000	23 100	20 440
Investment in Bremen GmbH		7 000	7 000		
Loan to Bremen GmbH		7 000	7 000		
Current assets					
Stock	Note 1	23 800	25 200	14 000	18 200
Trade debtors		13 720	14 000	13 440	14 560
Current account Bremen GmbH		1 792	2 100		
Cash		280	93 072	9 800	29 680
		39 592	134 372	37 240	62 440
Creditors due within one year					
Trade creditors		2 800	3 360	2 520	2 800
Current account Peach plc				4 480	4 200
		2 800	3 360	7 000	7 000
Net current assets		36 792	131 012	30 240	55 440
Assets less current liabilities		81 592	173 012	53 340	75 880

		Peach plc		Bremen GmbH	
		1991	1992	1991	1992
		£000	£000	000DM	000DM
Creditors due after one year:					
Borrowings	Note 2			7 000	7 778
Loan from Peach plc	Note 3			17 500	14 000
		81 592	173 012	28 840	54 102
Capital and reserves:					
Called up share capital		70 000	70 000	28 000	28 000
Profit and loss account		11 592	103 012	840	26 102
		81 592	173 012	28 840	54 102

Note 1: Peach plc sold goods to Bremen GmbH and there were unrealized profits in the stock held by Bremen GmbH as follows:

At 1 December 1991 unrealized profit was	£1 400 000
At 30 November 1992 unrealized profit was	£1 680 000

Note 2: The borrowings consist of a loan of 35 000 000 francs raised by Bremen GmbH on 1 December 1990 and is denominated in francs.

Note 3: The loan from Peach plc to Bremen GmbH is regarded by the parent company as part of its net investment and is denominated in £s.

Exchange rates have been as follows:

On date investment was made by Peach in Bremen	£1 = 4DM
On date loan was made by Peach to Bremen	£1 = 4DM
On date of purchasing the fixed assets	£1 = 3.616DM
On date of purchasing the stock held at 1.12.91	£1 = 2.701DM
At 1.12.91	£1 = 2.5DM
At 1.12.91	5 francs = 1DM
The profit and loss account balance has been translated for the 1991 consolidated accounts at	£1 = 3DM
At 30.11.92	£1 = 3DM
At 30.11.92	4.5 francs = 1DM

Required

(a) Prepare, using the closing rate method:
   (i) a consolidated balance sheet as at **1 December 1991** supported by workings showing clearly the consolidation adjustments and an analysis of the exchange difference;
   (ii) a calculation of the profit or loss on the loan denominated in francs and explain how it would be treated in the consolidated accounts for the year ended 30 November 1992;
   (iii) the consolidated reserves as at 30 November 1992 showing clearly the effect of consolidation adjustments and an analysis of the exchange difference;
   (iv) the consolidated balance sheet at **30 November 1992**.

(b) Explain how the auditor would determine whether the closing rate method is appropriate for translating the financial statements of Bremen GmbH.

ACCA Paper 13 Pilot
(Requirement (a) (iv) added)

11 ▷ Sundry regulations and topics

Objectives

After completing this chapter you should be able to:

- describe the situations in which a subsidiary is required or permitted to be excluded from consolidation and contrast the regulations in the Companies Act with those in FRS 2;
- describe the key feature of regulations that define subsidiaries and explain what is meant by a quasi-subsidiary;
- explain why provisions for future losses became a controversial issue in the fair value exercise and apply the rules in FRS 7 regarding these provisions;
- calculate fair values on an acquisition by applying the rules in FRS 7;
- prepare consolidated accounts when the subsidiary's share capital includes preference shares and apply the rules in FRS 4 on balance sheet presentation.

Introduction

There are a number of important regulations and topics that were excluded from previous chapters because they would have added little to the task of learning how to prepare group accounts. The topics concerned can be summarized as follows:

- exclusion of subsidiaries from consolidation;
- exemptions from the requirement to prepare group accounts;
- quasi-subsidiaries;
- fair values in acquisition accounting;
- preference shares in a subsidiary.

They are all important aspects of group accounts. Most of them are discussion topics but there are some, such as fair values on acquisition and preference shares in a subsidiary, that do have an impact on the quantitative aspect of preparing group accounts. The applicable accounting standards are FRSs 2, 4, 5 and 7 but in view of the variety of topics being covered in this chapter, there is no appendix with extracts from the regulations.

Exclusions and exemptions

There are provisions in the Companies Act 1985 that allow subsidiaries to be excluded from consolidation when certain conditions apply. There are also provisions that exempt companies from the requirement to prepare consolidated accounts. Both sets of provisions are covered in FRS 2 but with a different emphasis regarding the exclusion of subsidiaries from consolidation.

Exclusion of subsidiaries from consolidation

The Companies Act 1985 describes four situations where it is permissible to exclude a subsidiary from the consolidated accounts, and one case where the subsidiary must be excluded. FRS 2 requires (rather than permits) that the subsidiary should be excluded in two cases where exclusion under the Companies Act is permissive. The criterion under which subsidiaries may (or must) be excluded according to the Companies Act, and the way that FRS 2 affects each of these, is shown in the following summary. This will have more meaning after studying the details under each heading.

Companies Act 1985	FRS 2
Required exclusion:	
1. Different activities	Exclusion unlikely to apply
Permissive exclusions	
2. Severe long-term restrictions	Must be excluded
3. Investment acquired for resale	Must be excluded. Treat as current asset
4. Delay/expense in obtaining information	Not condoned
5. Subsidiary is immaterial in aggregate	Standards do not apply to immaterial items

The ASB took the view that Criterion 4 (disproportionate expense or undue delay in obtaining information about a subsidiary) was not an appropriate reason for excluding that subsidiary from consolidation and FRS 2 does not allow subsidiaries to be excluded on these grounds. The concept of materiality (Criterion 5) applies to all accounting standards and so there is no conflict with the Companies Act if an immaterial subsidiary is excluded from consolidation. The situations that require discussion are those identified under items 1 to 3 in the above summary.

Different activities

Although FRS 2 adopts the same approach as the Companies Act 1985, it does make it clear that 'cases of this sort are so exceptional that it would be misleading to link them in general to any particular contrast of activities' (para. 78).

The invoking provision in the Companies Act states that subsidiaries should be excluded 'where the activities of one or more subsidiary undertakings are so different from those of other undertakings [. . .] that their inclusion would be incompatible with the obligation to give a true and fair view' (Section 229).

The Act does, however, state that exclusion on the grounds of different activities does not apply 'merely because some of the undertakings are industrial, some commercial and some provide services, or because they carry on industrial or commercial activities involving different products or provide difference services'.

FRS 2 takes the view that the different activities of the various undertakings are best shown by segmental information (SSAP 25) rather than by exclusion. This is in keeping with an international trend towards full consolidation of all subsidiaries with disclosure of segmental results as supplementary information.

Different activities in most organizations tend to complement each other and in order to assess overall performance, the results of each activity should be combined. For example, many department stores provide credit card facilities operated through the medium of a finance subsidiary. To some extent the sales turnover and interest earned on the provision of credit card facilities are inter-related. To exclude the results of the subsidiary on the grounds that financing activities are different to trading activities is misleading when assessing the overall performance of the group.

In the past, it was often the separation of financing and trading activities that resulted in some subsidiaries being excluded from consolidation. For example, Marks & Spencer plc excluded finance subsidiaries from consolidation up to 31 March 1990. In subsequent accounts the results of the finance subsidiaries have been consolidated. If you refer to the published accounts for 1993 you will find that turnover includes the amount of interest earned from financial activities. Segmental analysis is provided in notes to the accounts in accordance with SSAP 25.

If a subsidiary is excluded on the grounds of different activities (even though it is difficult to imagine a situation where this applies) both FRS 2 and the Companies Act require the subsidiary to be recorded in the group accounts by using the equity method of accounting.

Severe long-term restrictions

The Companies Act permits a subsidiary to be excluded from consolidation where 'severe long-term restrictions substantially hinder the exercise of the rights of the parent company over the assets or management of that under-taking' (Section 229). FRS 2 insists that the subsidiary is excluded if this condition applies. The reasoning in FRS 2 for this is that the requirement to consolidate the results of another company rests on whether the parent company is able to control that company. If control has been lost or severely restricted, the results of the subsidiary should not be consolidated.

There are two common situations in which this might apply, namely:

- where a subsidiary is subject to an insolvency procedure and control over that company has passed to an appropriate official such as a receiver or liquidator;
- when a subsidiary operates in a foreign country and the political situation is such that restrictions are placed on the ability of that subsidiary to remit profits to the UK, or freedom to exercise control over the subsidiary is limited.

Activity 11.1

A subsidiary company in Pogolivia has been unable to remit profits to its UK parent for the last two years due to exchange control restrictions imposed by the government. As a result, the subsidiary has accumulated large cash resources which, if they were translated into sterling. would amount to £2 000 000.

State why it would be misleading to shareholders in the UK parent company for the results of the Pogoland subsidiary to be consolidated in the group accounts.

The requirement in FRS 2 for subsidiaries excluded on the grounds of severe long-term restrictions is that the subsidiary must be recorded in the group accounts at its equity value at the time the restrictions came into force. This is a frozen value and should not be adjusted by taking account of the subsidiary's subsequent results so long as the restrictions remain in force. In some cases it might be necessary to make a provision for a permanent diminution in value.

If the restrictions should subsequently be removed, the results of the subsidiary for the excluded period should be included as a separate item in the profit and loss account for the year in which control is resumed. This should also include the release of any provisions for loss in value that are no longer required.

Investment acquired for resale

This exclusion does not apply where the parent company intends to sell a subsidiary that had previously been consolidated in the group accounts. It applies only when a group acquires a subsidiary with the intention of selling it shortly after acquisition. The Companies Act refers to an investment held exclusively with a view to subsequent resale but makes it clear that the exclusion is not justified if the parent company has previously consolidated the results of the subsidiary.

Apart from exploiting an investment opportunity (buying and selling a company) the most likely situation where this exclusion will apply is when the parent company has acquired a subsidiary as a result of enforcing a loan security. FRS 2 differs from the Companies Act in that it requires (rather than permits) subsidiaries acquired with the intention of resale to be excluded from consolidation. The investment should be presented in the group accounts under current assets at the lower of cost and net realizable value.

Exemption from requirements to produce group accounts

The two most important situations where a group is exempt from the requirement to produce group accounts are as follows:

- where the group is classified as a small or medium-sized group;
- where the parent company is a subsidiary of another company.

A group is classified as small or medium-sized if two out of three specified limits are not exceeded. The limits specified are aggregate turnover, balance sheet totals, and number of employees. Since the limits for these items can be changed by Statutory Instrument, and have been changed from time to time, there is little point in stating the limits at the time of writing this book. Readers should refer to the latest regulations. Although the Companies Act specifies limits for both small and medium-sized groups, the figures for small groups are irrelevant for the purposes of exemption since the exemption applies to all amounts up to the limits imposed for medium-sized groups. Exemption is not available to groups that include public companies, banking institutions and insurance companies.

If a parent company is itself a subsidiary of another company it is exempt from the requirement to produce consolidated accounts. The accounting practices for this type of situation were discussed in Chapter 8. Since the introduction of the Companies Act 1989 (and FRS 2) it is no longer necessary for the intermediate parent to be wholly owned for this exemption to apply. If there are minority shareholders in the intermediate parent, there are provisions in the Companies Act that give them the right to request their company to prepare consolidated accounts. The exemption can be affected by the country in which the companies are incorporated but this aspect is outside the scope of subjects covered by this book.

Subsidiaries and quasi-subsidiaries

Throughout most of this book we have assumed that a subsidiary is a company where the majority of its ordinary shares are owned by the parent company. Although this was adequate enough when learning how to prepare the accounts, it is by no means adequate when studying the legal definition of a subsidiary.

In the first place, the Companies Act refers to a majority of the voting rights rather than a majority of ordinary shares. This is in keeping with all of the legal definitions that are based on the ability of one company to control another. Owning a majority of the voting rights in another company will certainly give the owner the power to control that company but there can be different types of ordinary share and the voting rights are likely to differ for each type of share. It is the ownership of voting rights that needs to be considered in these cases.

Secondly, the Companies Act 1989 completely changed the way that subsidiaries were defined by former legislation. To some extent the new definitions can be seen as anti-avoidance provisions and some were needed in order to harmonize practices with other EC countries. Before these regulations were introduced, some companies had found ways of conducting a part of their activities through the medium of a separate entity that they could control but which escaped being classed as subsidiary under the law. The new definitions attempt to cover various forms of control other than that which arises through the holding of a majority of the voting rights.

But the problem with legal definitions is that the words are cardinal. If someone can find a way of constructing a separate entity that falls outside of the words used to describe a subsidiary, it does not have to be consolidated despite the intentions of those who drafted the legislation and despite the commercial reality of the relationship that exists. This kind of avoidance is not restricted to separate entities that escape being consolidated; it has been fair game for a variety of creative accounting devices. In many cases these avoidance tactics have been aimed at keeping loss-making activities out of the group accounts, and in ensuring that certain types of loan finance are left out of the balance sheet.

In order to combat this kind of avoidance, the ASB issued an accounting standard in April 1994 known as *FRS 5: Reporting the substance of transactions*. This standard takes a conceptual approach by defining assets and liabilities and by linking transactions with the effect that they have on the assets and liabilities of the reporting entity. In the case of subsidiaries it defines what is known as a quasi-subsidiary in the following way:

> A quasi-subsidiary of a reporting entity is a company, trust, partnership or other vehicle that, although not fulfilling the definition of a subsidiary, is directly or indirectly controlled by the reporting entity and gives rise to benefits for that entity that are in substance no different from those that would arise were the vehicle a subsidiary (paragraph 7).

The standard then requires (in para. 15) that 'where the entity has a quasi-subsidiary, the substance of the transactions entered into by the quasi-subsidiary should be reported in the consolidated financial statements'.

As with the provisions in the Companies Act, the distinctive feature that needs to be considered is whether one entity is controlled by another. FRS 5 defines control of another entity as: 'the ability to direct the financial and operating policies of that entity with a view to gaining economic benefits from its activities'. The explanatory notes state that control can include the ability to restrict others from directing major policies (para. 97). Although FRS 5 has extended the legal provisions on the type of entity that must be consolidated, this is justified on the grounds of the special circumstances in the 'true and fair override' contained in Section 227(6) of the Companies Act 1985.

FRS 5 also considers quasi-subsidiaries in the context of the various circumstances in which a subsidiary can (or must) be excluded from consolidation, as discussed in pp. 276–279 above. The standard states that it is appropriate to exclude a quasi-subsidiary from consolidation in one situation only, namely where the quasi-subsidiary is held exclusively with a view to resale and its results had not previously been consolidated with those of the reporting entity (para. 101).

Fair values in acquisition accounting (FRS 7)

Provisions for future losses

FRS 7 was published in September 1994 and although it contains a number of detailed rules on the way that fair values should be determined for particular types of asset, its main impact on accounting practices is likely to be the way that reorganization costs are dealt with. This particular area was open to abuse before FRS 7 and allowed companies to make provisions for future losses and reorganization costs as a part of the fair value exercise on acquisition. This provided a convenient way of shielding post-acquisition profits from the impact of these costs.

A previous attempt to deal with the problem was a revision to SSAP 22 (*Accounting for goodwill*) in 1989. This required disclosure of information on the allocation of fair values over the various types of asset and liability in the acquired entity. Amounts provided for future trading losses and other provisions had to be specified. This, however, was merely a requirement to disclose the provisions – it did not prevent companies from making them. This kind of abuse is no longer possible under the rules in FRS 7: all post-acquisition costs and losses must be dealt with as post-acquisition items. The rules in FRS 7 on this are quite clearly summarized in one of the opening paragraphs to the standard which reads as follows:

> The liabilities of the acquired entity should not include provisions for future operating losses. Changes in the assets and liabilities resulting from the acquirer's intentions or from events after the acquisition should be dealt with as post-acquisition items. Similarly, costs of reorganization and integrating the business acquired, whether they relate to the acquired entity or the acquiring group, should be dealt was as post-acquisition costs and do not affect the fair values at the date of acquisition.

Fair values of specific items

The specific rules in FRS 7 regarding fair values of different types of asset and liability will not have such a significant impact on accounting practices as the rules on provisions. To a large extent the rules can be seen as a codification of best practices. Some areas are left open to doubt; the most troublesome area is concerned with identifiable intangibles such as trade names and brand names. It is likely that we shall have to wait for the ASB to publish a new accounting standard on the subject of goodwill before this problem is resolved. At the moment there is nothing to prevent assets such as brand names from being treated as an identifiable asset and excluded from the amount treated as goodwill. The ASB's discussion paper on this subject proposes that all intangible assets on an acquisition should be included with the amount classified as goodwill.

The rules on fair values for specific items can be summarized as follows:

1. **Fair value** is defined as: 'the amount at which an asset or liability could be exchanged in an arm's length transaction between informed and willing parties, other than in a forced or liquidation sale'. This is similar to the original definition in SSAP 22 (which it replaces) but with some additional clauses.

2. **Tangible fixed assets**. Fair value should be based on market value if assets similar in type and condition are bought and sold on the open market. In other cases, depreciated replacement cost can be used. The fair value should not exceed the 'recoverable amount' which is defined as being the lower of two amounts, namely:

    -   net realizable value;
    -   value in use, being the present value of future cash flows obtained by using the asset and those from the ultimate disposal of the asset.

3. **Identifiable intangible assets**. Fair value should be based on replacement cost, which is normally the estimated market value.

4. **Stocks and work-in-progress**. Normal trading stocks should be based on the lower of replacement cost and net realizable value. Replacement cost must be considered from the viewpoint of the acquired entity. Commodity stocks should be valued at current market price.

5. **Quoted investments**. These should be valued at market price, adjusted if necessary to reflect special factors such as the size of the holding.

6. **Monetary assets and liabilities**. In general terms these must be valued at the amounts expected to be received or paid.

7. **Contingencies**. These items are not normally included as assets or liabilities in the balance sheet except where SSAP 18 requires a contingent loss to be accrued. They must, however, be measured and included as assets or liabilities in the fair value exercise required by FRS 7. Reasonable estimates of expected outcomes may be used.

8. **Surpluses and deficiencies in pension schemes**. The allocation of fair values should include an asset in respect of a surplus in a funded scheme and a liability in respect of a deficiency. These assets and liabilities are a substitution for any existing prepayments and provisions that have been made under the requirements of SSAP 24. The effect of this is similar to contingencies on an acquisition. In both cases the assets or liabilities concerned are not normally recognized in financial statements but they must be included as a part of the fair value exercise. For example, SSAP 24 does not allow a surplus to be recognized as an asset but requires it to be recognized systematically over the average remaining service lives of employees. This involves

setting up a provision in the year (or years) when the company's contributions are reduced and releasing this to profit and loss account when normal contributions are resumed.

9. **Deferred tax**. Deferred assets and liabilities for taxation must be recognized by considering the enlarged group as a whole.

Period of hindsight

FRS 7 requires all investigations and measurements to be completed, if possible, by the date on which the first set of post-acquisition accounts is approved by the directors. If it has not been possible to do so, provisional valuations should be made. These should then be amended, if necessary, in the next financial statements with a corresponding adjustment to goodwill.

Acquisition cost

The cost of the acquisition is the amount of cash paid together with the fair value of any other consideration given by the acquirer. Certain incremental costs such as fees paid to merchant banks and accountants should be included in the cost of the acquisition but any internal costs of the acquirer that have been allocated to the acquisition must be charged to the profit and loss account.

| Preference shares in a subsidiary |

Purchasing preference shares in a subsidiary

Since preference shares do not normally carry any voting rights it would be unusual to find a group where the parent company had purchased any of the preference shares of its subsidiary under the terms of the acquisition. There is no doubt that this could happen but it probably occurs more in examination questions than it does in real life. The accounting issues involved are relatively straightforward.

Consolidation differences in so far as they concern the preference shares will simply be the difference between the purchase cost and the nominal value of the shares acquired. But there is no need for this to be calculated separately; the goodwill calculation can be based on the combined cost of the ordinary shares and the preference shares, as in the following illustration:

Details
Parent Ltd acquired 80% of the ordinary shares and 50% of the preference shares in Sub Ltd. The capital and reserves of Sub Ltd at the date of acquisition were as follows:

	£
Ordinary share capital	500 000
Fair value revaluation reserve	40 000
Profit and loss reserve	60 000
	600 000
Preference shares	50 000
	650 000

The total purchase cost of the ordinary shares was £500 000 and the cost of the preference shares was £20 000.

Goodwill calculation

	£	£
Cost of investments (£500 000 + £20 000)		520 000
Adjusted capital and reserves at acquisition:		
As above	650 000	
Less minority interests:		
20% × £600 000	(120 000)	
50% × £50 000	(25 000)	
		505 000
Goodwill		15 000

If you care to analyse this total you will find that positive goodwill of £20 000 can be attributed to the acquisition of ordinary shares and the preference shares were acquired at an amount that was £5000 less than their nominal value. No purpose is served, however, in making this analysis since the total amount of goodwill to be recorded and dealt with in the group accounts for this acquisition is £15 000.

The way in which the minority interests in the above example should be presented in the group balance sheet has been regulated by *FRS 4: Accounting for capital instruments*. This aspect is dealt with in a moment.

A little care is needed when preparing the profit and loss account of a subsidiary which has preference shares. To the extent that these shares are owned by minority interests, there will be dividends paid to shareholders outside of the group. The amount paid is normally included in the amount shown as minority interests in the profit and loss account. The interests of ordinary shareholders in the profits of their company for the year must be based on the subsidiary's profit after deducting preference dividends.

Balance sheet presentation (FRS 4)

The main impact of FRS 4 is in connection with the way that borrowing costs are dealt with, particularly on instruments such as deep discounted bonds and zero interest bonds. These aspects are not subjects for a book that is primarily concerned with the principles of preparing group accounts. The provisions in FRS 4 that are relevant are those that are concerned with presentation in the balance sheet, particularly presentation of minority interests.

The rules on balance sheet presentation are fairly straightforward and merely require the following:

- shareholders' funds to be analysed between equity and non-equity interests;
- minority interests to be analysed in a similar way;
- liabilities to be analysed between convertible and non-convertible debt.

We can ignore the third item and concentrate on the first two. The definition of non-equity shares is quite widely drawn. The intention is that only true 'ordinary shares' with a residual interest in the company should be classed as equity. Preference shares (as has always been the case) are non-equity shares.

Having adopted an activity-based learning approach through most of the book, we will end with a simple activity relating to the balance sheet presentation of minority interests. Good luck with your future studies, exams and professional development.

Activity 11.2

The balance sheet of a subsidiary in which the parent company has an 80% interest but does not own any of the preference shares has the following capital and reserves:

	£
Ordinary shares of £1.00 each	200 000
Revaluation reserve	10 000
Profit and loss account	400 000
	610 000
7% preference shares of £1.00 each	50 000
	660 000

Show how the figure for minority interests should be presented in the consolidated balance sheet.

Summary

The topics covered in this chapter are quite broad and to some extent the relevant text has been composed in summary form. The key learning points relate to the following:

- both the Companies Act and FRS 2 contain provisions that permit or require certain types of subsidiary to be excluded from the consolidation;
- the Companies Act has one required exclusion and four permitted exclusions;
- FRS 2 accepts the required exclusion (different activities) but makes it clear that the exclusion is unlikely to apply and the best interests of users are served by consolidating different activities and publishing segmental information;

- FRS 2 requires, rather than permits, exclusion on the grounds of severe long-term restrictions and in the case of an investment that was acquired for resale;
- FRS 2 does not consider the delay and expense in obtaining information as an appropriate reason for excluding the subsidiary;
- small and medium-sized companies are exempt from the requirement to produce consolidated accounts, as is an intermediate parent unless the rules of the country in which it is incorporated require such accounts to be prepared or the minority interests (if any) serve notice on the company requesting the accounts to be prepared;
- the key feature in the regulations regarding the definition of a subsidiary is based on control; in most cases control rests on owning the majority of voting power;
- FRS 5 extends the legal definitions of a subsidiary to include quasi-subsidiaries;
- FRS 7 has stopped the practice of treating provisions for future costs and losses as a part of the fair value exercise; all such items must be treated as post-acquisition costs;
- FRS 7 contains detailed rules on the fair values to be attributed to specific classes of asset and liability, including contingencies and pension fund surpluses and deficits;
- FRS 4 requires minority interests to be analysed between equity interests and non-equity interests such as preference shares.

Key to activities

Activity 11.1

The group accounts would give a misleading picture of the cash resources since they include a large amount of cash over which the parent company has no control.

Activity 11.2

Minority interests

	£
Equity interests (20% × £610 000)	122 000
Non-equity interests	50 000
	172 000

Questions

Questions for self-assessment

Answers to self-assessment questions are given at the end of the book.

11.1 FRS 7 – Fair values in acquisition accounting

The following shows the allocation of fair values and the calculation of goodwill following a recent acquisition of a new subsidiary by a group:

	£	£
Tangible fixed assets:		
at market value	500 000	
at depreciated replacement cost	100 000	
		600 000
Identifiable intangible assets		
Brand name at estimated market value		100 000
Stocks and work in progress at		
the lower of cost and net realizable value where cost		
is determined on a last in first out (LIFO) basis		200 000
Quoted investments at market price		90 000
Net monetary assets		
at book values less appropriate provisions		40 000
Contingencies:		
Contingent gain (expected to be recovered on court		
case)		50 000
Contingent loss (uncalled amounts on shares)		(10 000)
Pension fund surplus		80 000
Deferred tax (as adjusted to recognise enlarged group)		(50 000)
Provision for future reorganization costs		(100 000)
		1 000 000
Acquisition cost:		
Cash paid	700 000	
Nominal value of shares issued	300 000	
Acquisition costs:		
Agency and consultancy fees	60 000	
Company's administration costs	40 000	
		1 100 000
Goodwill		100 000

Required

The above calculation contains four (deliberate) instances where the principles applied are in contravention of the rules in FRS 7. Identify these four instances and describe why they contravene the rules in FRS 7.

11.2 Scotty plc

You are the group accountant of Scotty plc and need to make adjustments to the draft accounts for the year ended 30 June 19X9 to reflect the acquisition of a subsidiary. Information in respect of the new subsidiary is as follows:

1. On 1 October 19X8, Scotty plc acquired a 90% interest in Sulu Inc, a US corporation. The consideration of £2 450 000 comprised £1 500 000 satisfied by the issue of 5 000 000 25p ordinary shares in Scotty plc, and cash of £950 000 payable by two instalments. £750 000 cash was paid at completion and £200 000 is payable on 1 October 19X9.
2. Based on the financial statements of Sulu Inc at 30 September 19X8 the fair value of net identifiable assets was $4 370 000 before deducting costs totalling $380 000 in respect of redundancies which were identified at acquisition and subsequently paid.
3. At a board meeting to approve the acquisition, the directors of Scotty plc were informed that an investment in plant machinery would be required by Sulu Inc of $300 000 in the period to 30 June 19X9.
4. Professional fees for advice in respect of the acquisition amounted to £30 000 and your finance director has estimated that the time and expenses incurred by the directors of Scotty plc in negotiating and completing the deal amounted to £20 000.
5. Sulu Inc valued stocks on the LIFO (last in first out) method in its financial statements. On 30 September 19X8 these stocks would have been $150 000 greater if valued on the FIFO method consistent with that used by Scotty plc.
6. The exchange rate at 1 October 19X8 was £1 = $1.8.
7. Scotty plc amortizes goodwill arising on consolidation over a three year period.

Required

(a) Calculate the fair value of Sulu Inc at 1 October 19X8 giving justifications for your treatment of:

   (i)   redundancy costs
   (ii)   investment in plant and machinery
   (iii) professional fees and directors' time and expenses
   (iv)   stock

(b) Calculate the goodwill arising in the consolidated balance sheet of Scotty plc that would be carried forward at 30 June 19X9.

ICAEW PE II (part)

Question without answer

An answer to this question is published separately in the *Teacher's Manual*.

11.3 Leopard plc

During 1995, Leopard plc made two significant investments:
1. 90% of the issued share capital of Winter Ltd was acquired in two stages as follows:

   On 1 January 1995, 60% acquired for £2m being £1m in cash and £1m by way of the issue of 400 000 10p ordinary shares at market value (£2.50 each).

   On 1 July 1995, 30% acquired for £1.2m being £600 000 in cash and £600 000 by way of the issue of 200 000 10p ordinary shares at market value (£3.00 each).

   In taking the decision to invest in Winter Ltd the board of Leopard plc were aware that heavy trading losses were envisaged for Winter Ltd for some months. The agreed budget for Winter Ltd for the period 1 January 1995 to 30 September 1995, drawn up when take-over negotiations were under way, was for losses after tax of some £500 000. In the event, losses have been worse than expected, as demonstrated by the summary balance sheets for Winter Ltd as follows:

	1.1.95 £000	1.7.95 £000	30.9.95 £000
Fixed assets	2100	2200	2250
Net current assets/(liabilities)	790	70	(190)
Long-term creditors	(190)	(170)	(160)
Deferred tax	(200)	(200)	(200)
	2500	1900	1700
Share capital	300	300	300
Profit and loss account	2200	1600	1400
	2500	1900	1700

The only movements on the profit and loss account in the period were in respect of post-tax losses. The fair values of the identifiable assets and liabilities of Winter Ltd are approximately equal to their book values shown above.

2. On 1 April 1995, Leopard plc put fixed assets it already owned and have a book value (which was approximately equal to market value) of £500 000, together with 'know-how' and £100 000 cash, into a newly formed joint venture company, Lawrie Ltd, in return for 25% of the equity share capital in Lawrie Ltd. At 1 April 1995, the net assets of Lawrie Ltd were £2.6m. Because of the other shareholdings in Lawrie Ltd, Leopard plc is not able to exercise a dominant influence over Lawrie Ltd.

    Audited management accounts for Lawrie Ltd for the period 1 April 1995 to 30 September 1995 show profit before taxation of £450 000. No dividends have been paid or declared and there have been no changes in share capital since 1 April 1995.

Before accounting for the investments in Winter Ltd and Lawrie Ltd, the draft accounts of Leopard plc show that earnings available for ordinary shareholders in year ended 30 September 1995 were £2 080 000 and in year ending 30 September 1994 these earnings were £1 830 000. Throughout both years the number of ordinary shares in issue prior to the issue of shares on the acquisition of Winter Ltd was 10 000 000.

The directors of Leopard plc are anxious regarding the impact of the losses being sustained by Winter Ltd on the group's earnings per share. They see it as very important that the group accounts should show an improvement in earnings per share and have suggested to you, the group accountant, that it might be possible to deal with this problem in either of two ways, as follows:

1. Exclude the accounts of Winter Ltd on the grounds of different activities. The main activities of Leopard plc are in the manufacture of household furniture whereas the activities of Winter Ltd are mainly concerned with double glazing.
2. Since the price paid for the acquisition of Winter Ltd on 1 January 1995 took into account the projected loss of £500 000, this amount should be deducted from the fair values of the identifiable net assets and treated as a provision for future losses. This provision can then be used to write off all but £300 000 of the post-acquisition losses. The directors mentioned that this practice is specifically authorized by paragraph 14 of SSAP 22.

The directors have indicated that they are unsure regarding the impact on earnings per share of any goodwill arising from the acquisitions.

Required

Draft a memorandum to the directors dealing with the following:

(a) Their suggestions for the treatment of the acquisition of Winter Ltd.

(b) The calculation of goodwill arising on the acquisition of Winter Ltd, suggesting how this could be dealt with in the group accounts bearing in mind the directors wish to keep earnings per share as high as possible.

(c) A description and calculation to show how the investment in Lawrie Ltd must be dealt with in the group accounts.

(d) A calculation of earnings per share for years ending 30 September 1994 and 30 September 1995 after taking account of your recommendations on the treatment of Winter Ltd and Lawrie Ltd.

Assume a rate of corporation tax of 35%.

ICAEW PE II (revised and modified)

Answers to self-assessment questions

Chapter 1

1.1 Group structures

(a) The figures in the column headed 'Company' relate to the parent company; Imperial Chemical Industries plc. This company is a separate legal entity and its assets include investments in subsidiary companies with a carrying value of £5 800m. Figures for the 'Group' are a consolidation of the accounts of the parent company and its subsidiaries. Although the group has no separate legal status, it is treated as a single economic entity for accounting purposes. As a single economic entity, it cannot own investments in itself.

The basic consolidation process involves replacing the parent company's investments in subsidiaries with the underlying assets and liabilities of those subsidiaries. These assets and liabilities are combined with similar classes of assets and liabilities in the parent company's accounts. This provides the members of the parent company with more useful information than would be available from the separate accounts of their own company.

(b) The two points could be:

(1) The carrying values of investments in associated undertakings owned by the parent company are based on the amounts paid for those investments. In the group balance sheet the carrying value of these investments is based on their equity value. Equity values are calculated by taking a proportion of the net assets of the associated undertaking according to the proportion of equity shares owned. If an associated undertaking has earned and retained profits since the investment in it was made, the equity value of that investment will be higher than its cost.

(2) It could be that other companies in the group (the subsidiaries) own shares in associated undertakings. These are investments by the group in companies outside of the group and so they must also be presented in the group accounts at their equity value.

(c) Minority interests are shareholders in a subsidiary other than the parent company. A parent company and subsidiary relationship exists when one company (the parent) is able to exercise control over another company (the subsidiary). In the majority of cases, the ability to exercise control of another company is derived from the ownership of an investment that provides the owner with a majority (more than 50%) of the voting rights in that other company. If a parent company does not own the entire share capital of a subsidiary, there will be shareholders in that subsidiary other than the parent company. These shareholders are called minority interests.

1.2 Significant investments

The type of investment mentioned in the question is a substantial asset and yet it will simply be reported in the balance sheet of the investor at original cost. This does not provide the user of the investor's accounts with any information regarding the financial affairs of the investee. If the investment had been in an associated undertaking or a subsidiary, a user of the investor's accounts receives some information about the financial affairs of the investee company through the equity accounting or consolidation process.

Since no information regarding the financial affairs of the investee company is provided, the law ensures that the investor company publishes sufficient information in its annual report to enable a user to trace a copy of the financial statements of the investee company. In most cases these financial statements can be obtained from some kind of central registry, such as the Registrar of Companies in England and Wales. Most countries have similar facilities, hence the requirement to publish the country of incorporation.

1.3 Shareholder voting control

(a) The position regarding voting rights owned by Jasmin (Holdings) plc can be summarized as follows:

	Issued shares	Voting rights	%	Jasmin's proportion shares	votes
A Ordinary	6 000 000	6 000 000	80%	4 800 000	4 800 000
B Ordinary	4 000 000	8 000 000	10%	400 000	800 000
	10 000 000	14 000 000		5 200 000	5 600 000

The proportion of voting rights owned by Jasmin is, therefore, (5 600 000/ 14 000 000) 40% and on this basis Fortran plc should not be treated as a subsidiary, even though Jasmin owns 52% of Fortran's share capital.

(b) On the basis of voting control it appears that Jasmin's investment in Fortran plc should be treated as an associated undertaking and reported in the group accounts at its equity value.

Chapter 2

2.1 Kilgour group

Workings:

1. *Goodwill*

	Lynn Ltd £000	£000	Norr Ltd £000	£000
Cost of investment		1000		500
Capital and reserves				
Share capital	800		300	
Revenue reserves	400		150	

	Lynn Ltd		Norr Ltd	
	£000	£000	£000	£000
	1200		450	
Less minority interests	360		180	
		840		270
Goodwill at acquisition		160		230
Amortization		(4/10) 64		(1/10) 23
		96		207

2. Consolidated reserves

	£000
Kilgour	3700
Lynn Ltd 70% × (£200 − £400) *date*	(140)
Norr Ltd 60% × (£160 − £190)	(30)
Goodwill amortized (£64 + £23)	(87)
	3443

Consolidated balance sheet at 30 June 1994

	£000	£000
Fixed assets		
Intangible		
Goodwill (£96 + £207)		303
Tangible (per question)		7 700
		8 003
Current assets	14 400	
Current liabilities	6 500	
		7 900
		15 903
Capital and reserves		
Called up share capital		12 000
Revenue reserves		3 443
		15 443
Minority interests (30% × £1 000) + (40% × £400)		460
		15 903

2.2 Pagg group

Workings

1. Goodwill

	Ragg Ltd		Tagg Ltd	
	£000	£000	£000	£000
Cost of investment		3 000		1 000
Capital and reserves				
Share capital	1 000		500	
Profit and loss account	600		100	
	1 600		600	
Minority interests	(20%) 320		(40%) 240	
		1 280		360
Goodwill on acquisition		1 720		640
Amortized	(5/20)	430	(1/20)	32
		1 290		608

2. Consolidated profit and loss account

	£000
Pagg plc	1000
Ragg Ltd 80% × (£200 − £600)	(320)
Tagg Ltd 60% × (£150 − £100)	30
Goodwill amortized (£430 + £32)	(462)
Unrealized profit on stock 60% × 1/6 × £60	(6)
	242

3. Minority interests

	£000
Ragg Ltd 20% × £1200	240
Tagg Ltd 40% × (£650 − £10)	256
	496

Note on unrealized profit. The profit of £10 000 was recorded by Tagg Ltd. The effect of workings 2 and 3 is to charge the parent company's interest with 60% of the profit and to charge the remaining 40% to Tagg's minority interests – in accordance with FRS 2.

4. Cancellation of inter-company balances

	Pagg Ltd £000	Ragg Ltd £000	Tagg Ltd £000	Total £000
Debtors	3 000	200	300	
Less inter-company		200	35	
	3 000	—	265	3 265

	Pagg Ltd £000	Ragg Ltd £000	Tagg Ltd £000	Total £000
Creditors	4 000	270	400	
Less inter-company	200	35		
	3 800	235	400	4 435

Consolidated balance sheet at 31 March 1990

	£000	£000
Fixed assets		
Intangible – Goodwill (£1 290 + £608)		1 898
Tangible		3 500
		5 398
Current assets		
Stocks (£1 300 + £350 + £100 – £10)	1 740	
Debtors (Working 4)	3 265	
Cash	270	
	5 275	
Current liabilities		
Creditors (Working 4)	4 435	
		840
		6 238
Capital and reserves		
Called up share capital		5 500
Profit and loss account (Working 2)		242
		5 742
Minority interests (Working 3)		496
		6 238

Chapter 3

3.1 Primer

Consolidated balance sheet at 31 December 19X1

	£	£	£
Fixed assets			
Tangible (£30 000 + £80 000 + £3 000 – £300)			112 700
Investments:			
Interest in associated undertakings (25% × £70 000)			17 500
			130 200
Current assets			
As per question (£34 000 + £18 000 – £500)		51 500	
Dividend receivable from Ass Ltd (25% × £4 000)		1 000	
		52 500	

	£	£	£
Current liabilities			
Creditors (£10 000 + £3 000)	13 000		
Proposed dividends:			
Parent Ltd's shareholders	16 000		
Minority interests (40% × £5 000)	2 000		
		31 000	
			21 500
			151 700
Capital and reserves			
Called up share capital			80 000
Share premium			8 000
Profit and loss account (Working 2)			26 820
			114 820
Minority interests 40% × (£90 000 + £3 000 − £300 − £500)			36 880
			151 700

Workings

1. Goodwill
(a) On acquisition of Sub Ltd

	£	£
Cost of investment		50 000
Adjusted capital and reserves:		
Share capital	50 000	
Share premium	2 000	
Profit and loss account	20 000	
Revaluation adjustment	3 000	
	75 000	
Minority interests (40%)	30 000	
		45 000
		5 000
(b) On acquisition of Ass Ltd		
Cost of investment		12 000
Share of net assets 25% × (£40 000 + £4 000)		11 000
		1 000

2. Consolidated profit and loss account

	£
Hold Ltd:	
Balance per question	12 000
Dividend receivable from Sub Ltd (60% × £5 000)	3 000
Dividend receivable from Ass Ltd (25% × £4 000)	1 000
	16 000

	£
Sub Ltd 60% × (£38 000 − £20 000 − £300 − £500)	10 320
Ass Ltd 25% × (£30 000 − £4 000)	6 500
	32 820
Goodwill written off (£5 000 + £1 000)	6 000
	26 820

3.2 Court group

Consolidated profit and loss account for year ended 31 December 1991

	£000
Turnover	1410
Costs	920
Profit before taxation	490
Taxation	190
Profit after taxation	300
Minority interests (40% × £120)	48
Profit for the financial year	252
Dividends	150
Retained profit for the financial year	102

Consolidated balance sheet at 31 December 1991

	£000	£000	£000
Fixed assets			2 300
Current assets		820	
Current liabilities			
Creditors	800		
Proposed dividend	150		
		950	
Net current liabilities			130
			2 170
Capital and reserves			
Called up share capital			1 500
Profit and loss account (Working 2)			462
			1 962
Minority interests (40% × £520)			208
			2 170

Workings

1. Goodwill on acquisition

	Trial Ltd £000	Trial Ltd £000	Jury Ltd £000	Jury Ltd £000
Cost of investment		300		200
Capital and reserves				
Share capital	300		100	
Profit and loss account	100		70	
	400		170	
Minority interests	160		—	
		240		170
		60		30

2. Consolidated profit and loss account

	£
Court Ltd	500
Trial Ltd 60% × (£220 − £100)	72
Jury Ltd 100% × (£50 − £70)	(20)
	552
Goodwill written off (£60 + £30)	90
	462

Tutorial note:
Although the question did not require a statement showing movements on the profit and loss reserve for the year, you will find it quite helpful to prepare one. In order to prepare this statement it is necessary to ascertain the post-acquisition profits retained in the subsidiaries at the beginning of the year. The figures would be:

Movements on consolidated profit and loss reserve:

	£000
Balance at 1 January 1991 £450 + (60% × £0) + (100% × £0)	450
Retained profit for the financial year (as per profit and loss account)	102
	552
Less goodwill written off	90
	462

Chapter 4

4.1 Carver plc

Consolidated cash flow statement for year ended 30 September 1994

	£000	£000
Net cash inflow from operating activities (Note 1)		440
Returns on investments and servicing of finance:		
Dividends received from associated undertakings (Working 1)	250	
Dividends received from other investments (£200 – £45)	155	
Interest paid (£30 + £150 + £40)	(140)	
Dividends paid by Carver plc (£200 + £400 – £300)	(300)	
Dividends paid to minority interests (Working 2)	(48)	
		(83)
Taxation:		
Corporation tax paid (Working 3)		(318)
Investing activities:		
Purchase of machinery (£1 565 – £500 – £3 000)	(1 935)	
Sale of machinery	500	
		(1 435)
Net cash outflow before financing		(1 396)
Financing:		
Issue of ordinary shares (£3 940 + £2 883 – £2 220 – £2 164)	2 439	
Issue of loan capital (£2 410 – £870)	1 540	
		3 979
Increase in cash and cash equivalents		2 583

Notes to the cash flow statement

1. *Reconciliation of operating profit to net cash inflow from operating activities.*

	£000
Operating profit	1485
Depreciation (Buildings £125 + Machinery £200)	325
Profit on sale of machinery	(100)
Increase in stocks	(943)
Increase in debtors	(547)
Increase in trade creditors	220
	440

2. *Analysis of changes in cash and cash equivalents during the year:*

	£000
Balance at 1 October 1993	1 932
Net cash inflow for the year	2 583
Balance at 30 September 1994	4 515

Workings:

1. *Dividends received from associated undertakings*

Carrying value at 1 October 1993	1 000
Share of profits after tax (£495 – £145)	350
	1 350
Carrying value at 30 September 1994	1 100
Dividends received	250

2. *Dividends paid to minority interests*

Opening balance	63
Share of profit	100
	163
Closing balance	115
Dividends paid	48

3. *Corporation tax paid*

Opening balances (£167 + £135 + £13)	315
Charge in profit and loss account (£391 + £104)	495
	810
Closing balances (£375 + £87 + £30)	492
Tax paid	318

Chapter 5

5.1 A plc

Tutorial note: The question did not state the accounting policy adopted for goodwill under acquisition accounting. In these circumstances it is quite reasonable to show goodwill as a negative balance in the capital and reserves section of the balance sheet. If this approach is adopted, the net asset side of the balance sheet can be prepared fairly quickly. Most of the consolidation calculations under acquisition accounting (goodwill, consolidated profit and loss account, and minority interests) are dealt with in the capital and reserves section of the balance sheet.

Very few workings are provided for the following answer since most calculations are relatively straightforward. In situation (iv) the figure for 'other current assets' is reduced in order to recognize that (96% × 1 250 000 × £0.10) £0.12m has been paid out in cash by A plc.

(a) Acquisition accounting

	Situation			
	(i) £m	(ii) £m	(iii) £m	(iv) £m
Fixed assets				
Tangible:				
Land and buildings	3.25	3.25	3.25	3.25
Plant, fixtures and furniture	3.50	3.50	3.50	3.50
Vehicles	1.77	1.77	1.77	1.77
	8.52	8.52	8.52	8.52
Current assets				
Stocks and WIP	1.09	1.09	1.09	1.09
Debtors	0.89	0.89	0.89	0.89
Other assets	0.65	0.65	0.65	0.53
	2.63	2.63	2.63	2.51
Creditors	1.80	1.80	1.80	1.80
Net current assets	0.83	0.83	0.83	0.71
Net assets	9.35	9.35	9.35	9.23
Capital and reserves				
Called up share capital	4.80	5.40	4.40	4.80
Merger reserve	2.40	3.60	1.60	2.40
Revaluation reserve	0.60	0.60	0.60	0.60
Profit and loss account	1.65	1.65	1.65	1.65
Goodwill	(0.24)	(2.04)	0.96	(0.36)
	9.21	9.21	9.21	9.09
Minority interests	0.14	0.14	0.14	0.14
	9.35	9.35	9.35	9.23

(b) Merger accounting

	Situation			
	(i) £m	(ii) £m	(iii) £m	(iv) £m
Fixed assets				
Tangible:				
Land and buildings	2.75	2.75	2.75	2.75
Plant, fixtures and furniture	3.55	3.55	3.55	3.55
Vehicles	1.80	1.80	1.80	1.80
	8.10	8.10	8.10	8.10
Current assets				
Stocks and WIP	1.10	1.10	1.10	1.10
Debtors	0.90	0.90	0.90	0.90
Other assets	0.65	0.65	0.65	0.53
	2.65	2.65	2.65	2.53
Creditors	1.80	1.80	1.80	1.80
Net current assets	0.85	0.85	0.85	0.73
Net assets	8.95	8.95	8.95	8.83

| | Situation | | | |
	(i) £m	(ii) £m	(iii) £m	(iv) £m
Capital and reserves				
Called up share capital	4.80	5.40	4.40	4.80
Revaluation reserve	0.60	0.60	0.60	0.60
Profit and loss account (note)	3.43	3.43	3.43	3.43
Difference on consolidation	—	(0.60)	0.40	(0.12)
	8.83	8.83	8.83	8.71
Minority interests (note)	0.12	0.12	0.12	0.12
	8.95	8.95	8.95	8.83

Note: Figures for the profit and loss account and minority interests have been rounded. The actual figures are as follows:

Profit and loss account £1.65m + (96% × £1.85m)	£3.426m
Minority interests 4% × £3.10m	£0.124m

5.3 Dinos and Nivis

(a) Consolidated balance sheet – acquisition accounting

	£000
Fixed assets (Working 1)	3 626
Net current assets (£1 218 + £265)	1 483
	5 109
Capital and reserves	
Called up share capital (£3 000 + £400)	3 400
Merger reserve (400 000 × £2.50)	1 000
Profit and loss account (Working 3)	709
	5 109

Workings (all figures in £000s)

1. *Fixed assets*		
Nivis per balance sheet	920	
Unrecorded revaluation	270	
	1 190	
Additional depreciation	29	
	1 161	
Dinos per balance sheet	2 465	
	3 626	

2. *Goodwill*		
Cost of investment (400 000 × £3.50)		1 400

Adjusted capital and reserves at acquisition:

Share capital	600	
Profit and loss account	300	
Revaluation reserve	270	
	1 170	
	230	

3. Consolidated profit and loss reserve

Dinos (£540 + £143)	683
Nivis (£285 – £29)	256
	939
Less goodwill written off	230
	709

(b) Consolidated balance sheet – merger accounting

	£000
Fixed assets (£2,465 + £920)	3 385
Net current assets (as before)	1 483
	4 868
Capital and reserves	
Called up share capital (as before)	3 400
Profit and loss account (£683 + £585)	1 268
Consolidation difference (£600 – £400)	200
	4 868

(c) See pages 119–120 of the text book. The reasons behind the regulations in FRS 6 are to ensure that merger accounting is used only in the case of a genuine merger – as defined. If an acquisition is considered to be a take-over, acquisition accounting must be used even if the entire consideration given is in the form of equity shares in the acquiring company.

Chapter 6

6.1 Friendly plc

(a) Consolidated balance sheet at 30 June 19X8

	£000
Net tangible assets (£738.5 + £240 + £560)	1 538.5
Capital and reserves	
Share capital	731.5
Share premium	540.0
Profit and loss account (Working 2)	43.0
	1 314.5
Minority interests (40% × £560)	224.0
	1 538.5

Workings (all figures in £000s):

1. Goodwill on acquisition of Tolerance Ltd

Total cost of investment (£160 + £373)		533.0
Capital and reserves at 31 March 19X8		
Share capital	100.0	
Share premium	100.0	
Retained earnings	250.0	
	450.0	
Minority interests (40%)	180.0	
		270.0
		263.0

2. Consolidated profit and loss account

Friendly plc		400.0
Patience 100% × (£190 − £120)		70.0
Tolerance 60% × (£360 − £250)		66.0
		536.0
Goodwill written off:		
Patience (given in question)	230.0	
Tolerance – as in Working 1	263.0	
		493.0
		43.0

(b) If a stepped (or proportional) basis had been allowed for the acquisition of Tolerance Ltd, the calculations would have been as follows:

Goodwill on acquisition of Tolerance Ltd:

Acquisition date	31 October 19X7		31 March 19X8	
Percentage control obtained	18%		42%	
	£000	£000	£000	£000
Cost of investment		160		373
Capital and reserves at acquisition:				
Share capital	100		100	
Share premium	100		100	
Profit and loss reserve	200		250	
	400		450	
Applicable to control obtained	18%	72	42%	189
		88		184

Consolidated profit and loss reserve:

	£000	£000
Friendly plc		400
Patience Ltd (as before)		70

	£000	£000
Tolerance Ltd		
18% × (£360 – £200)	28.8	
42% × (£360 – £250)	46.2	
		75
		545
Goodwill written off:		
Patience (as before)	230	
Tolerance (£88 + £184)	272	
		502
		43

As can be seen from the above, the final balance on the consolidated profit and loss reserve is the same as in part (a). Goodwill on the acquisition of Tolerance Ltd is £9 000 greater under the proportional basis and the amount of post-acquisition profit consolidated for Tolerance Ltd is £9 000 greater. (The £9 000 represents 18% of the £50 000 retained profit for the period 31 October 19X7 to 31 March 19X8.) However, since goodwill is being written off against the balance on the profit and loss account, the final balance on this account does not change. The situation would have been different if goodwill had been treated as an asset and amortized over a number of years.

Generally speaking FRS 2 does not permit the proportional basis. This is in keeping with the requirements in Schedule 4A of the Companies Act 1985. The FRS does recognize that there will be some (rare) circumstances where the proportional basis should be applied in order to show a true and fair view. This might apply when an investment in an associated company is increased to the point where it becomes a subsidiary.

(c) See page 37 for details. A note should have been made that the only reserve available for immediate write off in the case of Friendly plc is the profit and loss reserve. It should also have been noted that although the immediate write off policy was adopted for the acquisition of Patience Ltd, there is no requirement for the same policy to be adopted in the case of Tolerance Ltd. Companies can choose either policy for each acquisition. The way in which the accounting policy for goodwill affects 'distributable' profits is discussed on page 212 (Chapter 9) but this has little significance for group accounts since groups do not make distributions.

Chapter 7

There was no self-assessment question at the end of this chapter.

Chapter 8

8.1 Apple, Banana and Cherry

Although the situation in this question was not complex, it is a good idea to get into the habit of setting out a diagram of the group. In this case the diagram could be as follows:

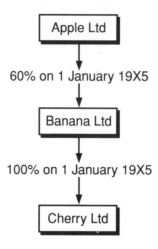

Apple Ltd

60% on 1 January 19X5

Banana Ltd

100% on 1 January 19X5

Cherry Ltd

The next stage is to set out a schedule of proportional interests, as follows:

		Banana Ltd	Cherry Ltd
Apple Ltd	direct	60%	0%
	indirect	0%	60% × 100% 60%
		60%	60%
Minority interests (balance)		40%	40%
		100%	100%

Next, set up a working schedule to allocate balances between goodwill, minority interests and consolidated profit and loss account. This could be as follows:
In the following schedule, debit balances are shown in brackets.

	Goodwill £000	Minority interests £000	Profit and loss account £000
1. Allocate cost of investments:			
in Banana Ltd	(1500)		
in Cherry Ltd	(850)		
Transfer 40% of investment in Cherry Ltd to minority interests	340	(340)	
2. Allocate share capital			
in Banana Ltd	600	400	
in Cherry Ltd	360	240	
3. Allocate revaluation reserve			
in Banana Ltd	270	180	
4. Allocate profit and loss account			
in Apple Ltd (£563 + £157)			720
in Banana Ltd (£300 + £120 – £90)		132	198
in Cherry Ltd (£100 + £60)		64	96
5. Transfer pre-acquisition profits to goodwill			
Banana Ltd (60% × £300)	180		(180)
Cherry Ltd (60% × £100)	60		(60)
	(540)	676	774

The question did not give the accounting policy for goodwill. In the following answer it is assumed that goodwill will be written off immediately against reserves.

Consolidated balance sheet at 31 December 19X5

	£000
Fixed assets at book value (£800 + £600 + £700 + £450 − £90)	2 460
Net current assets (£270 + £470 + £310)	1 050
	3 510
12% Long-term loans (£650 + £500 + £250)	1 400
	2 110
Capital and reserves:	
Share capital	1 200
Profit and loss account (£774 − £540)	234
	1 434
Minority interests	676
	2 110

8.2 HRS

1. Group structure:

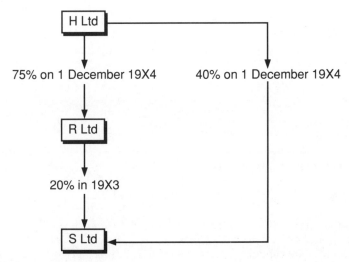

75% on 1 December 19X4   40% on 1 December 19X4

20% in 19X3

2. Proportional interests

	R Ltd	S Ltd
H Ltd direct	75%	40%
indirect		15%
	75%	55%
Minority interests (balance)	25%	45%
	100%	100%

3. Consolidation adjustments in H Ltd for dividends and unrealized profit

	Cost of Investment in R Ltd £	Profit and loss account £
Balance per question	367 500	180 250
Dividend from pre-acquisition profits (75% × £35 000)	(26 250)	(26 250)
Unrealized profit on stocks (recorded by H Ltd) 20% (£12 500 + £10 400)		(4 580)
Revised balances for group accounts	341 250	149 420

4. Allocation of profit and loss accounts in subsidiaries

It is possible to adopt the approach used in the allocation schedule for 8.1 but in view of the profit and loss deficits it might be easier to sort out the profit allocation as a separate working. Using brackets to indicate deficits, this working could be as follows:

	R Ltd £		S Ltd £
Goodwill 75% × £35 000	26 250	55% × (£35 000)	(19 250)
Minority interests 25% × £17 500	4 375	45% × (£17 500)	(7 875)
Profit and loss 75% × (£17 500 − £35 000)	(13 125)	55% × ((£17 500) − (£35 000))	9 625
Balances per question	17 500		(17 500)

5. Allocation schedule

	Goodwill £	Minority interests £	Profit and loss account £
1. Allocate cost of investments:			
H in R	(341 250)		
H in S	(49 000)		
R in S	(24 500)		
Transfer 25% of R's investment in S to minority interests	6 125	(6 125)	
2. Allocate share capital			
in R	315 000	105 000	
in S	96 250	78 750	
3. Allocate profit and loss accounts			
H (Working 3)			149 420
R (Working 4)	26 250	4 375	(13 125)
S (Working 4)	(19 250)	(7 875)	9 625
4. Allocate 'other reserves'			
S (25% × £70 000)		17 500	
	9 625	191 625	145 920

6. Debtors and creditors

	H Ltd £	R Ltd £	S Ltd £	Total £
Debtors:				
Debtors per question	241 920	129 680	29 750	
Less cash in transit	(8 000)			
Less owing by R				
(£25 500 – £8 000)	(17 500)			
	216 420	129 680	29 750	375 850
Creditors:				
Creditors per question	(95 480)	(86 645)	(88 605)	
Invoice for goods in transit		(12 500)		
Owing to R (£5 000 + £12 500)		17 500		
	(95 480)	(81 645)	(88 605)	(265 730)

Consolidated balance sheet at 30 November 19X7

	£
Fixed assets	
Land and buildings (£447 500 + £230 950 + £52 000)	730 450
Plant and machinery (£600 500 + £61 750)	662 250
Fixtures and fittings (£54 500 + £41 000 + £8 800)	104 300
	1 497 000
Current assets	
Stocks (as per question + £12 500 – £4 580) 783 520	
Debtors (Working 6) 375 850	
Cash and bank balances (per question + £8 000) 109 030	
1 268 400	
Creditors due within one year	
Creditors (Working 6) 265 730	
	1 002 670
	2 499 670
Capital and reserves	
Share capital	1 750 000
Other reserves £350 000 + (75% × £70 000)	402 500
Profit and loss account (Working 5)	145 920
Negative goodwill (Working 5)	9 625
	2 308 045
Minority interests (Working 5)	191 625
	2 499 670

Chapter 9

9.1 Brompton plc

(a) Correction of trainee's draft accounts.

Disposal of entire holding on 1 July 19X8
Three basic mistakes made by the trainee accountant are:
  (i)   The gain on disposal for the consolidated accounts has not been calculated. The amount of £740 000 shown in the consolidated accounts is simply the gain in the parent company's accounts.
  (ii) The gain has been reported as an extraordinary item.
  (iii) No provision has been made for the tax payable of £222 000
The gain on disposal for the group accounts is as follows:

	£000
Gain in Brompton plc's accounts	740
Less post-acquisition profits (£1000 − £560)	440
Gain before tax in the group accounts	300
Tax on ordinary profits must be increased by (as stated in question)	222

Budgeted consolidated profit and loss account year ended 30 June 19X9

	£000
Profit before tax (as in question)	3 020
Gain on disposal of subsidiary	300
Ordinary profit before tax	3 320
Taxation (£1 427 + £222)	1 649
Profit after tax for the financial year	1 671

The following details for the consolidated profit and loss reserve ignore the effect of goodwill on acqusition since no data on this was provided in the question. If goodwill on the acquisition of both subsidiaries had been written off against the balance on the profit and loss account in the group accounts, it would be necessary to reduce the consolidated balance brought forward by the amount of this goodwill. An adjustment should then be made for the reinstatement of the goodwill relating to Doulidge.

Consolidated profit and loss reserve

	£000
Balance brought forward (£2 900 + £970 + £440)	4 310
Profit for the year	1 671
Balance carried forward	5 981
Reconciliation of balance carried forward:	
Brompton plc (£4 815 − £222)	4 593
Chieftan (£970 + £418)	1 388
	5 981

Disposal of entire holding on 1 January 19X9
The same mistakes as above have been made. In addition:

(i)   The consolidated profit and loss account should only include profits of Doulidge up to the date of disposal.
(ii) FRS 3 requires separate disclose of profits and losses from discontinued activities.

The loss on disposal for the group accounts is as follows:

	£000	£000
Gain in Brompton plc's accounts		740.0
Less post-acquisition profits:		
as before	440.0	
plus 6/12 × £929	464.5	
		904.5
Loss before tax in group accounts		(164.5)

Budgeted consolidated profit and loss account year ended 30 June 19X9

	Discontinued activities £000	Continuing activities £000	Total £000
Profit as per question	672.0	3 020.0	3 692.0
Loss on disposal of subsidiary	164.5		164.5
Ordinary profit before tax	507.5	3 020.0	3 527.5
Taxation (£1 427 + £207.5 + £222)			1 856.5
Profit after tax for the financial year			1 671.0

Movements on the consolidated profit and loss reserve, and its reconciliation, will be the same as in (a), subject to the reservations mentioned regarding goodwill.

(b) (i) A sale of 600 000 ordinary shares will leave Brompton with an interest in Doulidge of (900 000/1 500 000) 60% and so it will still be a subsidiary following the disposal. In the accounts of Brompton the gain on disposal will be calculated by deducting 6/15 of the cost of the investment from the sale proceeds of £1 300 000. This will give a gain before tax of £140 000. Corporation tax on this gain is payable by Brompton.
  A strict interpretaion of FRS 2 requires the gain in the group accounts to be calculated by comparing the following:

  Brompton's interest in the net assets of Doulidge prior to disposal, with the sale proceeds, plus Brompton's interest in the net assets of Doulidge after the disposal.

However, in the case described it is quite likely that Brompton's interest in the net assets of Doulidge after the disposal will be based on a direct proportion of its interest prior to the disposal. In these circumstances the gain for the group accounts can be calculated in a manner similar to that used in (a). The gain of £140 000 recorded by Brompton will be reduced in the group accounts by (6/15 × (£1 000 000

– £560 000)) £176 000. This produces a loss for the group accounts of £36 000 before tax.

The consolidated profit and loss account should consolidate 100% of each item in Doulidge's profit and loss account down to profit after tax. An adjustment should then be made for Doulidge's 40% minority interests. The consolidated balance sheet will include 40% of the adjusted capital and reserves of Doulidge under minority interests.

(ii) A disposal of 1 350 000 shares will leave Brompton with a 10% interest. The gain on disposal in Brompton's accounts, and in the group accounts, will be calculated in manner similar to that described for (i). The main problem in the group accounts concerns the carrying value of the investment following the disposal. A fairly common approach to this problem is to carry the investment at its equity value on the date of disposal. This is treated as a frozen value except where it becomes necessary to make a provision for any permanent diminution in value. Income from the investment is reported in the group accounts on the basis of dividend income.

(c) It is assumed that comments are required in respect of the choice between selling the entire holding in Doulidge on 1 July 19X8 and selling it on 1 January 19X9. As can be deduced from the calculations in part (a), the earnings per share (EPS) in the group accounts will be the same whichever date for the disposal is adopted.

This would not have been the case prior to FRS 3, where the gain or loss in the group accounts for the disposal of a subsidiary was treated as an extraordinary item, because extraordinary items were excluded when calculating EPS. Since EPS in the group accounts does not change by delaying the date of disposal, there is little point in losing the investment potential of £3 640 000 for the period from 1 July 19X8 and 1 January 19X9.

Chapter 10

10.1 Somco plc

Transaction A

	£
(a) Gross profit (not applicable)	
Exchange gain/loss:	
Original liability recorded as (N130 000 ÷ 0.65)	200 000
Payment made (N130 000 ÷ 0.50)	260 000
Exchange loss	60 000

(b) Include under **other operating expenses**. This is a settled transaction that has already been reflected in cash flows

Transaction B

	£
(a) Sale recorded as (the sterling amount)	68 000
Cost of sales (as recorded in sterling)	46 000
Gross profit	22 000

	£
Debtor originally recorded as (the sterling amount)	68 000
Proceeds of settlement:	
The wording suggests that the transaction was denominated in Krams. This is sometimes done in order to encourage exports because it protects the purchaser from the risks of exchange rate movements. The purchaser would have recorded a debt of (£68 000 × 7.0) K476 000.	
The Kram proceeds would realise (K476 000 ÷ 6.7)	71 045
Exchange gain	3 045

(b) Include the exchange gain under **other operating income**. This is a settled transaction and the gain has already been reflected in cash flows

Transaction C

		£
(a)	Sale recorded as (the sterling amount)	24 000
	Cost of sales (as recorded in sterling)	17 000
	Gross profit	7 000

	£
On the assumption that the transaction was denominated in Sarils:	
Debtor originally recorded (Sarils = £24 000 × 2 224 = 53 376 000)	24 000
Debtor restated at 31 December 1989 to (S53 376 000 ÷ 2 250)	23 723
Exchange loss in 1989	277

	£
Restated debtor	23 723
Saril proceeds would realize (S53 376 000 ÷ 2 306)	23 147
Exchange loss in 1990	576

(b) Include both losses under **other operating expenses** for the respective year. Although the exchange loss in 1989 was on an unsettled transaction, it will shortly be reflected in the company's cash flow (when settled). SSAP 17 on post balance sheet events specifically gives changes in exchange rate as an example of a non-adjusting event. Consequently, there is no requirement to restate the debt at 31 December 1989 to £23 147.

Transaction D

		£
(a)	Gross profit (not applicable)	
	Loan recorded as (R426 000 ÷ 1.5)	284 000
	Repayment would cost (R426 000 ÷ 1.8)	236 667
	Exchange gain	47 333

(b) This could be included under **other interest receivable and similar income** or treated as a reduction of **interest payable and similar charges**. Either way the gain must be reported in the profit and loss account under ordinary activities because the transaction has been settled and the gain has been reflected in the company's cash flows.

Transaction E

The equity investment (being a non-monetary asset) would not normally be translated after its initial recording except where the 'offset' policy is being adopted. In order to take advantage of the offset policy permitted by SSAP 20, there is no requirement for the loan to be obtained from the same country as the equity investment. The loan must be retranslated at each balance sheet date even if the offset policy is not adopted. This practice is justified in SSAP 20 as being consistent with the accruals concept. Gains or losses on retranslating the loan must be reported as a part of ordinary profit except where the offset policy is adopted. If the offset policy is adopted, the gains and losses are as follows:

	£
Exchange gains or losses for 1988:	
(i) Equity investment:	
Original sterling cost (K196 000 ÷ 7.3)	26 849
Restated at 31 December 1988 to closing rate (K196 000 ÷ 6.9)	28 406
Exchange gain	1 557
(ii) Nidar loan:	
Originally recorded as (N15 000 ÷ 0.56)	27 786
Restated at 31 December 1988 to closing rate (N15 000 ÷ 0.52)	28 846
Exchange loss	2 060
Exchange gains and losses for 1989:	
(i) Equity investment:	
Balance at 1 January 1990 (as above)	28 406
Restated at 31 December 1989 to (K196 000 ÷ 7.5)	26 133
Exchange loss	2 273
(ii) Nidar loan:	
Balance at 1 January 1990 (as above)	28 486
Restated at 31 December 1990 (N15 000 ÷ 0.54)	27 778
Exchange gain	1 068

In order to see whether or not the company would have claimed the 'cover or offset' method permitted by SSAP 20, it is necessary to take a view of what the position would have been in 1988.

Exchange gains/(losses)	1988	1989
Equity investment	1 557	(2 273)
Hedging loan	(2 060)	1 068
Net gain or (loss)	(503)	(1 205)

These figures suggest that the offset policy would be adopted in 1988. Failure to do so would require the company to include an exchange loss of £2 060 as part of profit from ordinary activities, whereas the gain on the investment would be ignored. By adopting the offset policy the equity investment can be retranslated and the gain treated as a reserve movement. The loss on the loan can then be set against this reserve up to a maximum of £1 557. The balance of the loss (£503) must be included in ordinary profit (e.g. under **interest paid and similar charges**).

Assuming the offset policy was adopted in 1988, the company would not be able to report the gain on the loan of £1 068 in 1989 as part of ordinary profit. The offset policy must be continued and this would result in a reserve movement for the net translation loss of £1 205.

Transaction F

Tutorial notes: The examiner's comment that the branch is treated as independent and financed in local currency suggests that the closing rate basis (rather than the temporal basis) should be used for translation of the Rolad figures. Strictly speaking this information is inadequate but there is no other basis that can be used for the details provided. Note that where the closing rate basis is adopted, SSAP 20 does **permit** the profit for the year to be translated at an average rate even though the balance sheet must be translated at closing rate.

The branch current account in the head office books usually contains two cash columns, one for the local currency and one for sterling. This account can be used to ascertain the translation gain or loss, as follows:

Branch current account

Details	Rolads	Rate	£	Details	Rolads	Rate	£
Balance b/d	638 000	1.6	399 125	Bank	207 300	Act	116 727
Profit and loss a/c	423 400	1.7	249 059	Bal c/d	854 700	2.0	427 350
				Loss on			
				translation			104 107
	1 062 000		648 184		1 062 000		648 184

The loss (to be debited to reserves) arises because the investment is in a country whose currency is weakening against the pound. Although the above figures have been set out in the form of a 'T' account, it is easier to see how the loss arises if they are set out as follows:

	£	£
Net investment at the start of the period		399 125
Add: profit recorded	249 059	
Less: remittances received	116 727	
		132 332
		531 457
Net investment at end of period		427 350
Loss on translation		104 107

Chapter 11

11.1 FRS 7 – Fair values in acquisition accounting

The four deliberate errors are as follows:

(1) The cost of stock has been determined on a last in first out (LIFO) basis. This contravenes the requirement in FRS 7 that the cost of stock should be based on 'replacement cost'. These replacement costs should be considered from the viewpoint of the acquired entity and take account of the current sources and prices available to it. Costs determined under a LIFO basis are unlikely to reflect these current replacement costs. (Note how this answer refers to the provisions in FRS 7. The question is not adequately answered by referring to provisions in SSAP 9 regarding the use of LIFO.)

(2) A provision for future reorganization costs has been made. This contravenes the provisions in FRS 7 which state that the liabilities should not include such provisions. Any future costs or losses should be dealt with as post-acquisition items. Prior to the introduction of FRS 7, the practice of making these provisions was encouraged by paragraph 14 of SSAP 22 (now superseded by FRS 7). The argument put forward at that time was that these future costs would have been taken into account when arriving at the purchase price. This was, however, a strange argument because the price paid would also have taken account of the future profit potential of the acquired entity. It is hardly likely that anyone would have argued that an asset should be set up for expected future profits.

(3) The acquisition cost includes shares issued by the parent company at nominal value. In the situation described, merger relief under Section 131, Companies Act 1985 would not apply and the share issue must be recorded at fair value of the shares issued.

(4) Acquisition costs include an apportionment of the company's own administration costs. This is specifically prohibited by the rules in FRS 7.

Note that the assets for a contingent gain of £50 000 and a pension fund surplus of £80 000 are correctly dealt with in the fair value table. FRS 7 requires these items to be treated as assets even though they are not recognized as such under SSAPs 18 and 24 (see page 282).

11.2 Scotty plc

(a) The calculation of fair value for Sulu Inc at 1 October 19X8 should deal with the four items mentioned in the question as follows:

(i) **Redundancy costs**. Although FRS 7 is quite strict on not allowing provisions to be set up for future costs or losses, it does not insist that no provisions are made as part of the fair value exercise. The FRS recognizes (particularly in Paragraph 38) that an acquired entity might have commitments at the date of acquisition which have not been reflected in its own accounts as liabilities. In these circumstances it is quite reasonable to recognize such commitments as an identifiable liability at the date of acquisition. In the circumstances described in the question it seems that the redundancy costs were a definite commitment at the date of acquisition and as such a provision for the identifiable liability should be made.

(ii) **Investment in plant and machinery**. This is a future commitment at the date of acquisition and as such no provision should be made. In any event, the mere mechanics of double-entry suggest that if the liability is recognized the asset should be recognized also. If both the asset and the liability were recognized, the total fair value would not change.

(iii) **Professional fees and directors' costs**. These items do not relate to the fair value of the acquired entity but to the fair value of the consideration. FRS 7 allows the costs of external professional fees (£30 000) to be added to the consideration but not the internal costs of £20 000. These internal costs are not the result of a market transaction and are incapable of objective measurement.

(iv) **Stock**. The cost of stock in Sulu Inc was determined on a last in first out (LIFO) basis. This policy is permitted in a US corporation but it contravenes a provision in FRS 7 that requires the cost of stock to be based on 'replacement cost'. These replacement costs should be considered from the viewpoint of the acquired entity and take account of the current sources and prices available to it. Costs determined under a LIFO basis are unlikely to reflect these current replacement costs. It is assumed that costs based on FIFO will give a fair reflection of current replacement costs.

Fair value of Sulu Inc at acquisition

	$	$
Fair value of net identifiable assets prior to adjustments		4 370 000
Adjustments as described above		
(i) Redundancy costs	(380 000)	
(ii) Stock adjustment	150 000	
		(230 000)
		4 140 000

Translation of the total fair value into sterling is ($4 140 000 ÷ 1.8) £2 300 000

(b) Balance of goodwill that could be carried forward at 30 June 19X8

	£	£
Fair value of consideration – as per question		
(see Note 2)	2 450 000	
Add professional fees	30 000	
		2 480 000
Fair value of net identifiable assets in Sulu Inc (90% × £2 300 000)		2 070 000
Total goodwill on acquisition		410 000
Amount amortized (£410 000 ÷ 3 × 9/12)		102 000
Balance carried forward at 30 June 19X8		308 000

Notes:
1. Although the acquisition satisfies the conditions for merger relief, it is unlikely that the situation is such that merger accounting will be permitted by FRS 6. In these circumstances the share issue will have to be recorded at fair value, although the difference between nominal value and fair value can be credited to a separate reserve such as a 'merger reserve' rather than the share premium account.
2. The consideration of £2 450 000 shown in the above calculation includes a deferred cash payment of £200 000. FRS 7 requires deferred cash payments to be discounted to their present value. The appropriate discount rate is a rate at

which the acquirer could obtain a similar borrowing taking into account its credit status and any security given. This aspect could not be applied to the answer because no interest rates were given. Students should note that this particular aspect is one of the few instances where UK accounting regulations require the time value of money to be recognized when reporting items in financial statements.

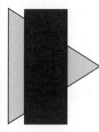

Index of references to accounting regulations

This index gives page numbers on which references to various accounting regulations can be found. There is a separate 'index of extracts from accounting regulations' set out in subject order.

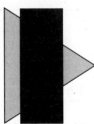

Index of extracts from accounting regulations

This index refers to pages in the book where extracts from legislation and accounting standards can be found. Most extracts are in appendices but some are included as part of the text.

Subject index

This index refers to pages in the book where the main text on specific subjects can be found. Page references do not include the appendices containing extracts from relevant regulations. There is a separate subject index for locating extracts from accounting regulations.